Denkart Europa

Schriften zur europäischen Politik, Wirtschaft und Kultur | 26

herausgegeben von der ASKO EUROPA-STIFTUNG, Saarbrücken und der Europäischen Akademie Otzenhausen gGmbH.

Hartmut Marhold [ed.]

Europe in Trouble

Developing under the Constraint of Crises

 **Nomos**

These Policy Papers were published online between September 2015 and July 2016 by the Research Department of the Centre international de formation européenne (CIFE), with the financial support of the European Commission.

© Coverpicture: fotolia.com

The Deutsche Nationalbibliothek lists this publication in the Deutsche Nationalbibliografie; detailed bibliographic data are available on the Internet at http://dnb.d-nb.de

ISBN   978-3-8487-3530-3 (Print)
        978-3-8452-7863-6 (ePDF)

British Library Cataloguing-in-Publication Data
A catalogue record for this book is available from the British Library.

ISBN   978-3-8487-3530-3 (Print)
        978-3-8452-7863-6 (ePDF)

Library of Congress Cataloging-in-Publication Data
Marhold, Hartmut
Europe in Trouble
Developing under the Constraint of Crises
Hartmut Marhold (ed.)
208 p.
Includes bibliographic references.

ISBN   978-3-8487-3530-3 (Print)
        978-3-8452-7863-6 (ePDF)

1. Edition 2016
© Nomos Verlagsgesellschaft, Baden-Baden, Germany 2016. Printed and bound in Germany.

Preface

In the period between mid-2015 and mid-2016 Europe and the European Union were in serious trouble: Not yet fully recovered from the financial, economic and state debt crisis (even now unresolved), still challenged by the Ukraine war and Russian foreign policy, two more crises exploded in the face of the Europeans:

Some two million or more refugees reached the heartlands of Europe, travelling through the Balkans, towards Germany and Scandinavia, in particular, where the readiness to welcome and integrate them in order to avoid a humanitarian catastrophe on European soil triggered a wave of protest, amplified and exploited by right wing populists and demagogues.

And terror not only caused the deaths of hundreds of European citizens, in France and Belgium, in Paris, Brussels and Nice, but also profoundly shocked our societies, and played further into the hands of irresponsible political adventurers, who now seem to represent, at least in some countries, a real threat to democracy and trust at the European level/in Europe.

Partly as a result of these destabilising developments and events, partly owing to yet another critical event where a majority of the British electorate voted in favour of a "Brexit" in June 2016, the European Union was finally plunged into an unprecedented crisis: Never before had a member state asked to leave the EU (or the European Communities). Where this will lead is still totally uncertain in this summer 2016 – everybody seems to have seized the opportunity to put forward his or her project for a European Union acceptable to everybody, but these projects are contradictory and plead for either more or less integration.

The scale of these crises means that we are in danger of overlooking/ neglecting other important issues on the European and global agenda, which also need to be addressed, and deserve political attention - issues ranging from the preparation of the electoral campaign for the new US president to China's economic growth and internal and external political attitudes.

CIFE has continued, for a second year, to publish, twice a month, policy papers on a wide range of these challenges, in the two dominant working languages of the institute, French and English. Again, twenty scholars, members of CIFE's research team and guest authors from other universities and institutes, from many countries and scientific disciplines, have analysed and assessed these issues. The series does not pretend to give a systematic, representative account of world history between summer 2015 and summer 2016, but all of these papers deal with relevant issues of European integration and international affairs, in a readable way.

The picture we paint is one of a Europe in trouble – but an active Europe, ready to engage in serious combat to maintain its unity, its values, its interests, and even, as so often in history, under the constraint of the current crises, to continue in its development.

Hartmut Marhold, July 2016

Table of Contents

Europe's polity and policies

Comment désigner des biens publics, collectifs ou communs en Europe?

Jean-Claude Vérez

Les concepts de biens publics, biens collectifs, biens communs sont poly-sémiques et ne recouvrent pas de facto les mêmes définitions selon qu'ils soient analysés par des philosophes, des juristes ou des économistes. Au sein des sciences économiques, les débats sont nombreux et, selon les écoles de pensée, il existe de fortes disparités quant à leur champ respectif, leur mode de régulation, leur financement, leur réglementation etc. Dans les théories de l'économie de la réglementation, les questions clés tournent autour de la propriété, de la tarification, de l'incitation ou du rationne-ment. Qui ou quelle institution détermine qu'un bien est public ou com-mun ? Comment inciter les acteurs à le respecter en évitant les comporte-ments de passager clandestin ? Les mesures incitatives (impôt négatif) sont-elles préférables aux mesures coercitives (taxes) ?

Les questions d'efficacité et/ou d'équité sont omniprésentes et nous renvoient au champ de l'intervention publique : est-elle plus adaptée que le libre marché pour régler, par exemple, les problèmes de pollution ? Le service public est-il remis en cause par la déréglementation ou, au contraire, la réglementation est-elle avant tout un instrument de redistribu-tion ? A priori, la supériorité de l'intervention publique pour remédier aux défauts de marché n'est pas acquise. Il faut l'aborder au cas par cas. Transposée au niveau européen, on est tenté de considérer que l'interroga-tion est encore plus fondamentale du fait de réglementations nationales hé-térogènes. La diversité des territoires, la taille du marché européen et la pluralité des acteurs rendent la question plus complexe.

Essayons dans un premier temps de dissocier les biens. Un *bien collec-tif* est un bien non rival et non excluable tel l'éclairage public, quiconque ne peut individualiser la consommation de cet éclairage. La définition, au sens strict, d'un bien public est différente : un *bien public* est un bien à la fois produit et fourni par la puissance publique, soit par exemple en France l'école publique mais celle-ci peut être excluable. Comme la production des biens collectifs n'est pas optimale dans le cadre du marché (coût d'en-trée élevé, rendement incertain), ces biens sont souvent produits et fournis par la puissance publique et sont donc souvent aussi des biens publics mais il n'existe pas de relation nécessaire entre les deux types de biens : un bien collectif n'est pas forcément un bien public et vice-versa. Il ne faut donc pas préjuger du mode de production et de gestion de ces biens, qui peuvent être publics, communautaires voire privés.

Dès le 18è siècle, Adam Smith avait relevé les défauts de marché. Si les intérêts individuels ou égoïstes doivent être respectés au sein du libéralisme, ils ne correspondent pas nécessairement -malgré la main invisible- aux intérêts de tous. L'auteur soulignait par exemple les avantages procurés par les routes, les ponts, les travaux publics tout en admettant qu'aucun particulier (voire quelques-uns) ne saurait obtenir un retour sur investissement eu égard au coût initial puis au coût d'entretien de telles infrastructures. Le concept de défaut de marché nous renvoie à l'impossibilité de satisfaire les intérêts privés des consommateurs et des producteurs et la satisfaction de l'intérêt général.

Outre les biens collectifs et publics, on dissocie encore les biens de club ou les biens communs. *Les biens de club* sont exclusifs et non rivaux (abonnement à une chaîne de TV par exemple) ; diverses communautés ont ainsi des intérêts en commun avec comme interrogation majeure la taille de leur communauté ou association. On les distingue *des biens privés* non accessibles à tous et consommés par un individu et un seul.

Les propriétés de rivalité et de non exclusion définissent *les biens en commun*. On les différencie des biens publics dont l'objet est d'accroître le bien-être collectif, après avoir désigné ce type de bien (qui ne serait généralement pas produit s'il était laissé à l'initiative des individus). Un bien commun est un bien partagé pour lui-même et résulte des interactions individuelles comme par exemple un ballet de danse classique. Il a pour objet de procurer du bien-être. Ainsi, contrairement au bien public, c'est plus le fait de le produire en commun qui crée des externalités positives que le bien en tant que tel. Et c'est en raison de ces externalités et pour cette qualité qu'il convient de le désigner.

Quand un bien est élevé au rang de bien commun, la question de sa protection devient cruciale. Si, par exemple, les chasseurs d'un pays chassent un animal en voie de disparition, ils mettent en danger sa reproduction. Pour éviter une disparition complète, les autorités peuvent élever au rang de bien commun l'espèce menacée. Ce choix implique une réglementation d'où la nécessité pour l'économiste (sans que cela lui soit exclusif) de réfléchir à la « meilleure » réglementation. On peut privilégier une réglementation préoccupée par l'efficacité et non par les problèmes de redistribution, respectant en cela la tradition de l'économie publique. Ce qui compte tient à la dissociation de l'efficacité (objet de l'analyse économique) et de la redistribution (à la charge des institutions publiques). C'est parce qu'il existe un défaut de marché qu'il devient possible de désigner un bien commun ou collectif ou public, mais il faut veiller à ce que cette solution soit réellement efficace ce qui inclut une autonomie pour le réglementeur afin qu'il puisse échapper à toute forme de pression ou de lobbying.

C'est justement pour pallier à ces pressions que l'économie politique se dissocie de l'économie publique en matière de réglementation. On peut admettre d'une part, que les partis politiques sont mus par des considérations électorales et que, d'autre part, les entreprises, bien que favorables a priori au libéralisme et aux règles du marché, tentent d'être protégées de la concurrence de sorte que les intérêts des uns et des autres peuvent parfaitement être compatibles. Pour cette raison, la nouvelle économie publique cherche à pointer les défauts du réglementeur et la manière de les corriger.

On peut encore mobiliser les travaux de l'économie institutionnelle qui s'appuie sur les travaux de Coase (1960), lequel critique en partie les raisons de l'intervention publique développée par Pigou dans les années 1930. Pour mémoire, Pigou est le père de l'économie du bien-être qui s'intéresse à la manière d'augmenter la satisfaction des individus. L'auteur aborde les externalités tant positives que négatives et tant des producteurs que des consommateurs. Chaque acte individuel peut influer positivement ou négativement sur la situation d'un autre agent, sans que cette relation fasse l'objet d'une contrepartie monétaire. Prenons l'exemple d'un de mes voisins qui dispose d'un beau jardin, fleuri et qui me réjouit (si j'aime les fleurs) lorsque je passe devant, à l'opposé d'un autre voisin qui transforme son jardin en dépôt de pièces détachées avec à la clé des réparations sources de nuisances sonores et de pollution. Pigou considère que les externalités ne sont pas prises en compte par le marché et si, chacun poursuit son seul intérêt, on s'éloigne d'une situation optimale : le premier voisin ne mettra pas assez en valeur son jardin quand le second polluera trop. Cette situation justifie donc chez Pigou l'intervention publique tandis qu'elle interpelle davantage Coase en raison des coûts de transaction.

Outre la question de la réglementation, la problématique des biens collectifs, publics ou communs pose également la question des droits de propriété ? Quel est le système de droits de propriété le mieux adapté pour assurer de manière efficiente la production et la gestion des biens communs ou des biens collectifs ? On dissocie le régime d'accès libre où il n'y a ni droit, ni contrôle à l'opposé du régime de propriété privée. On distingue encore le régime communautaire (ou de club) avec un accès restreint aux membres de la communauté et le régime de propriété publique où l'État contrôle l'accès aux ressources et leur mode de régulation.

C'est en raison de ces différents régimes de propriété et des diverses conceptions de la réglementation que le débat sur les biens collectifs, communs ou publics au sein de l'Europe est complexe. Autant l'UE-28 est globalement d'accord sur la nécessité de la Défense ou de la protection contre les risques de conflit à l'échelle du continent afin de préserver le bien européen le plus précieux, la paix, autant les manières d'y parvenir, les moyens à allouer, les stratégies à déployer suscitent de nombreuses controverses. En outre, ce qui a trait aux questions de défense ou de sécurité (contre le terrorisme par exemple) ne s'arrête pas aux frontières de l'Europe ? Quelle serait l'efficacité d'une défense comme bien commun si aux frontières extérieures, la menace étrangère devait frapper ? Idem en matière environnementale : la pollution ne s'arrête pas au continent européen. S'il y a une différence essentielle entre ces deux exemples dans la mesure où la Défense doit être conçue, financée, dotée d'une politique de recrutement et de formation, l'environnement n'est pas à construire mais à préserver, il n'en reste pas moins vrai que ces deux biens exigent de régler leur mode de gouvernance, de régulation soit, in fine, leur mode de réglementation.

La temporalité et la territorialité étendues de l'espace européen ainsi que la pluralité des acteurs ne garantissent en rien un accord à 28. L'Union européenne n'a pas de facto une vision commune à propos du champ de l'espace public et du choix des biens collectifs ou des biens communs. Si, malgré tout, les 28 pays venaient à être d'accord sur le choix de l'un d'entre eux, le seraient-ils sur le mode de financement du bien, sur la réglementation à adopter et à faire respecter, sur l'accès totalement ouvert au bien ? Les réponses communes à ces questions permettraient d'avancer vers la détermination des biens communs dont l'Union européenne a urgemment besoin. On aura compris que ce type d'accord exige des compromis politiques autour de la question de la souveraineté nationale, nécessairement limitée face à l'interrogation posée et aux défis à relever.

(publié en ligne mi-octobre 2015)

Equal pay for equal work in the same place!

Isabelle Weykmans

Introduction

The free movement of persons and services within the EU is one of the major achievements of European integration. The mobility of workers and services is generally a good thing for employees and employers and gives Europe's economy a competitive advantage. Directive 96/71/EC concerning the posting of workers was adopted on 16 December 1996 with the aim to guarantee free competition and the rights of posted workers. Now, some 20 years later, EU expansion, numerous decisions by the European Court of Justice and the courts of the Member States, as well as experience and the negative developments seen in various sectors, such as the construction sector and the transport sectors, show that this directive is no longer able to meet needs. Social dumping and social theft are now an everyday phenomenon in the EU and the principle of equal work, equal rights at the same place is no longer possible. For me, as a firm liberal and European, I cannot and will not accept that employers and employees have to suffer from this unfair and at times fraudulent competition in Europe which is sometimes tolerated. Today's economic reality and the inconsistent enforcement of the Directive concerning the posting of workers are contrary to all of the fundamental principles of the Union and of liberal philosophy.

With this publication, I would like to first highlight the shortcomings, provide some examples and attempt to briefly outline the problem. This will show that what we are dealing with is not a classical labour conflict, but instead that the fundamental principles of the Union are at risk and that the support of EU citizens for the EU is dwindling increasingly. Finally, taking Belgium and the Benelux as an example, I want to show how we can address this matter and what a European solution should look like.

Stock-taking

The aim of the Directive concerning the posting of workers is to guarantee a minimum level of protection for temporarily posted workers while at the same time observing the provision contained in Article 56 of the Treaty on the Functioning of the European Union regarding the free movement of services. In practice, this means that every employer is obliged to apply the minimum criteria of the country to which the employee is posted. The minimum criteria must be defined for each sector in legal texts and collective agreements. They determine working hours rules, holiday time rules, minimum wage, etc.

Even with the few, admittedly good, adjustments which have been made by the European legislator, such as the prior checking in the country of origin or the expansion of the employer's responsibility, today's situation remains unsatisfactory and, despite everything, paves the way for social dumping and social fraud.

What does this mean in practice?

There are still legal loopholes.

The directive concerning the posting of workers stipulates that the employer's costs must, however, be paid in the country of origin subject to such country's terms and conditions. This leads to a distortion of competition and, put briefly, means a clear disadvantage for those countries that have a healthy and strong social security network. Furthermore, the country of origin is responsible for adherence to the directive and also for prior checking. There are enormous differences to be found here when it comes to the quality and effectiveness of public authorities and this, once again, puts the other European countries at a disadvantage. The collective agreements in the construction sector, for instance, not only provide for legal claims but also for compensation measures which employers can grant when maximum working hours are temporarily exceeded. If the posted employee exceeds the maximum working hours without receiving any compensation, this too is a distortion of competition.

The fact that there are no provisions for the self-employed nor any penal provisions and sanctions is another legal loophole. A further example of the inconsistency of the directive is the discretionary interpretation of its language.

In an expert report initiated by the European Commission, the Commission criticizes a law from 2012 which permits the Belgian inspection services and courts who detect social fraud to suspend the certificate that enables, for instance, the employer from the country of origin to post his employee. The Commission is of the opinion that this is not in line with the directive concerning the posting of workers. Instead, it believes that only the country of origin can do so. But this is not what happens in practice. Belgium sees this matter differently and is certainly of the opinion that it can work against social fraud on its own territory. The case is underway.

Concrete fraudulent practices:

- The minimum wage is not paid, especially in the cleaning, transport and construction sectors.
- Fictitious companies are set up in other European countries so that employees can be posted at a low wage.
- Brief but regular stays by the posted employee.
- Fake self-employed individuals are hired because they are not subject to the directive.

Some figures from Belgium's National Social Security Office:

The number of foreign or posted employees rose by 20% between 2012 and 2014. The comparison of employees who are posted from Belgium and those who come to Belgium shows a negative result amounting to -88%. In Poland, this figure totals +1389%. This does not include those who are not registered, i.e. illegal workers as well as "self-employed" workers who know nothing about minimum wages. 10% of self-employed workers today are not from Belgium.

The sectors affected are calling attention to the fact that the social fraud practices and competition distortion are having a strong impact on the employment situation in Belgium. Jobs in the transport sector have declined by 4,000 since 2008 and more than 12,000 jobs were lost in the construction sector over the past two and a half years.

This list of examples is endless. The result is that small and medium-sized enterprises are suffering from what is at times unfair competition and that employees, especially from the countries of origin, sometimes have to suffer inhumane conditions.

Belgium's answer and that of the Benelux countries

For some years now, the Belgian state has been very active and is attempting to resolutely fight social fraud by improving Belgian laws, spending more on inspection services and through targeted activities in co-operation with the sectors hardest hit. But these measures, however, only address the tip of the iceberg. Belgium is a pioneer in technological solutions based on joint databases which are used primarily by public agencies and authorities in order to better co-ordinate inspection work. Belgium has good networks with public authorities in other European Member States and co-operates closely with professional and industrial associations. A so-called action plan was adopted last year by the federal government.

On 13 February 2014, Belgium together with the Benelux partners also agreed to assume a leading role in Europe in the fight against social fraud. The idea here is to offer and use the system for electronic recording of worker mobility across borders (LIMOSA) and the experience gained with it, and to offer this to the Benelux and the EU and to expand the system further. Furthermore, sanctions across borders are also to be improved. A European system is also envisaged which would make it possible to trace and verify social security contribution payments in the interest of employees in all EU countries.

Conclusion

Belgium is calling upon the European Commission to make use of or to introduce the above, but also to get to the root of the problem, i.e. to adapt the directive concerning the posting of workers in order to combat social fraud and social dumping and to hence protect the fundamental values of the EU, to strengthen Europe's economy, to protect the rights of European workers and to step up its activities, especially here, in order to improve its image. In mid-June 2015, Belgium's Minister for Labour, together with his colleagues from the Netherlands, Luxembourg, Germany, France, Austria, Sweden and Denmark demanded that the European Commission revise the current directive. A maximum stay period is to be defined for posted workers, the concept of equal work for equal pay is to be applied, and greater co-operation between inspection services is to be achieved through a joint technological solution at European level. The Commissioner in charge has stated that the directive is to be adapted.

It's high time!

In addition to the challenges currently facing our monetary union, it will be the matter of healthy economic development that will put the EU to the test. After all, without economic success, our society will not be able to develop our society further. If we are to efficiently deploy the strengths of the Union on the global economic market, then we will have to put an end to this vicious circle.

And even if the current situation appears to be "helpful" for some individuals, in the medium-term and from a global perspective it will be disastrous for Europe. We have to act in the interest of healthy social and economic development for our Union which serves the interests of its citizens.

(published online early November 2015)

Migration is not the real problem

Hartmut Marhold

The media, and in its wake, public opinion considers the influx of migrants into the European Union as a huge problem, potentially challenging the well-being of the Europeans as a whole, putting into question the way of life we are used to in the European welfare states. Historical comparisons with the migration period, or "Barbarian Invasions" in the late Roman Empire, are frequent; "the boat is full" is a widespread standard phrase for the refusal of more refugees, a (usually unconscious) quotation from a member of the Swiss government, who coined this phrase when opposing more Jews crossing the border from Nazi Germany[2], the "limits of our absorption capacity"[3] have been reached, most of the tabloid press tells us. But what is the real size of the problem in 2015?

The real size of the problem

Most often, absolute figures, varying from single to double, are advanced: one or two million immigrants in the EU, 800.000 or one million in Germany alone, the country which takes in by far the majority of them – in terms of absolute figures. In fact, in proportion to its population, Sweden takes in more immigrants. On face it, figures can seem impressive - but figures are useless and don't tell us anything about the real size of the problem (as already illustrated by the short reference to Germany and Sweden). Figures gain their meaning only in comparison – to other figures about migration, to other figures about demography, population, employment, GDP etc.

On a global scale, there are about 60 million people are refugees currently on the move, according to the UNHCR, at the end of 2014. Close to 40 million of them did not cross the borders of their home country. This is to say that most of the refugees worldwide are living in developing countries and are unable or unwilling to leave their home country.

That is even the case for Syria, where approximately half of the populations, i.e. more than 10 million people, were forced out of their homes;

about 40% of these 10 million left Syria, half of them stayed in Turkey, another quarter in Lebanon, many others in Jordan. 95% of the 2.6 million Afghans who left their country live in Pakistan. Second lesson: Most of those who finally do leave their country end up in the immediate neighbourhood.[4]

Starting from the perspective of the global "refugee crisis", the first conclusion is that 5% of the refugees come to Europe. To put it another way: There might be a huge refugee crisis – but Europe is at the margins of this crisis, and encounters only a very small share of the whole problem.

But we can also look at the numbers of migrants as well from the European side, and start to assess the size of the problem with comparisons between those 5% of global refugees reaching Europe and other European figures, with reference to demography etc.. How big is a figure of one or two million refugees compared to the European population, to national populations? The European Union has approximately 500 million citizens – 2 million (to calculate with the higher estimates of the figures put forward) join them. This is one refugee for every 250 Europeans. In order to make the figures more vivid, we could imagine a beer garden, where 250 people are sitting under the trees, chatting, drinking, eating – one additional guest arrives, looking for a chair and a place at one of the tables. This is the real size of the "problem".

As we know, one of the crucial questions is how to distribute the refugees over the European Union; many member states are reluctant to take any refugees at all. That is why the Council of the European Union voted with a QMV (qualified majority) a distribution plan for 120.000 refugees, on the 22 September, against the opposition of four East Central European countries (Hungary, Slovakia, Czech Republic, Romania)[5]. We should not lose sight of the comparative magnitude: 120.000 refugees for every 500 million Europeans mean approximately one refugee for every 4000 European citizens.

Sweden and Germany are the countries which receive most of the refugees, Sweden proportionally, Germany in absolute figures: Some 190.000 refugees may arrive in Sweden this year, i.e. approximately 2 for every 100 Swedish citizens – twice the rate of Germany, which is expecting between 800.000 and 1 million, i.e. roughly one refugee per 100 citizens. Other countries which do take refugees – like the Netherlands and France – are far below these rates.

So again – this is the realistic picture, the real size of the "problem".

Media driven perception

The media tells us another story, as if it was relating a totally different reality. To start with, the Swedish case, as reflected by the German foreign
broadcast network "Deutsche Welle", looks like this: "Sweden has reached
the breaking point. [...] Sweden has now reached the limit. [...] An extraordinary 190,000 refugees are now expected to arrive in Sweden this year -
double what the agency expected at the start of the year, and more people
than live in Uppsala, the country's fourth largest city. If the predictions are
correct, Sweden will take 20,000 asylum applications per million people
in 2015, double the rate even of Germany. [... Deutsche Welle quotes Anna Kinberg Batra, the leader of Sweden's center-right Moderate Party:] "If
we do not act now, we will have a collapse in the system".[6]

The British "Express" and the Bavarian "Bayern Express" have already
been quoted. An interesting investigation has been conducted on behalf of
Migazin, a network of researchers on "Migration in Germany", addressing
the use of metaphor in media reports on migration.[7] One of the central
findings is that very link to the above quoted phrase "the boat is full":
Many journalists take refuge in metaphors like "waves", "flooding",
"streams" of migrants[8]: "Migrants stream into Croatia in a bid to bypass
Hungary", „Europe is Facing a ‚Great Wave' of Immigration", „Staggering interactive map shows waves of migrants flocking to Europe each day.
The flow of more than a million migrants into Europe has been shown in
these amazing interactive maps", and many more examples are easily
available.

All of these metaphors suggest that migrants are a kind of a natural
catastrophe which nobody can control and which will inevitably do much
damage to those who are exposed to the risk. Moreover, this qualification
(categorisation) of immigration allows us to escape from a proper assessment of the problem – it is presented as a simply overwhelming phenomenon, out of reach and unmanageable by the people, by the Europeans.

It is obvious that the real size of the problem – 250 Europeans receiving
one refugee – is totally different from the media driven perception of public opinion: "Europe is facing a Great Wave of Immigration". The gap between reality and perception is simply staggering.

Politicians' reactions

Politicians in many European countries are visibly tempted to follow the media driven hysteria, instead of reacting according to the real size of the problem. Even the Swedish moderate Anna Kinberg Batra could not withstand this temptation, as quoted above. David Cameron declared: „Britain would be 'overwhelmed' if it opened its doors to every refugee"[9]; Viktor Orban, Hungarian Prime Minister, who erected an armed border wall against migrants, goes one step further and taps into the arsenal of war metaphors: "Refugees 'look like an army', says Hungarian PM Viktor Orban"[10]. It comes as no surprise that Marine le Pen, leader of the French "Front National" takes of this opportunity to affirm her stance: "France is about to be 'submerged' in a 'terrifying' wave of migrants who represent only a 'burden.'"[11] The German leader of the so-called Christian Social Union, the Bavarian branch of the Christian Democratic Party, Horst Seehofer, calls the policy of the Chancellor a "predictable disaster"[12], as various German media recall.

Angela Merkel seems to stand alone with her "welcome policy" (except for representatives of the European Union). When she declared on the 5th of September that the German borders would be open to any refugee, she triggered enthusiasm in a large part of the German public, but, after a short moment of wonder, disenchantment among most of her colleagues all over Europe.

The real big problem, revealed by immigration, is… us

What the comparison between the real size of immigration on the one hand and media driven, politically endorsed perception on the other reveal is that the real problem does not lie with immigration, but with the European Union, its member states, its political class, its media and its societies.

Jean-Claude Juncker is right when he says in his "State of the Union address" before the European Parliament: „It is time to speak frankly about the big issues facing the European Union. Because our European Union is not in a good state. There is not enough Europe in this Union. And there is not enough Union in this Union. We have to change this. And we have to change this now."[13]

Look at the problem under a different, opposite hypothetical premise: If the EU were to be a community of self-confident states and societies, if they would live up to their ambition to act in a united way, pursuing the declared values of the Union – like human dignity, freedom, respect for human rights – showing solidarity ... then the one refugee joining 250 Europeans would not be considered as a problem. In other words, immigration, as it stands, is not the big problem itself, it reveals a big problem within the European Union and its members – they do not have a problem, they are the problem.

Recommendations

A logical consequence of the above is, in the first instance, to turn our perception around and look at Europe and its member states; the big problem lies at their level. Of course, this is not a plea to leave the immigrants without a solution for their lives – there must be an integrated approach to deal with immigration. But it is not very difficult to sketch out such an approach: Their immediate needs (accommodation ...) have to be satisfied, they need education (professional and cultural!), they need jobs ... and this is the best way to integrate them into our societies in a way which would be beneficial for both sides. Even the implementation of this strategy is not just about solving a problem, but about investing in a better performing society.

The really big problems, however, lie with the Europeans themselves, and the main plea of this analysis is to allocate attention to this side of the affair. There is no doubt that the media has to be free in European countries, but there is undeniably a problem with the perceptions of contemporary problems they create. We have to address the problem of media driven false perceptions, which are misleading the behaviour of our societies and their political representatives. One of the problems which contribute to the hysterical overestimation of some problems is the outrageous competition on the market for information. Responsible information should not only be submitted to the rules which apply to any other merchandise. The media should commit itself to rules which curb the run for ever more dramatic, exaggerated and in the end false assessments of real problems.

Secondly, political leadership is required in order to overcome the dramatic shift of large parts of the electorates in many European countries to populist (and worse) parties. It does not come as a surprise that those parties benefit from fear and the perception of threat. They are therefore interested in fostering these attitudes, be it at the price of wrong information, exaggeration and lies. "Listening to the people" has all too often degenerated into an excuse for a lack of leadership and accommodating populist parties, an electoral strategy which is not only immoral, but rarely successful. The original is always more attractive than the copy, and the ones to benefit from this strategy will always be the populists themselves.

Thirdly, and closely linked with the previous recommendation, there is no other way toward a sustainable societal and political future of Europe than to take the commitment to values, which all member states convened upon, seriously. Article 2 (Title 1, Common Provisions) of the Treaty on European Union is as binding as all other articles of a duly ratified and implemented treaty:

The Union is founded on the values of respect for human dignity, freedom, democracy, equality, the rule of law and respect for human rights, including the rights of persons belonging to minorities.

Governments and European institutions have to act in accordance with this (and similar) provisions – the current attitude vis-à-vis the so-called immigration crisis is far from corresponding to this requirement.

Open borders are among the most appreciated achievements of European integration. Freedom of movement is one of the highest values for Europeans, it must go hand in hand with value-based solidarity at the common borders and cannot be sacrificed for the sake of a misguided perception of immigration, for the sake of populist electoral considerations.

Finally, the immigration problem reveals that Europeans, to a large extent, close their eyes to the real world outside the European borders. This has to change, too – globalisation is an irreducible fact, and Europe greatly benefits from it. But there is no way to deny the consequences: Europe has to act united beyond its borders, in order to prevent the societal and political failure of a whole neighbouring region (the Mediterranean, the Middle East, and beyond). There is no way Europe can retrench behind new iron curtains, and there is no reason to do so: Europe is strong enough to turn globalization to its advantage, if it is willing to do so.

References

1) Migration understood as the sum of immigrants, asylum seekers, and refugees – there is not the difference between these categories, of relevance here.

2) Eduard von Steiger, 30 August 1942.

3) Express, 29 September 2015; http://www.express.co.uk/news/world/608656/ Germany-migrant-backtrack; Bayernkurier, 14 October 2015; https:// www.bayernkurier.de/inland/6650-grenzen-setzen

4) UNHCR: World at War. Global Trends. Forced Displacement in 2014; http:// unhcr.org/556725e69.html; UNHCR: http://data.unhcr.org/syrianrefugees/region-al.php, as of 23 June 06 2015; more recent UNHCR data, especially for the Mediterranean: http://data.unhcr.org/mediterranean/regional.php

5) The Financial Times called the vote, which conforms with the procedures agreed upon and implemented with the European Treaties "EU Ministers force through refugee quota plan"; ft.com/cms/s/0/76c2dd9e-6111-11e5-9846-de406ccb37f2.html; for the Council decision see the Commission's press release: http://europa.eu/rapid/ press-release_STATEMENT-15-5697_de.htm

6) Deutsche Welle: Sweden hits refugee crisis zero hour; 20 November 2015; http:// www.dw.com/en/sweden-hits-refugee-crisis-zero-hour/a-18863702

7) http://www.migazin.de/2015/11/18/metaphern-fluechtlinge-wir-wellen-flut/

8) Express again is at the forefront of this type of journalism: „Staggering interactive map shows wave of migrants flocking to Europe each day. The flow of more than a million migrants into Europe has been shown in these amazing interactive maps"; Express 30 October 2015; http://www.express.-co.uk/news/world/615542/Stagger-ing-interactive-map-shows-wave-of-migrants-flocking-to-Europe-eachday;
France24 is another example: http://www.-france24.com/en/20150926-migrants-stream-croatia-serbia-hungary-refugees, and there are many more. An American one is Nicholas M. Gallagher: The European Immigration Crisis: Europe is Facing a "Great Wave" of Immigration; The American Interest, 28 August 2015;http:// www.the-american-interest.com/2015/08/28/europe-is-facing-a-great-wave-of-im-migration/

9) The Independent, 7 October 2015; http://www.independent.co.uk/news/uk/politics/ david-cameron-britain-would-be-overwhelmed-if-it-opened-its-doors-toevery-refugee-a6684541.html

10) The Guardian, 23 October 2015; http://www.theguardian.com/world/2015/oct/23/ refugees-look-like-an-army-says-hungarian-pm-viktor-orban

11) Quoted (for linguistic reasons) from The New York Times, 5 October 2015; http:// www.nytimes.com/2015/10/06/world/europe/for-marine-le-pen-migration-is-a-ready-made-issue.html?_r=0

12) Horst Seehofer: Kollaps mit Ansage, 3 October 2015, quoted by Focus, Spiegel online, N24 and others.

13) Jean-Claude Juncker: State of the Union 2015, 9 September 2015; http:// ec.europa.eu/priorities/soteu/- docs/state_of_the_union_2015_en.pdf

(published online mid-November 2015)

Penser le fédéralisme dans un monde globalisé

Frédéric Lépine

Depuis une quinzaine d'années, le fédéralisme semble connaître un renouveau dans la réflexion politique. Après avoir été cantonné pendant longtemps, sur le plan analytique à l'étude comparée des États fédéraux, et sur le plan européen à un idéal dont il était inutile de construire les contours précis, la réflexion s'est ensuite largement étendue sur ce qu'il fallait entendre par fédéralisme dans le contexte actuel de globalisation des sociétés post-industrialisées, sur le plan culturel, économique, et finalement politique. Cependant, cette réflexion est loin d'être encore aboutie. Comme l'indiquent Gaudreault-DesBiens et Gélinas :

> Le fédéralisme est pour ainsi dire condamné à évoluer et à se complexifier, à mesure que l'État auquel il est associé lui aussi évolue et se complexifie. […] Peut-on […] séparer conceptuellement ces frères siamois que sont le fédéralisme et l'État et que la doctrine classique déclarait jadis inséparables ? Pareille interrogation renvoie à la nécessité de penser, ou plutôt d'*impenser*, le phénomène fédéral dans un cadre théorique qui serait plus large que celui, essentiellement institutionnel, de la réflexion sur l'organisation de l'État.[1]

C'est à cette démarche que souhaite s'atteler le présent article, en ouvrant quelques portes sur les nouvelles façons d'envisager le fédéralisme à l'ère du monde globalisé, et d'en identifier certains écueils.

Impenser le fédéralisme

De manière générale, depuis la Seconde Guerre mondiale et jusqu'à la première décennie du XXIe siècle, l'approche du fédéralisme s'est faite à partir des États fédéraux et de leur comparaison. Cela correspond à une période historique. Au cours de cette époque, la souveraineté des États semblait un fait acquis, et les principales réalisations du fédéralisme s'inscrivaient dans le cadre de ceux-ci. En outre, l'idée de confédération, au moins dans l'utilisation de la terminologie, relevait du passé.

Ainsi, lorsque l'on évoquait le fédéralisme comme finalité de la construction européenne, on se référait à une idée générale — faisant parfois référence aux « États-Unis d'Europe » — et on insistait surtout sur le caractère original, *sui generis*, de cette construction, avant que la langue française puis la langue anglaise ne s'approprient le terme de « supranationalité ». Il est à noter, de surcroît, que les premières tentatives d'analyse des institutions issues de la construction européenne à partir d'une démarche relevant du fédéralisme comparé ne débutent, à l'exception de quelques pionniers, qu'à la fin des années 1980, et que leur intérêt est toujours contesté aujourd'hui.[2]

Pourtant, dès la fin de la Seconde Guerre mondiale, on pouvait trouver les signes clairs d'une transformation de l'organisation du monde, à travers le développement d'organisations internationales, comprises d'abord comme des forums de discussion, puis comme des organismes de coopération politique et économique. Cependant, le modèle de la séparation du monde en deux niveaux d'analyse, l'État-nation souverain d'une part, et les relations internationales entre États souverainement indépendants d'autre part, imprégnaient encore trop les esprits pour prendre pleine conscience de cette évolution.

Il faut donc reconstruire l'idée de fédéralisme dans un contexte qui dépasse celui, chronologiquement daté, de l'État-nation. C'est donc tout d'abord à une démarche de constructivisme historique qu'il faut procéder.

Pour cela, il est nécessaire de redéfinir le concept d'entité politique au-delà de l'idée d'État. Une réponse à cet égard est apportée par le concept innovant de Jean Baechler, qui propose une définition d'entité politique transhistorique, sous le néologisme de « politie ». La *politie* est « un groupe humain institutionnalisé, avec une tendance interne à la pacification et une virtualité externe à la violence ».[3] Une telle définition permet d'envisager les évolutions politiques sur le long terme, en se détachant du concept d'État. Il est alors possible d'envisager l'évolution historique du fédéralisme en rapport avec des agrégats politiques de nature différente, suivant les structures sociétales auxquelles ils doivent s'adapter.

Dans un premier temps, avant l'ère de la modernité politique dont on trouve les prémices dès la Renaissance, le fédéralisme se caractérise comme une union de polities. Ceci correspond à la racine étymologique du mot, qui renvoie au mot du bas latin *foedus*, signifiant contrat ou pacte. Dans cette première approche historique, le fédéralisme concerne des entités politiques qui s'unissent contractuellement, tout en préservant leurs spécificités sociales et culturelles, pour des raisons avant tout de défense militaire. L'économie n'entre pas encore en ligne de compte. En effet, la production de biens et services était jusqu'à la Renaissance principalement caractérisée par une économie de subsistance.

Avec l'entrée dans la modernité, et le développement d'États souverains, puis d'États-nations, une nouvelle forme d'organisation de nature fédérale va voir le jour : la *politie de polities*. Cette nouvelle approche du fédéralisme, adaptée au concept de souveraineté qui s'est peu à peu imposé, trouvera l'origine de son développement dans la Convention de Philadelphie de 1787 et la rédaction de la constitution des États-Unis d'Amérique. Ce qui n'était, dans l'esprit des négociateurs américains, qu'une forme de « marchandage » entre les partisans d'un seul État américain plus centralisé, et ceux qui défendaient les prérogatives des treize anciennes colonies britanniques, s'est transformé en modèle d'organisation politique qui s'imposera à chaque fois qu'il paraîtra nécessaire d'assurer, au sein d'un État souverain, une forme d'unité dans la diversité, ou, pour reprendre l'expression de Daniel Elazar, une combinaison de *self-rule* et *shared rule*.[4]

Dans le contexte historique à partir duquel nous opérons cette analyse, cette approche du fédéralisme reste encore dominante, le monde étant toujours juridiquement découpé selon les territoires de la souveraineté. Il semble toutefois nécessaire de sortir du « corset de la souveraineté » pour comprendre les effets du processus de globalisation du monde, avec toutes les interdépendances que cela crée (en particulier dans les pays les plus industrialisés) pour l'évolution des structures politiques.

Vers un réseau de polities : le troisième âge du fédéralisme

L'article fondateur de la réflexion sur le fédéralisme dans le monde contemporain de la globalisation est celui que Daniel Elazar rédigera pour la revue Publius en 1995. Son titre est en soi particulièrement évocateur : « From Statism To Federalism : A Paradigm Shift. »[5] L'auteur y évoque les changements du monde apparus depuis la fin de la guerre froide et la chute des régimes communistes en Europe. Il y perçoit une modification progressive et profonde de l'organisation du monde, où la souveraineté sera progressivement remplacée par un jeu de coopération entre acteurs multiples. On pourra synthétiser son approche par la métaphore du modèle matriciel, qu'il oppose au modèle de pouvoir pyramidal ou au modèle centre-périphérie, pour indiquer que, dans les nouvelles approches du monde contemporain, le pouvoir perdra de sa centralité et de sa hiérarchie, et tendra à se diffuser entre différents lieux de pouvoir non hiérarchisés.[6] Le décès de cet auteur, quatre ans plus tard, nous empêche cependant de savoir dans quel sens il aurait pu approfondir sa réflexion.

À la même époque, l'article de Gary Marks, « Structural policy and *Multi-level governance* in the EC »[7], propose une nouvelle terminologie pour aborder les évolutions des structures contemporaines, à travers le concept de gouvernance multiniveaux (multi-level governance). Le prétexte à la présentation de cette nouvelle approche se trouve dans la réforme des fonds structurels du traité de Maastricht, qui aborde pour la première fois la possibilité pour une entité supranationale d'entrer directement en contact avec une entité infranationale. À travers cette nouvelle terminologie, on peut cependant retrouver facilement une perception au sens large du fédéralisme. Marks et Hooghe confirmeront par la suite le lien entre fédéralisme et gouvernance multiniveaux[8], et divers auteurs accepteront l'idée d'une généalogie claire entre les deux idées, la gouvernance multiniveaux ne faisant que renvoyer, avec une nouvelle sémantique dépourvue de connotation négative, à une vision du fédéralisme incluant les relations entre les entités politiques incluses dans les états souverains et les organisations dites « internationales ».[9]

C'est à partir de ces deux articles fondateurs que nous pouvons évoquer l'idée que le fédéralisme entre dans un « troisième âge » comme un réseau de polities, en considérant la *gouvernance multiniveaux* comme une expression de sa plus récente évolution.

Le troisième âge du fédéralisme et ses nouveaux défis

Comprendre le fédéralisme, c'est d'abord dépasser l'idée que le fédéralisme doit être perçu comme un concept qui trouve son application principale dans le cadre des États modernes. De même, comprendre le fédéralisme, c'est accepter que les nouveaux modèles d'organisation que l'on peut appeler de gouvernance multiniveaux ou de supranationalité ne sont pas des réalités particulières *sui generis*, mais bien les premières concrétisations d'une nouvelle forme d'organisation politique qui trouve sa place dans la complexité de la globalisation, celle d'une organisation en réseaux, qui échappe progressivement à la stricte hiérarchie des organisations.

Le fédéralisme semble donc commencer un troisième âge, celui des réseaux de polities. En suivant Elazar, il ne s'agit pas ici de promouvoir une nouvelle forme d'organisation, mais simplement de constater un changement progressif dans les structures institutionnelles politiques et dans leur hiérarchie. On se fonde sur l'hypothèse que les sociétés post-industrialisées ont atteint un tel niveau de complexité communicationnelle qu'elles ne peuvent plus être gérées par l'organisation de l'État souverain, fondé sur une structure pyramidale légale-rationnelle inadaptée à la communication en réseaux.

Une fois posée l'hypothèse de l'entrée du fédéralisme dans un troisième âge — sans y voir une portée téléologique—, il est nécessaire d'envisager les nouveaux questionnements qui peuvent résulter de cette nouvelle forme d'organisation. Une nouvelles forme d'organisation suppose de nouveaux défis, et de nouvelles approches qui en résultent.

Le premier défi est celui de la *coopération* entre ces acteurs. Au sein de l'État souverain, ou dans les relations entre ceux-ci, le rapport contractualiste est avant tout fondé sur la volonté de coopération.[10] Si la volonté de coopération n'est pas présente dans l'ordre interne des États souverains, alors la hiérarchie du pouvoir s'impose. Dans l'ordre externe des relations internationales, c'est plutôt la fermeture des communications politiques qui s'impose ; et, dans le cas extrême, la guerre qui se substitue alors à la coopération.

Dans une structure politique en réseau, où l'idée de l'État souverain considéré comme autosuffisant s'estompe, les formes de coopérations s'imposent dans tous les domaines, sans que les polities en tant que telles ne puissent facilement imposer leur volonté, et sans qu'une autorité régulatrice suprême ne soit présente.

Le deuxième défi est celui de la *fonctionnalisation croissante* des relations en réseau. Un mode d'organisation en réseau utilise les différents lieux de pouvoir dans leur capacité à répondre à des besoins fonctionnels. Il crée notamment des institutions temporaires ou permanentes en fonction des nécessités. C'est ce que Hooghe et Marks identifient par la distinction entre la gouvernance multiniveaux de type I, qui s'appuie sur des institutions de compétence générale, et la gouvernance multiniveaux de type II, qui crée les instances en fonction des besoins.[11] Auprès de gouvernements de compétences générales, fondées sur un *demos* de nature politique — par exemple une nation — ou administrative, peuvent ainsi s'agréger une constellation complexe d'institutions (ou *agencies*) *ad hoc*, qui brouillent la capacité d'une gestion politique générale coordonnée.

Enfin, et complémentairement, un troisième défi est celui de la *transparence* et de la *responsabilité* de la gestion démocratique, rendues plus difficiles par la multiplication des instances de décision. Dans le contexte d'une organisation en réseau, l'absence d'instance régulatrice générale fondée sur un *demos* clairement identifié, peut faire disparaître en grande partie la responsabilité démocratique. Peters et Pierre évoquent ainsi l'existence d'un pacte faustien (*Faustian bargain*), où les valeurs fondamentales de la démocratie sont abandonnées au profit de la recherche de compromis, de consensus et d'efficacité.[12]

Les réponses à ces défis ne peuvent se trouver que dans une redéfinition des instances de contrôle démocratique, au risque de les voir disparaître dans un système de domination des groupes d'intérêt particuliers, susceptibles de communications informelles à même de contourner les instances de décision formalisées.

Conclusions

Au terme de ce bref parcours de l'évolution des structures fédérales, il peut être utile d'évoquer les objectifs des principaux pères fondateurs de la pensée fédéraliste au lendemain de la Seconde Guerre mondiale. Tous cherchaient à dépasser l'État-nation, considéré comme l'un des principaux vecteurs des conflits mondiaux. Pour Altiero Spinelli, dès le Manifeste de Ventotene, c'est la nature belliqueuse de l'État souverain qui est à l'origine des conflits mondiaux. Pour Alexandre Marc et Denis de Rougemont, c'est le carcan idéologique de l'État qui pose problème, en ce qu'il est réducteur et destructeur de l'identité de la personne humaine. Rougemont indiquera même que, contre toutes les idéologies réductrices, le « fédéralisme est l'amour de la complexité ».[13]

La complexité qui accompagne le processus de globalisation mondiale est cependant bien éloignée de ce que préconisait Rougemont. Les penseurs du fédéralisme de la construction européenne, s'ils voulaient réduire le rôle de l'État souverain, ont toujours envisagé l'existence d'une entité régulatrice supérieure en charge d'assurer un système de valeurs au sein de la fédération, quelle qu'en soit la forme.

La forme que semblent prendre les sociétés « postmodernes » se rapproche aujourd'hui davantage de la prédiction de Francis Fukuyama. Comme celui-ci le précisait dans un commentaire écrit plus d'une dizaine d'années après son ouvrage *The End of History and the Last Man* (1992) :

> The End of History was never linked to a specifically American model of social or political organisation. Following Alexandre Kojève, the Russian-French philosopher who inspired my original argument, I believe that the Eu-

ropean Union more accurately reflects what the world will look like at the end of history than the contemporary United States. The EU's attempt to transcend sovereignty and traditional power politics by establishing a transnational rule of law is much more in line with a "post-historical" world than the Americans' continuing belief in God, national sovereignty, and their military.[14]

On peut cependant se demander si Fukuyama n'a pas surestimé la capacité d'un système libéral à créer cet « État de droit transnational » et à conforter la démocratie libérale à travers le monde.

Le fédéralisme, à quelque époque que ce soit, n'est jamais qu'un principe d'organisation adapté à la complexité des structures sociétales dans lesquelles il se développe. Il se met au service de valeurs mais ne peut pas les définir par lui-même.

Ainsi, si l'on revient à la démocratie, et au-delà des discussions sur le devenir et l'importance de l'identité européenne, c'est avant tout une nouvelle forme de contrôle de la décision politique qu'il faut aujourd'hui inventer. Pour établir ces nouvelles formes de contrôle démocratique, il faut définir et imposer un système de valeurs à la fois hérité du passé et adapté aux nouvelles contraintes structurelles historiques. C'est tout l'enjeu de la définition du « bien public européen ».

Sources :

1. Jean-François Gaudreault-DesBiens and Fabien Gélina, eds., *The States and Moods of Federalism: Governance, Identity and Methodology - Le fédéralisme dans tous ses états : gouvernance, identité et méthodologie* (Cowansville [Quebec] : Éditions Yvon Blais [with Bruylant], 2005), 4.

2. R. Daniel Kelemen and Kalypso Nicolaidis, "Bringing Federalism Back In," in *Handbook of European Union Politics* ed. Knud Erik Jorgensen, Mark A. Pollack and Ben Rosamond (London: Sage Publication, 2007).

3. Jean Baechler, in : Vlad Constantinesco and Stéphane Pierré-Caps, *Droit constitutionnel*, 5e ed., Thémis Droit (Paris : Presses universitaires de France, 2011), 6

4. Par exemple: Daniel J. Elazar, *Exploring Federalism* (Tuscaloosa (AL): The University of Alabama Press, 1987).

5. Daniel J. Elazar, "From Statism To Federalism: A Paradigm Shift," *Publius: The Journal of Federalism* 25, no. 2 Spring (1995).

6. Elazar, *Exploring Federalism*, 35-38.

7. Gary Marks, "Structural policy and Multi-level governance in the EC," in *The State of the European Community: The Maastricht Debate and Beyond*, ed. Alan W. Cafruny and Glenda G. Rosenthal, State of the European Community; vol. 2 (Boulder (Colorado), Harlow (England): Lynne Rienner Publishers, Longman, 1993).

8. Liesbeth Hooghe and Gary Marks, "Unraveling the Central State, but How? Types of Multi-level Governance," *American Political Science Review* 97, no. 2 (2003), 236

9. Pour de plus amples informations sur le lien entre fédéralisme et gouvernance multi-niveaux, nous renvoyons à notre article : Frédéric Lépine, "A Journey through the History of Federalism: Is Multilevel Governance a Form of Federalism?," *L'Europe en formation* 53, no. 363 (2012).

10. Voir: Michael Burgess, *In Search of the Federal Spirit: New Theoretical and Empirical Perspectives in Comparative Federalism* (Oxford: Oxford University Press, 2012), 19-28. Frédéric Lépine, "Federalism: essence, values and ideologies," in *Understanding Federalism and Federation*, ed. Alain-G. Gagnon, Soeren Keil and Sean Mueller, Federalism Studies (Farnham (Surrey): Ashgate, 2015).

11. Hooghe and Marks, "Unraveling the Central State, but How?."

12. B. Guy Peters and Jon Pierre, "Multi-level Governance and Democracy: A Faustian Bargain?," in *Multi-level Governance*, ed. Ian Bache and Matthew Flinders (Oxford: Oxford University Press, 2004).

13. Denis de Rougemont, "L'attitude fédéraliste," *Rapport du premier congrès annuel de l'Union européenne des Fédéralistes* (Montreux, août 1947, Genève).

14. Francis Fukuyama, "The History at the End of History," *The Guardian*, 3 April 2007 http://www.guardian.co.uk/commentisfree/2007/apr/03/thehistoryattheendofhist.

(publié en ligne début décembre 2015)

L'avenir de l'Euro?

Jean-Claude Vérez

Cette note de réflexion[1] est un peu particulière puisqu'elle est inspirée de l'ouvrage de *Philippe Maystadt, L'Euro en question(s), paru en 2015 aux éditions Avant-propos*. L'auteur a pour objectif majeur d'apporter des réponses précises à ceux qui doutent et/ou critiquent l'euro. Il n'est pas interdit bien entendu de s'opposer à la monnaie unique ou de nier les problèmes rencontrés mais de là à considérer que les difficultés actuelles au sein de l'Union européenne et particulièrement de la zone euro sont dues à la monnaie unique, il y a un pas que Philippe Maystadt ne veut pas et ne peut pas franchir. D'emblée, il faut préciser que c'est l'UEM qui est au cœur des préoccupations de l'ouvrage et non l'UE à 28. De fait, le Brexit n'est pas abordé puisque la sortie éventuelle du Royaume-Uni ne concerne que l'UE.

Les faits sont là : la crise n'est pas finie, le chômage perdure, la croissance reste faible, la pauvreté ne recule pas. Il faut tenter de trouver des solutions pour un avenir européen plus prospère, plus solidaire, et qui doit éviter tout repli sur lui-même. La croissance ne suffira pas à résoudre les problèmes macroéconomiques cités. Il faut accompagner la politique monétaire commune de la zone euro par une discipline budgétaire plus volontariste, une union bancaire, l'instauration d'un budget de la zone euro, un traitement collectif de la dette, une convergence renforcée tout en apportant des progrès en matière sociale, démocratique dans un contexte de plus forte solidarité.

Il est utile de rappeler que les fondements de la monnaie unique s'inscrivent dans l'une des étapes des processus d'intégration régionale qu'est l'Union économique et monétaire. Le projet européen aurait pu « se contenter » d'une étape moins contraignante telle la zone de libre échange comme c'est le cas de l'ALENA. Le projet de l'UEM et de l'euro est plus ambitieux et de nature plus politique qu'économique. Les « arguments » dénonçant la perte de souveraineté dans le domaine monétaire du fait de la création de la BCE ne sont guère convaincants car la plupart des banques centrales européennes étaient depuis longtemps à la fois interdépendantes et « soumises » à la Bundesbank. Elles étaient encore tenues par la politique monétaire de la FED depuis que le système de Bretton-Woods avait choisi ou imposé le dollar comme monnaie centrale du nouveau SMI. Les débats après guerre entre l'américain White et le britannique Keynes à propos de la position asymétrique dont allait bénéficier l'économie et la monnaie américaine sont à cet égard riches d'enseignements. Le second proposait la création d'une monnaie mondiale et d'une banque centrale mondiale.

Une autre asymétrie se trouve au coeur de l'UEM : d'un côté, on a instauré une politique monétaire centralisée, de l'autre, on a laissé les politiques économiques aux mains des États-nations. Il y avait pourtant des voix qui proposaient d'introduire dans le traité de Maastricht l'idée d'un gouvernement économique. Les Allemands y voyaient une remise en cause de l'indépendance de la BCE. Ces divers points de vue nous renvoient à l'opposition entre les partisans et les détracteurs du « tout » marché. Ou du moins de son côté autorégulateur, qui est acquis pour les premiers et, inversement, un leurre pour les seconds. La crise récente déclenchée aux USA et étendue en Europe, montre les limites de la première option.

Pour aller de l'avant, il est souhaitable d'envisager une *discipline budgétaire* qui serait l'émanation des institutions européennes et non d'un seul État membre. Sans en faire un dogme, elle reste supérieure au laxisme d'où l'intérêt d'un encadrement européen renforcé des politiques budgétaires. Que ce soit à propos des dettes, notamment de leur évolution, des procédures (plus strictes) ou des sanctions (plus crédibles), les décisions récentes marquent un progrès. Pour autant, ce progrès ne suffit pas. Toute politique économique repose a minima sur trois piliers majeurs : une politique monétaire, une politique budgétaire et une politique fiscale. Viennent s'ajouter les politiques industrielle, sociale, etc. L'harmonisation ou la convergence des politiques budgétaires serait un pas important ; ce serait mieux encore si elle était suivie d'une harmonisation des politiques fiscales et sociales.

Une *union bancaire*, autre enjeu majeur, a été décidée par le Conseil européen du 14 décembre 2012, suite à la crise financière des années 2007-2008, au comportement laxiste de certaines banques et à la hausse considérable des risques systémiques. Sans qu'il soit nécessaire de rappeler qu'en la matière trop de régulation vaut mieux qu'une absence de régulation, les défis restent nombreux : améliorer la qualité de la supervision, rapprocher les normes prudentielles, instaurer un système commun de garantie des dépôts.

La discipline budgétaire et l'union bancaire exigent *un budget de la zone euro*, ne serait-ce que pour aider à absorber les chocs asymétriques. Une telle décision permettrait une convergence + ou a minima + un rapprochement des recettes budgétaires (soit des recettes fiscales) et des dépenses. Il n'y a pas d'avenir possible sans budget, que ce soit au niveau de l'UE ou de la zone euro ; il n'y a pas de budget sans politique fiscale ; la pertinence de celle-ci dans un contexte d'union monétaire est vaine si chaque pays membre reste souverain en matière fiscale. Le cas irlandais est de ce point de vue exemplaire : le taux d'imposition sur les sociétés, plutôt faible, décidé par les autorités pour attirer des capitaux diverge des taux français et allemand bien plus élevés. Cela n'empêche pas l'Irlande de bénéficier des transferts européens financés par le budget européen. En outre, quand la crise sévit, l'Irlande asphyxiée, demande aux européens une aide immédiate. Dans d'autres situations, on associerait un tel comportement à celui de passager clandestin (free rider).

Le défi budgétaire est indissociable du problème de *la dette*. Question épineuse s'il en est : elle est au coeur des préoccupations relatives à la souveraineté. Mais, dès lors que des pays ont décidé d'avoir une monnaie unique, comment imaginer un seul instant que l'un d'entre eux puisse + le cas échéant + mettre en péril la zone monétaire du fait d'une dette élevée, difficile à financer voire à rembourser ? Le poids différencié des dettes nationales rapporté au PIB est une préoccupation majeure. Outre le fait que les niveaux d'endettement ont des causes multiples, l'écart entre d'un côté, une monnaie unique et une BCE, et de l'autre, des politiques budgétaires, fiscales nationales est intenable. L'urgence est de contenir les dettes et de déployer une solidarité entre pays de la zone euro, sans inciter les comportements de passager clandestin. Une mutualisation des dettes publiques + limitée et temporaire + est une piste à creuser. Il conviendrait que les pays « riches » de la zone euro l'acceptent ou du moins l'entendent étant entendu que leur niveau de richesses provient en grande partie du commerce intra-européen !

La nouvelle architecture de la zone euro pourrait encore reposer sur *la convergence économique*. L'une des critiques justifiées à l'égard de la zone euro est le fait qu'une zone monétaire (et a fortiori une monnaie unique) ne peuvent aboutir que si et seulement si les rythmes de croissance et les niveaux de productivité se rapprochent. À défaut, les écarts se creusent et les positions asymétriques des économies domestiques membres de la zone et utilisant la même monnaie créent des déséquilibres majeurs. La convergence économique permettrait par ailleurs d'amortir les chocs cycliques et serait cohérente avec l'harmonisation des politiques budgétaires et fiscales.

Le futur du projet européen ne peut « se contenter » d'objectifs économiques. *La dimension sociale du projet, la solidarité entre les États et la légitimité démocratique doivent devenir des priorités.* En matière de dimension sociale, il est essentiel que les européens se sentent davantage concernés par la construction européenne. Le pragmatisme prévaut : l'UE pas plus que la zone euro n'a permis d'enrayer les inégalités, les pauvretés, l'exclusion, la misère, etc. Lutter contre ces fléaux passe entre autre par la réduction du chômage. Une fois cela précisé, il faut mener selon nous une grande réflexion sur les causes et les remèdes des maux cités afin qu'une politique sociale plutôt convergente ait des chances d'aboutir. L'avenir européen, peu peuplée, dans une économie mondialisée de plus en plus peuplée, n'a guère de perspectives s'il n'intègre pas ses jeunes. Leur taux de chômage est dramatique, notamment pour les moins diplômés et les moins qualifiés. Les mêmes interrogations valent pour les seniors, de plus en plus tôt exclus du marché du travail, faute de compétences supposées (ou avérées) insuffisantes, dans un contexte démographique par ailleurs vieillissant qui pose deux questions cruciales : le financement des retraites et la dépendance du quatrième âge. Il est possible de progresser si les autorités nationales et européennes coopèrent, si les partenaires sociaux sont davantage consultés, si la société civile s'en mêle. Il faut répondre à des questions clés : quelle politique sociale faut-il choisir pour limiter les problèmes cités ? Comment serait-elle financée ? Comment juger de son efficacité et/ou de son équité ?

La solidarité entre les États pourrait « copier » la solidarité des régions d'un même pays, comme c'est plutôt le cas en France ou en Allemagne où la « loi fondamentale » oblige la fédération à garantir des conditions de vie similaires partout dans le pays. On peut y opposer une autre conception pour laquelle les règles adoptées d'un commun accord doivent être respectées, ce qui évite ex post toute solidarité ? Dit autrement, si la Grèce avait respecté les critères de Maastricht comme d'autres pays, elle n'aurait pas subi pareille crise et n'aurait pas eu besoin de la « solidarité » européenne. C'est faute de responsabilité et de loyauté vis à vis de ses partenaires que la Grèce s'est retrouvée en quasi faillite. Si on ne peut légitimer l'irresponsabilité (c'est au contraire le principe de solidarité qui exige la responsabilité car il engage et concerne tous les partenaires), il reste que des chocs exogènes peuvent toujours survenir (cf. la crise financière) et frapper différemment les pays solidaires … ex ante !

Pour finir, l'auteur réclame « un renforcement du contrôle démocratique » et a le mérite de rappeler certains des propos ou remarques de Jürgen Habermas pour qui il y a urgence à dissocier souveraineté du peuple et souveraineté de l'État : dès lors que la première dépend conceptuellement de la seconde, elle bloque toute pensée, toute perspective. Si Philippe Maystadt n'est pas convaincu que l'approche intergouvernementale puisse satisfaire l'intérêt collectif européen car le réflexe national est « naturel », notamment en cas de litige, l'approche fédéraliste (qui permet un transfert des compétences étatiques à une instance supranationale) ne doit pas porter atteinte aux droits des citoyens. Il conviendrait donc de renforcer le contrôle parlementaire, de constituer une commission de la zone euro au sein du Parlement qui exercerait un contrôle sur les décisions de la Commission et du Conseil et, enfin, d'instaurer une conférence associant les représentants des commissions concernées des parlements nationaux et européens, une sorte de conférence interparlementaire de l'UEM.

L'avenir de l'Europe n'est pas acquis mais il n'est pas anecdotique : il est primordial. Il est notamment lié à la zone euro qui devrait être dotée d'instruments de prévention et de gestion des crises. Une Convention de l'UEM comprenant la pluralité d'acteurs cités pourrait aider à la décision dès lors que la non-ratification d'un traité par un État vaudrait notification de la volonté de quitter l'UEM.

[1.] Enrichie par les remarques d'Hartmut Marhold que je remercie.

(publié en ligne mi-avril 2016)

The European "Area of Freedom, Security and Justice" – three fundamental dilemmas

Hartmut Marhold

1. The "Area of Freedom, Security and Justice" – its way toward the heart of European integration

Three pillars, three crises. The European "Area of Freedom, Security and Justice" is at the heart of the latest EU crisis, the "migration" or "refugee" crisis – indeed, all three terms in the title are relevant here with this problem or, to be precise, all four: Because "area" itself is a doubtful category for a political system. If we apply the Maastricht pillar trilogy – still apparently well known - , one might say that the financial, economic and state debt crisis affected the first pillar, focusing on economic integration, whereas the Ukraine-Russia crisis had much to do with the second pillar, i.e. foreign, security and defence policy. The migration crisis, then, puts into question the third pillar, "Justice and Home Affairs", to use the Maastricht terminology – the "Area of Freedom, Security and Justice" (AFSJ), as it became known after the Amsterdam Treaty (1997/1999).

Schengen and Dublin. This "Area" of policy has come a long way before arriving at the core of the European Union. It started with just a few countries, and outside the then existing treaties. "Schengen" and "Dublin" are still in use to designate some of the central features of the system: "Schengen" started at that small Luxembourg border city in 1985 with five countries convening upon the abolishment of their borders with each other: France, the Federal Republic of Germany and the three Benelux countries. Five years later, they concluded a "Convention" laying down the principles of such an "area" without borders, and another five years later, in 1995, the border controls fell completely/once and for all: a hugely hailed achievement, visible and appalling for every citizen who crossed what was no longer a border after this moment. "Dublin" went a similar way: Launched in 1990, it aimed at common rules regarding asylum, i.e. the treatment of immigrants fleeing to Europe from threat, war, torture and distress.

From Maastricht's "Third Pillar" to the "Area of Freedom, Security and Justice". The Maastricht treaty took these perspectives already into account, by creating the "Third Pillar" without, however, including "Schengen" and "Dublin" in the treaty itself. It is only with the Amsterdam Treaty, in 1997, that two important steps were taken in order to integrate the open border and common migration/asylum policies into the EU Treaty: The "third pillar" was renamed more prominently "Area of Freedom, Security and Justice" and some of the various sectoral policies covered by this large denomination were transferred from a purely intergovernmental sphere into the so-called "community method", marked by the supranational decision making, which characterised the "first pillar". This move triggered four structural consequences of great impact: First, an extraordinary European Council meeting at the Finnish city of Tampere further developed a programme of implementation of the Amsterdam Treaty in general terms. Secondly, this implementation dynamic led to quinquennial "action programmes" – after Tampere in 1999, it was The Hague in 2004 and Stockholm in 2009. Thirdly, hundreds of legal acts trickled down from these action programmes, creating an important share of the "aquis communautaire". Fourthly, no less than nine "agencies" saw the light of day, mandated to execute, promote, control and survey the various policies in the field of AFSJ, among them such important ones as "Frontex" and "Europol".

Lisbon: AFSJ is fully submitted to the "community method". The last important step in the evolution of AFSJ toward the heart of the EU before the current crisis was the Lisbon Treaty, which fully integrated all AFSJ policies into the "ordinary legislative procedure", i.e. put a definite end to intergovernmental cooperation in this field. AFSJ is now submitted to decision making marked by the Commission's right of initiative, by Qualified Majority Voting (QMV) in the Council and the equal right of the European Parliament to vote any legal measure under Title V of the Treaty on the Functioning of the European Union, that is the "Area of Freedom, Security and Justice". Consequently, in 2014 – five years after the Stockholm action programme, but now under the provisions of the Lisbon Treaty – there is no more "action programme", but "strategic guidelines" laying down the project for ASFJ legislation for the ensuing five years.

Differentiated participation. However, whereas the full integration into the "community method" has been achieved, things are still much more difficult with regard to the participation of EU member states and other countries. Some EU member states do not participate in the open border system ("Schengen", those who stay apart are the UK and Ireland, in earlier years Denmark, too), some are member states, but are, for the time being, refusing to participate (Romania, Bulgaria, Croatia and Cyprus), whereas three European countries, which are not member states of the EU, do participate in "Schengen", that is Norway, Switzerland and Iceland.1

Intermediate conclusion. On the whole, the "Area of Freedom, Security and Justice" has come a long way and arrived at the centre of European integration at the very moment when the "refugee crisis" has confronted the EU with constraints, perceived as threats, which have the potential to jeopardize the whole achievement. At any rate, this crisis, as it has developed since summer 2015, reveals three fundamental dilemmas.

2. Three fundamental dilemmas

2.1 The European Union and its Member States

Common (European) area of freedom vs. borders under state sovereignty. The first of these dilemmas is only too well-known in nearly all other policy fields – it is nothing other than the unsolved question of who holds the sovereign rights, the Union or the member states. "Freedom", "security" and "justice" have not been transferred equally from the state level to the European one. Whereas the abolishment of borders has opened the European wide area for the free movement of all citizens who enter this space at any given time, the control of security remains largely with the member states. To put it more precisely than the terms of the treaty : Freedom in this context means exclusively "freedom of movement" (not freedom of religion, speech etc.), and the abolishment of borders between the participating (member) states amount to giving up sovereignty at the limits of national territories. But the emerging common territory, the "area" of free movement, has not been submitted to any common sovereign control. "Security", in this sense, means mainly border control (not security in the streets of a European city, even if the "strategic guidelines" of 2014 put the emphasis on new issues like data security), and this border control is still conferred upon the member states, i.e. those member states who have an external border along the outer border of the European "area".2 One might see an analogical situation in the field of Economic and Monetary Union, where the much-criticised imbalance between a fully-fledged Monetary Union, with a powerful and independent Central Bank, has no counterpart in the corresponding field of economic policy, which still remains under national sovereignty. It seems reasonable, however, to draw the consequences of the abolishment of internal borders and confer the security of the external borders to the authority which rules over the "area of freedom", and that is the European Union (with its differentiated membership, as indicated above).

The European Commission does openly recognize the problem: "At this moment in time, there are serious deficiencies in external border control caused by a lack of border surveillance and insufficient registration and identification of irregular migrants. As a consequence of the secondary movements triggered by these deficiencies, Member States have reintroduced internal border controls. These serious deficiencies therefore jeopardise the Schengen area as a whole, and are evidence of a threat to public policy or internal security in that area."3

Example: FRONTEX. A perfect example of this dilemma is the agency created by the member states and the European Union in 2004, and the name of the agency itself is sufficient to outline the whole problem – FRONTEX is the "European Agency for the Management of Operational Cooperation at the External Borders". First, the name does not explicitly mention which borders are concerned – the reason is that the differentiated participation of not only EU member states, but of some additional ones, makes it complicated to deliniate those borders. But that is a minor problem compared to the competences and mandate of FRONTEX: Far from being in charge of the external borders as such, the agency is only entitled to make the member states "cooperate", not to substitute a European border control in place of the multiple national ones. But even "cooperation" is downsized to its "operational" level, so that it is neither political nor strategic, and is even further away from sovereignty. And still this is not where restrictions end: Even the "operational cooperation" is not under the jurisdiction of FRONTEX, only its "management" lies within its mandate, a further retrenchment which ultimately leaves little space for this supposed counterpart to an area of freedom of movement for more than 400 million people – the poor 350 employees of FRONTEX may then indeed be sufficient in number for such a limited mandate. In the face of the current challenge,The Commission has ventured to bring an end to this dilemma by proposing a "European Border and Coast Guard", which would indeed solve the problem in favour of a European approach.

Implementation of EU law. Finally, treaties, action programmes, strategic guidelines and hundreds of ensuing legal acts (regulations, directives

…) are an impressive output of strategic thinking and planning, of primary and secondary law – but the real proof of their impact is the implementation of all these legal and political decisions by the member states themselves. Despite the fact that "Schengen" as well as "Dublin" provide rules for member states who wish to apply internal border controls and to postpone or interrupt the application of the "Dublin" rules in exceptional situations, the fragmentation of the "Area of Freedom, Security and Justice" is only too obvious today. Again, the European Commission has a clear stance on this issue: "The wave-through approach is incompatible with Schengen and Dublin rules. [...] Therefore, stopping the wave-through approach in a coordinated way is a requirement for the functioning of the Schengen and Dublin systems, as well as the relocation scheme."4 Last but not least, the relocation of 120.000 refugees decided by QMV in the Council, convened on the 22 September 2015 according (for the first time) to the Lisbon rules, has not been executed by the member states – until now, only 600 refugees have been redistributed over the member states up until spring 2016. This refusal to implement decisions which have been taken according to agreed rules, in line with the primary (treaty) law of the EU, is more than an incident – it is a fundamental threat to the reliability of the rule of law in the EU and amounts to a retreat of member states from Europe to national sovereignty.

2.2. *Freedom versus Security*

Freedom *"of movement", part of an overall free society*

"Freedom", in the context of the "Area of Freedom, Security and Justice", must be understood as "freedom of movement", as outlined above. But taken as it stands, "Freedom" does mean much more of course, for a society which, since World War II, draws its identity from the idea that it was part of the "free world", in opposition to authoritarian and dictatorial regimes, ranging from the Soviet Union and the Eastern Bloc to nearly all other continents, and for many years to some European countries, too, like Portugal, Spain and Greece. Freedom is therefore a fundamental value of the European Union and ranks just below the most supreme of all values, human dignity, in the European Charter of Fundamental Rights5, which itself owes its existence to the same exceptional European Council meeting at Tampere, where the AFSJ was transformed into a political programme.

And that is far from being an accident. On the contrary it is the affirmation that the AFSJ approach has something to do with this fundamental value of freedom, despite its limitation to freedom of movement in the narrower sense of the AFSJ. The link between the limited AFSJ understanding of freedom and the fundamental value of freedom is indirect, but undeniable. But "Freedom" is closely linked to "Security", at the European level as much as in many debates at the national level. In fact, the earliest origins of the AFSJ approach illustrate this link: The initial motivation to cooperate at the European level in the field of justice and home affairswas the threat of terrorism in the late 70s, in particular in Italy and Germany, and the initiative to make such sensitive bodies like the police and judiciary cooperate for the sake of better security led the heads of state and government at the time to already think about more freedom of movement for their citizens. The balance between freedom and security has always been, and still is, delicate, as the shifting back and forth of the "action programmes," starting with Tampere, illustrate: Whereas the late 90s were an era of enthusiasm about the huge steps toward an "ever closer Union" and laid the emphasis on more freedom, the terrorist attacks in New York, London and Madrid in the early 2000s recommended a shift towards what the The Hague action programme (2004) called a "balance between freedom and security"; Stockholm (2009) again restored the primacy of freedom, under the slogan of a "Europe of Rights", whereas the "Strategic Guidelines" (2014) aim at more data safety and security.

Freedom as a "negative" integration (abolition of borders)

Is it easier to provide for freedom than to assure security? It seems so, since "freedom" requires less effort , less legislation, less control than "security". The "negative" integration ("negative" in the sense of "abolishment", "cancellation") on the side of "freedom" has not in all respects been complemented by a "positive" integration ("positive" in the sense of "construction", "creation"), e.g. on the side of security at the (common) borders. Here, too, an analogy is obvious with other fields of European integration. The way to the Common Market is, according to a classical theory, marked by three steps – (1) the abolition of internal borders (customs, tariffs; this is then a "free trade area"), (2) the creation of a common tariff all around the common area (that is a "customs union"), and finally, (3) common rules for the behaviour of all actors on the common market, which is the crucial step, because it requires common legislation (and only then a common market emerges). The first step is relatively easy, because it is only "negative", whereas the third is the most difficult, because it requires common decision-making, something "positive" (the second stage is "positive" too, but does not require much of the national sovereignty to be transferred to the common level). Similarly, in the field of AFSJ, much more has to be done in the field of security if its effect is to amount to the same level of integration as the abolition of internal borders.

9 EU Agencies – for security, and for justice, but not for freedom

The range of EU agencies created under the umbrella of the "Area of Freedom, Security and Justice" illustrate this emphasis on security, and ‚respectively, justice. If one would categorize these agencies and relate them to either "freedom", or "security", or "justice", most of them would fall under the category of "security" (or maybe "justice"): That is the case with FRONTEX, EUROPOL (European Law Enforcement Agency)); CEPOL (European Police College); EUROJUST (The European Union's Judicial Cooperation Unit); ENISA (European Union Agency for Network and Information Security); EASO: European Asylum Support Office; The European Monitoring Centre for Drugs and Drug Addiction. Only two of them are more closely related to the ideas of „justice" seen as „rights", but none of them explicitly to "freedom": FRA (European Union Agency for Fundamental Rights) and EIGE (European Institute for Gender Equality). This does not necessarily mean that security is absolutely predominant in the EU approach to the AFSJ, just because of the argument advanced above: Freedom means to be free from control, supervision, legal constraints etc., whereas security (and justice) do require exactly e that whole range of rules and decisions. But it is a clear message that a European security (alongside justice) policy has widely spread at a level and in a sphere where there is not much transparency for citizens, and maybe even for parliaments.

2.3 Values versus utility

Roosevelt's 4 freedoms vs. 4 market freedoms. A final dual relationship relates "freedom" as a fundamental ethical value to "freedom" as a means, one among others, to implement the Single Market. Talk of the "Four Freedoms" has accompanied European integration as far back as the Rome Treaties (1957) and their core policy project, i.e. the creation of a common market for the member states of the European Economic Community. But the formula "Four Freedoms" goes even farther back in history: to the famous speech given by US President F.D. Roosevelt in January 1941, when the United States had to spell out their credo against Japanese and fascist aggression. In this sense, the four freedoms meant (1) freedom of speech, (2) freedom of worship, (3) freedom from want and (4) freedom from fear – four ethical requirements which have nothing to do with markets, remarkably. The European Economic Community and then, too, the European Union based their core policy project, the Single European Market, on a totally different understanding of "freedom", when they alluded to the "four freedoms" – in this context, it was all about free movement of the principle economic factors, which needed to be available without borders on a common market, i.e. goods, capital, services and workers. Freedom of movement in this respect was – and still is – a utilitarian, not an ethical idea.

Emancipation of ASFJ from Common Market. However, the ethical side of "freedom" of movement for citizens did not disappear, on the contrary: When the European Union achieved the political project of a common, or even single market, the idea of "freedom (of movement)" was on the way to emancipation from its utilitarian background. The decisive step was the Amsterdam Treaty, when the "Area of Freedom, Security and Justice" took shape and was conceived as a policy of its own, and no longer only at the service of any other political project. In the Lisbon Treaty, the two aspects of "freedom" as a useful means to establish the single market on the one hand and as the implementation of a fundamental right on the other, split decisively into two different series of provisions, spelled out in two different titles of the Treaty on the Functioning of the European Union: Part Three of the TFEU distinguishes between different "Titles" – Title IV elaborates on the policies aiming at "Free Movement of Persons, Services and Capital", in line with the market approach, whereas Title V is devoted to the "Area of Freedom, Security and Justice", which does not contain any hint as to its role for the single market, and stands therefore on its own.

"Back to Schengen". A Roadmap. As the treaty shows, both aspects of "freedom", the utilitarian and the ethical, are historically linked, but not systematically integrated – they dwell side by side in the TFEU, ignoring

each other. A last illustration of this ambiguity is the way in which the European Commission argues in favour of re-establishing the "Area of Freedom, Security and Justice", more precisely the Schengen Area, in its "Back to Schengen – A Roadmap"

communication, which has been quoted above. The twofold argument for freedom of movement – ethical and utilitarian – marks the whole text, starting with the introduction: "Schengen is one of the key means through which European citizens can exercise their freedoms, and the internal market can prosper and develop. [...] The stabilisation of the Schengen system through the use of its safeguard mechanisms is essential in order to ensure the subsequent lifting of all internal border controls. To fail to do so would not only deprive people of the huge benefits of free movement across borders, but it would impose major economic costs on the EU economy as a whole by damaging the Single Market. From an economic perspective, the Commission has estimated that full re-establishment of border controls to monitor the movement of people within the Schengen area would generate immediate direct costs for the EU economy in a range between €5 and €18 billion annually."

Conclusion

Obviously, the "Area of Freedom, Security and Justice" is a perfect example of how European integration works: pragmatic steps are taken under the premise of their usefulness, but with a hidden agenda – that is to turn them, sooner or later, into a value based foundation for a political union; these steps are incomplete and unbalanced, because national sovereignty does not allow for a reasonable implementation of a fully-fledged political entity at the European level, and the real challenges at any given moment in history do not require more; crises reveal these shortcomings and press for a more balanced, more logical, more complete construction; not all member states agree on such a dynamic, some withdraw from some of those steps, some of them join later, some stay apart. But a core majority of member states reluctantly accepts the need for a European solution of a transnational problem. The future will show whether this incremental method of community building will indeed continue to lead to an "ever closer Union".

References:

1. For „Dublin", the map is similarly split, but differently. And smaller issues (like the participation of Monaco, e.g.) make the picture even more complicated. All in all, ASFJ is worth a case study in „differentiated integration".

2. To some extent, this is of course true for all the participating states, since airports are points of entry into the „area" as much as land or sea borders.

3. European Commission: Back to Schengen – A Roadmap. Brussels, 4.3.2016 COM(2016) 120 final, p. 11; online: http://ec.europa.eu-/dgs/home-affairs/what-we-do/policies/borders   -and-visas/schengen/docs/communication-back-to-schengen -roadmap_en.pdf.

4. Back to Schengen, p. 8.

5. The second paragraph of the preamble of the Charter reads: „Conscious of its spiritual and moral heritage, the Union is founded on the indivisible, universal values of human dignity, freedom, equality and solidarity; it is based on the principles of democracy and the rule of law. It places the individual at the heart of its activities, by establishing the citizenship of the Union and by creating an area of freedom, security and justice."

(published mid-May 2016)

L'Union européenne face aux défis de l'économie de la connaissance et de la migration des cerveaux

Jean-Claude Vérez[1]

L'économie de la connaissance est plutôt récente, à moins qu'elle ne fût dénommée autrement il y a des décennies. Elle est caractérisée par la progression des emplois hautement qualifiés, des savoirs, des dépenses en recherche et développement (R&D) et des brevets. Elle est aussi caractérisée par le développement des apprentissages, plutôt expérimentaux que routiniers.

Dans les années 1990, elle s'est constituée comme une spécialité à partir d'un double phénomène : d'une part, l'accroissement des ressources consacrées à la production et à la transmission des connaissances (éducation, formation, R&D), d'autre part, l'avènement des Nouvelles technologies d'information et de communication (NTIC). Cette économie traduit la part croissante de l'immatériel dans la production des richesses.

Au niveau des entreprises, l'avantage compétitif (plus que comparatif comme le soulignait David Ricardo) repose essentiellement sur les compétences de ses ressources humaines et sur la capacité à se doter d'une organisation apprenante. Le salarié schumpétérien qui se substitue au salarié fordiste ou tayloriste, est plus autonome, apte à la décision, innovateur. Le partage des savoirs devient crucial ainsi que la nécessité de préserver les « cerveaux ».

La part croissante du capital intangible et du travail intellectuel n'aurait pu émerger sans qu'il n'y ait eu en amont de lourds investissements dans les systèmes éducatifs. Les familles y participent avec une forte demande d'éducation et, du côté des entreprises, les exigences en formation professionnelle redoublent d'intensité. Du côté de l'offre d'éducation et de la formation, les programmes en alternance se multiplient.

Ces tendances sont mondiales et de fait, les diplômés, les compétences, les talents sont très recherchés au point de bouleverser les flux migratoires. La crise de 2008 a accentué cette tendance, notamment au sein de l'UE, de sorte que nous sommes peut-être à la veille de déséquilibres démographiques d'un genre nouveau. Certains pays assistent à l'expatriation de leur jeunesse la plus talentueuse faute d'emplois domestiques et en cela, les déplacements de population n'ont rien de commun avec ceux de l'après guerre. Le phénomène actuel d'émigration a des caractéristiques qui le distinguent des vagues précédentes : d'une part, il concerne davantage d'êtres humains du fait de la taille de la population mondiale (et donc européenne) et de l'accès d'un plus grand nombre de jeunes à des niveaux supérieurs d'études et de formation. D'autre part, plusieurs pays sont concernés simultanément par l'émigration économique (Grèce, Irlande, Portugal). Enfin, sur un plan qualitatif, on aura compris que ceux qui quittent leur pays sont les plus diplômés, les plus qualifiés, les plus « entrepreneurs », sans que la pratique des langues étrangères ne soit un obstacle.

Au sein de l'UE, outre les pays cités et touchés par les départs, on distingue les pays attrayants comme l'Allemagne, la Grande-Bretagne, les Pays-Bas (ou la Suisse en dehors de l'UE) ainsi que certaines zones géographiques comme l'Italie du nord (au détriment de l'Italie du sud). On peut encore souligner que quelques pays incitent activement les talents des pays en crise à venir s'installer chez eux comme l'Allemagne de sorte qu'on peut opposer les politiques d'émigration non désirées aux politiques d'immigration plutôt actives et, à terme, des déséquilibres démographiques facteurs d'aggravation des disparités économiques existantes. Si l'on s'accorde en effet sur le fait que la croissance économique dans les pays industrialisés repose majoritairement sur les connaissances, les déplacements de la main d'oeuvre qualifiée ont un impact positif sur les économies des pays d'accueil et négatif sur les économies des pays d'origine.

Le cas de l'Irlande est révélateur de ce risque : alors que c'était un pays d'immigration durant les dix années qui ont précédé la crise, période faste en terme de croissance économique et d'attrait des capitaux, la dite crise a inversé la tendance au point où une partie des expatriés rentre depuis dans leur pays d'origine, ce qui n'est pas sans conséquence sur le rythme de la croissance. Rappelons qu'il s'agit de salariés, d'actifs indépendants et autres chefs d'entreprise à fort potentiel. Ce retour dans le pays d'origine pourrait avoir un impact positif sur le nivellement des qualifications entre les pays dans la mesure où les actifs concernés sont dotés a minima de capacités et de pratiques enrichies durant leur expatriation. Mais c'est oublié que la main d'œuvre la plus qualifiée ne revient pas nécessairement dans son pays d'origine, soit en raison des niveaux de salaire, soit en raison des opportunités professionnelles ou de carrières, soit en raison de la composition de la famille.

L'évolution de ces flux migratoires dans un cadre d'économie de la connaissance suscite des interrogations au sein de l'UE :

1/ Si les rythmes de croissance divergent alors que le projet européen visait leur convergence, il faudra repenser la solidarité entre pays européens, à moins de formuler un autre projet. Il semble difficile de concevoir une Union avec des économies à fort potentiel de main d'oeuvre, capables par exemple de participer à la production d'Airbus, d'innover, de déposer des brevets, et d'autres économies à dominante agricole ou de petits services ou de « petits boulots ».

On pourrait assimiler ce contexte à un effet centre-périphérie, effet (ou inquiétude) déjà évoqué au moment de la création du Marché commun (Acte unique, 1987) qui, à l'époque, avait suscité grâce à Jacques Delors une vraie politique régionale, dotée de fonds importants. Faudra-t-il s'inspirer de ce modèle pour l'appliquer au secteur de l'éducation, des connaissances, des compétences ?

2/ Les pays européens qui ont connu pendant une dizaine d'années un boom économique (Irlande, Espagne) ou, au moment de leur intégration, un rattrapage économique (Portugal, Grèce) n'auront pas nécessairement une seconde « chance ». On s'est aperçu par exemple que la croissance espagnole était en partie superficielle via la spéculation immobilière. Quant aux aides de l'UE pour les nouveaux pays intégrés, elles seront plus limitées en raison notamment de la crise et des niveaux d'endettement.

3/ Selon l'ampleur des départs et des arrivées, le financement des systèmes de solidarité nationale pourrait être remis en cause dans un contexte de vieillissement démographique ; pour certains pays européens, il faudra réfléchir à la manière de concilier une baisse des cotisations (liée aux départs des jeunes diplômés) et une hausse des dépenses sociales (inhérente au poids croissant des troisième et quatrième âges du fait de l'espérance de vie qui augmente régulièrement dans la majorité des pays européens). A terme, selon les pays, c'est le modèle social qui pourrait être impacté avec un rôle accru des compagnies d'assurances privées comme substitut au financement public des dépenses sociales.

4/ Les déplacements de travailleurs qualifiés au sein de certains pays européens engendrent des interactions culturelles qui vont elles-mêmes modifier les comportements liés au management et aux cultures professionnelles des pays d'accueil. Ces faits vont sans doute rejaillir sur les processus de formation avec un double défi : d'une part, former des jeunes aptes à se déplacer et, d'autre part, capables d'exercer des métiers en grande partie méconnus à un horizon de dix ou quinze ans, compte tenu des progrès technologiques.

5/ Il est possible que ces tendances incitent les pouvoirs publics à réviser le niveau de leurs dépenses publiques et la répartition de ces dépenses publiques. Pourquoi former des jeunes futurs actifs qualifiés si ils finissent par exercer leur talent en dehors de leur pays d'origine ? A court terme, l'impact peut être positif sur les finances publiques ; à moyen et long terme, l'impact pourrait être désastreux avec une catégorisation des pays à trois dimensions : les uns produiraient de la connaissance, les autres la codifieraient, les derniers « suivraient ».

On comprend in fine que l'UE a plutôt intérêt à s'inscrire dans l'économie de la connaissance. Face aux sociétés transnationales américaines et chinoises (de plus en plus nombreuses), qui investissent dans l'immatériel, financent les dépenses en R&D, déposent des brevets et attirent les talents, l'UE ne peut pas se replier sur elle-même mais doit au contraire être offensive. Les autorités chinoises ont envoyé pendant une assez longue période leurs étudiants dans le reste du monde, dans les meilleures universités ou autres instituts de formation, avant de les « inviter » à rentrer au pays. Si les pays européens n'instaurent pas une politique harmonieuse en matière de formation, d'accès à la connaissance et de partage des savoirs, ils courent à la catastrophe. Et que l'on ne confonde pas les échanges entre étudiants via les projets Erasmus et la circulation ou la captation des actifs qualifiés et très qualifiés. Le défi européen dont la population tend à vieillir consiste à poursuivre des investissements dans l'éducation, la formation, tout au long de la vie, et ce sans renforcer la concurrence intra-européenne mais, au contraire, de manière à faire face à la concurrence des pays du reste du monde en matière de capital humain, d'innovations et de connaissances.

[1] Merci à Hartmut Marhold pour ses remarques et suggestions pertinentes.

(publié en ligne mi-juin 2016)

Europe and its member states

Gestion de la dette publique grecque: mode d'emploi

Laurent Baechler

La question de la soutenabilité de la dette

La dette publique forme avec l'impôt l'alternative qui se présente à tout Etat pour financer ses dépenses. La situation est donc tout à fait différente de ce qu'elle est pour les agents privés, puisque la dette publique est un substitut à l'impôt prélevé sur le revenu courant (le Produit Intérieur Brut, PIB), alors que pour les agents privés, l'endettement est un substitut au revenu futur, qui permettra ultérieurement le remboursement. L'affaire se complique évidemment lorsque l'Etat est surendetté, qu'il est incapable de rembourser sa dette par prélèvement de l'impôt, et que les nouvelles dettes contractées servent à rembourser les échéances passées. C'est peu ou prou la situation dans laquelle se trouvent actuellement de nombreux Etats, essentiellement des pays dits riches, le cas grec en étant une illustration pathétique. Tout dépend donc des conditions dans lesquelles la dette publique est accumulée et gérée, de ce que l'on appelle couramment la soutenabilité de la dette. De manière évidente, une dette publique bien gérée est considérée comme moins risquée, entretient un coût de financement plus faible et génère un cercle vertueux. A l'inverse une dette insoutenable se répercute sur son coût et peut déboucher sur une situation extrême dans laquelle le poids de la dette ralentit la croissance économique et fait exploser les coûts de refinancement, obligeant l'Etat exclu des marchés de la dette à faire appel à l'aide extérieure, comme c'est le cas de la Grèce actuellement, et pour longtemps encore.

L'objectif principal de la gestion de la dette publique (GDP) est de satisfaire les besoins de financement de l'Etat et ses obligations de paiement au moindre coût possible à long terme, tout en maintenant le risque à un niveau raisonnable[1]. Dans cette optique les paramètres clé de la GDP vont bien au-delà des critères évidents de ratio d'endettement (dette/PIB) ou de capacité de remboursement (comme par exemple le solde de la balance commerciale/PIB). Ils incluent principalement la structure de la dette et sa dynamique. Autrement dit un niveau de dette élevé ou une faible capacité de remboursement ne caractérisent pas nécessairement un surendettement.

Dans ces conditions déterminer le niveau soutenable d'une dette publique est une affaire extrêmement compliquée, qui fait effectivement l'objet de controverses acharnées entre spécialistes de la question. Tentons d'y voir plus clair.

La structure de la dette publique

La structure de la dette publique fait référence à sa composition, autrement dit sa maturité (court ou long terme), son mode de paiement (à taux fixes ou variables), son libellé (en monnaie nationale ou étrangère), et son origine (nationale ou extérieure). Ainsi une dette à long terme est considérée comme plus facilement gérable qu'une dette à court terme, pour la raison simple qu'elle laisse à l'Etat davantage de temps pour trouver des solutions de financement. Parmi les solutions envisagées pour alléger le fardeau de la dette publique grecque figure ainsi l'allongement de sa maturité, qui est déjà en moyenne beaucoup plus longue que pour les autres membres de la zone euro avec une moyenne de 16 ans contre 7 (avec de surcroit des différences de maturité importantes entre des institutions comme le FMI ou la Banque centrale européenne aux règles rigides, et les partenaires de la zone euro plus flexibles et disposés à accepter des maturités supérieures à 30 ans).

Une dette à taux variable ou libellée en devises crée un risque de marché lié à la variabilité des taux d'intérêt et des taux de change. Ce risque est quasi-inexistant pour la Grèce, du fait que sa dette est à taux fixes et libellée presqu'exclusivement en euro. Ce ne serait plus le cas si la Grèce devait sortir de la zone euro et revenir à la drachme, avec une monnaie nationale fortement dévaluée (probablement de l'ordre de 50%) et une dette en euro alourdie en proportion (autrement dit multipliée par deux).

Enfin une dette contractée vis-à-vis d'agents nationaux est considérée comme davantage viable qu'une dette extérieure (le paramètre est différent de celui du libellé de la dette dans le cas grec, dans la mesure où la dette grecque est libellée dans une monnaie partagée avec les pays créanciers). Le cas emblématique en la matière est celui du Japon qui, en dépit d'une dette publique avoisinant les 250% du PIB (contre près de 180% pour la Grèce, et 92% en moyenne pour la zone euro), ne fait jamais parler de lui comme d'une bombe financière à retardement, alors même que l'économie japonaise combine dette élevée et faible croissance (donc faible capacité de remboursement) depuis plus de deux décennies. L'explication semble résider dans le fait que la dette publique japonaise est presque intégralement nationale, autrement dit que les japonais se sont endettés vis-à-vis d'eux-mêmes. Ce à quoi il faut ajouter que près de la moitié de cette dette est détenue par des organismes publics (et se substitue donc à l'impôt), et qu'enfin une grande partie est entre les mains de la Banque centrale japonaise, un cas extrême de monétisation de la dette sans inflation apparemment soutenable (puisque le Japon est en quasi-déflation sur la même période), et dont certains économistes voudraient bien que la BCE s'inspire... La Grèce est de ce point de vue dans la situation difficile de devoir près de 80% de sa dette à des agents extérieurs, principalement ses partenaires de la zone euro, la BCE et le FMI.

La dynamique de la dette publique

La dynamique de la dette fait référence à l'articulation entre le niveau de cette dette, son coût, et la capacité de remboursement de l'Etat, déterminée principalement par la croissance économique, autrement dit la croissance du revenu national sur lequel sont prélevés les impôts. Une première approche grossière indiquerait que la dette est soutenable tant que le coût de son financement, le taux d'intérêt, reste inférieur à la capacité de financement de l'Etat, c'est-à-dire la croissance économique. De fait les épisodes de désendettement des Etats dans l'histoire correspondent souvent à des périodes au cours desquelles les taux de croissance économique excèdent les taux d'intérêt des dettes publiques, comme ce fût le cas pendant les « trente glorieuses » qui ont permis d'éponger une bonne partie des dettes de la Deuxième Guerre mondiale. Mais ce calcul est trop sommaire, car il ne tient pas compte des spécificités de chaque situation nationale qu'il faut étudier au cas par cas, en analysant l'articulation entre les paramètres de la dynamique de la dette et les facteurs institutionnels qui peuvent peser sur la capacité de gestion de cette dette par l'Etat.

Les études en la matière sont récentes et donnent des résultats controversés. L'une des plus connues est celle proposée par K. Rogoff et C. Reinhart, dont les résultats ont amorcé une discussion animée entre économistes sur le niveau de soutenabilité des dettes publiques. Les auteurs trouvent sur les deux derniers siècles un écart de taux de croissance de 4,2 points en moyenne entre ce qu'ils considèrent comme des pays faiblement endettés (avec un niveau de dette publique inférieur à 30% du PIB) et des pays fortement endettés (plus de 90% du PIB)[2]. Une autre étude du FMI trouve qu'une hausse de 10 points de pourcentage du ratio de dette publique (par exemple un passage de 30 à 40% du PIB) réduit le taux de croissance du PIB réel par habitant de 0,2 point par an, avec un impact d'autant plus sévère que le ratio lui-même est plus élevé[3].

Le paramètre institutionnel est bien évidemment décisif pour expliquer la capacité de gestion de la dette par l'Etat. Interviennent ici la capacité à lever l'impôt et à lutter contre la fraude fiscale, la fiabilité des politiques macroéconomiques, l'indépendance de la Banque centrale pour réduire les risques de monétisation de la dette, les dérapages de dépenses publiques liés à la corruption, ... et une infinité d'autres paramètres qui font de chaque situation nationale un cas particulier. La Grèce semble se distinguer par ses piètres performances dans nombre de ces domaines, ce qui explique la trajectoire divergente qu'elle a suivie ces dernières années par rapport aux autres pays de la zone euro gravement affectés par la crise financière à partir de 2010, et qui ont malgré tout pu revenir vers les marchés internationaux de la dette publique récemment, principalement l'Irlande et le Portugal.

Une préoccupation récente porte sur l'articulation entre la dette publique et le niveau de la dette privée des ménages et des entreprises. Certaines études vont même jusqu'à considérer que la dette publique ralentit la croissance économique principalement dans les cas où elle est associée à un surendettement privé[4]. De fait celui-ci est caractéristique de la période récente, et dans des proportions encore plus alarmantes que pour la dette publique (126% en zone euro contre 92% pour la dette publique). Nombreux sont ceux pour qui le véritable problème est là, non seulement du fait de son ampleur et de son caractère généralisé, mais surtout parce que les agents privés ne bénéficient pas des mêmes moyens de gérer leur dette que les Etats.

Finalement, on ne peut comprendre la crise des dettes souveraines dans la zone euro sans faire référence au rôle des Banques centrales dans la gestion des dettes publiques. L'euro est une monnaie sans Etat, ce qui conduit au fait que la BCE ne peut jouer le rôle de prêteur en dernier ressort (c'est-à-dire de garant que la dette publique sera remboursée, en dernier recours par émission monétaire) que les Banques centrales peuvent jouer dans d'autres contextes nationaux, et ce en dépit de leur indépendance supposée et de leur mission de gardiennes de la stabilité des prix. La Grèce n'est pas plus concernée que les autres membres de la zone euro par ce phénomène, mais il est indéniable que l'absence de cette possibilité a entretenu la spéculation sur les taux d'intérêt de la dette publique grecque, et a pesé sur les primes de risque exigées par les marchés financiers.

La combinaison de ces paramètres fait de la dette publique grecque un fardeau insoutenable, en augmentation, et qui n'a aucune chance de se voir réduire dans un avenir proche ou même lointain, tant le cercle vicieux croissance faible-augmentation de la dette publique semble impossible à inverser, le poids de la dette grecque ayant augmenté de plus de 20 points de PIB depuis le déclenchement de la crise en 2010 pour atteindre près de 180%. Le fait est reconnu par certains des principaux créanciers de la Grèce, au premier rang desquels figurent le FMI et désormais la BCE. Les Etats membres de l'UE ne peuvent le reconnaître aussi facilement pour des raisons politiques qui ont leur propre logique, mais cet état de fait ne pourra pas être éludé indéfiniment.

La gestion de la dette publique

Il existe en tout et pour tout trois moyens de gérer la dette publique : l'inflation, l'austérité, le défaut (partiel ou total).

L'inflation (c'est-à-dire la réduction du poids réel de la dette par diminution progressive du pouvoir d'achat des sommes empruntées) présente l'immense avantage de permettre de ronger la dette « en douceur », de manière presque indolore. De fait les Etats y ont eu recours en masse au cours du 20ème siècle, et l'on peut soupçonner que certains soient actuellement tentés par le stratagème, tant les politiques monétaires sont devenues accommodantes ces dernières années pour gérer les effets de la crise, aux Etats-Unis ou au Royaume-Uni notamment[5]. Mais la recette est extrêmement risquée, car l'on sait bien que l'idée de « piloter » l'inflation à loisir (à un taux de 5% l'an par exemple, considéré comme raisonnable) pour dégonfler la dette est parfaitement illusoire. Le risque est plutôt de voir l'inflation s'emballer et devenir incontrôlable, comme ce fût le cas dans les années 1970, auquel cas les politiques nécessaires pour revenir à la situation antérieure peuvent devenir encore plus coûteuses que la dette elle-même. Il n'y a de fait aucun exemple historique d'une telle stratégie maîtrisée, et tous les exemples révèlent un recours à l'inflation accepté en désespoir de cause.

La zone euro s'interdit de toute façon cette possibilité, la BCE ayant pour mission le maintien d'une inflation faible et stable proche de 2%. Dans les conditions déflationnistes actuelles qui caractérisent la zone, il n'est même pas certain que la stratégie puisse être couronnée de succès. Elle est donc à exclure quoi qu'il en soit.

L'austérité est la deuxième possibilité. Il s'agit en l'occurrence de dégager des excédents budgétaires suffisants et sur une période suffisamment longue pour que l'Etat puisse rembourser sa dette. Le seul exemple de dette publique comparable à celle de la Grèce gérée de cette manière est celle du Royaume-Uni au 19ème siècle, dans une période sans inflation, au lendemain des guerres napoléoniennes[6]. Dégager des excédents budgétaires ne peut se faire qu'en réduisant les dépenses et/ou en augmentant les recettes de l'Etat. Le succès de cette stratégie est loin d'être garanti tant ces deux mesures risquent d'aggraver la situation de l'Etat endetté. On parle alors de politique pro-cyclique, c'est-à-dire de mesures qui amplifient l'effet récessif de la dépression économique qui a déclenché la crise de la dette, en un cercle vicieux austérité-dette publique impossible à inverser une fois installé. C'est exactement ce qui s'est produit dans le cas de la Grèce, ce qui n'a pas empêché ses créanciers de continuer de lui demander des efforts budgétaires et fiscaux déraisonnables, qui consistent plus précisément à exiger des excédents budgétaires annuels de 4% du PIB sur une période prolongée à partir de 2017, ce que personne ne peut considérer comme réaliste, même en espérant une sortie de crise pour la Grèce. D'autant que parallèlement, ces mêmes créanciers continuent de prêter des sommes gigantesques à la Grèce, ce qui devrait logiquement déboucher sur des exigences encore plus lourdes à l'avenir…

Reste finalement la possibilité du défaut, partiel ou total, négocié avec les créanciers ou non. La dette peut également être restructurée en allongeant les périodes de remboursement ou en diminuant les taux d'intérêt, mais il est à craindre que cela soit totalement inutile dans le cas grec, qui nécessite vraisemblablement un allègement de la dette publique. Ainsi les dispositions prises jusqu'ici par les créanciers pour rendre la dette supportable à court terme[7] ne règleront en rien le fond du problème. Un premier effort a bien été demandé en 2012 aux créanciers privés de la Grèce, qui ont dû accepter une décote de 50 à 70% de leurs créances, représentant l'un des allègements de dette les plus importants de l'histoire, de l'ordre de 115 milliards d'euros. Mais un quasi-consensus existe entre économistes pour considérer qu'il faudra faire davantage d'efforts pour sauver la situation. Bien entendu cela n'est pas sans risques. Au-delà de celui de l'éjection des marchés financiers de la dette pour une période prolongée, le risque de contagion aux autres pays dans le contexte spécifique de la zone euro (par le biais du secteur bancaire notamment) est bien réel, et explique en grande partie les blocages récents.

L'histoire ne manque pas d'exemples de défauts négociés. Certains aiment à rappeler l'ironie du cas de l'Allemagne qui en a bénéficié dans des proportions inédites après la Deuxième Guerre mondiale, la conférence de Londres de 1953 débouchant sur une annulation de sa dette, dont l'ordre de grandeur était le niveau de son PIB de l'époque... soit presque exactement le niveau actuel de la dette publique cumulée des pays de la zone euro en difficulté (Portugal, Italie, Irlande, Grèce et Espagne)[8]. La comparaison entre la Grèce actuelle et l'Allemagne des années 1950 est tronquée du fait des particularités du projet européen et de la gouvernance de la zone euro[9], mais la référence au cas allemand permet de rappeler qu'une annulation de dette peut être le début d'un rebond économique (ce qui ne garantit en rien que ce serait le cas pour la Grèce). A ce titre des études récentes estiment que ramener la dette grecque à 100% du PIB (contre près de 180 aujourd'hui) pourrait coûter presque deux fois moins cher qu'une sortie non contrôlée de la Grèce de la zone euro. Quant à l'argument selon lequel la répudiation de la dette publique est un remède de pays en développement, il est balayé par un examen attentif de l'histoire[10].

Thomas Piketty, dans son best-seller « Le capital au 21ème siècle », propose une dernière solution qui vient enrichir le débat : un impôt progressif sur le capital. Partant de l'idée que l'équivalent d'un impôt exceptionnel proportionnel de 15% sur tous les patrimoines privés européens permettrait de rembourser intégralement l'ensemble des dettes publiques européennes, la proposition permet d'imaginer des aménagements moins radicaux autorisant des allègements de dettes utiles. La solution s'apparente bien à une répudiation de la dette publique, dans la mesure où l'Etat se fait rembourser par les contribuables. Elle est néanmoins hautement préférable selon Piketty, car plus juste (l'impôt progressif permet de faire payer ceux qui en ont les moyens, alors que la situation actuelle frappe aveuglément toutes les couches de population), transparente (les gouvernements annoncent clairement comment se répartit le fardeau du remboursement), et efficace (selon le principe qu'une dette allégée permet le rebond économique). Il va sans dire que la proposition donne lieu à controverse, car il est loin d'être évident pour tout le monde que l'équité consiste à faire payer « les riches » pour tout le monde, ou qu'une annulation ou même un allègement de la dette grecque soit compatible avec une mise en œuvre des réformes institutionnelles indispensables, et sans lesquelles les mêmes causes risqueraient de produire à l'avenir les mêmes effets.

Il est inévitable que la dette publique grecque soit un jour restructurée, et plus probablement annulée en partie[11]. La seule vraie question est quand et dans quelles conditions ? Y apporter des réponses rapidement permettrait d'éviter d'avoir à se retrouver plus tard à regretter les décisions prises depuis plusieurs mois ou années, et qui consistent à augmenter davantage le niveau d'endettement d'un pays déjà largement surendetté, en attendant qu'il fasse les réformes indispensables pour que la situation ne se reproduise plus à l'avenir...

Notes:

(1) Voir à ce sujet les « Directives pour la gestion de la dette publique », Banque mondiale et Fonds monétaire international, 2001. Accessible sur http://www.imf.org/external/np/mae/pdebt/2000/fra/pdebtf.pdf

(2) Carmen M. Reinhart et Kenneth S. Rogoff, « This Time is Different: Eight Centuries of Financial Folly », Princeton University Press, 2009. Les critiques adressées aux auteurs portent sur le fait qu'ils expliquent peu le pourquoi de cette situation, et se contentent de constater ces régularités statistiques. Le seuil de soutenabilité de la dette publique établi à 90% du PIB fait ainsi débat.

(3) Voir Manmohan S. Kumar et Jaejoon Woo , « Public Debt and Growth », IMF Working Paper, juillet 2010. Accessible sur https://www.imf.org/external/pubs/ft/wp/2010/wp10174.pdf.
Egalement S. Ali Abbas, Nazim Belhocine, Asmaa El Ganainy et Mark Horton, « A Historical Public Debt Database », IMF Working Paper, novembre 2010. Accessible sur http://core.ac.uk/download/pdf/6476905.pdf.

(4) Voir The Economist, 26 octobre 2013, accessible sur http://www.economist.com/news/finance-and-economics/21588382-euro-zone-blighted-private-debt   -even-more-government-debt-debtors

(5) Un calcul rapide indique qu'avec une inflation de 5% l'an, contre une norme actuelle de l'ordre de 2% dans les pays riches, la valeur réelle de la dette en pourcentage du PIB est réduite de 15% sur cinq ans, toutes choses égales par ailleurs.

(6) Thomas Piketty rappelle qu'il aura fallu un siècle d'excédents budgétaires annuels de 2-3 % du PIB pour se débarrasser de l'énorme dette publique héritée des guerres de l'époque. Voir « Le capital au 21ème siècle », 2013, p 893.

(7) La Grèce bénéficie notamment jusqu'en 2023 d'un moratoire sur ses dettes vis-à-vis de ses partenaires européens et du Fonds Européen de Stabilité Financière, qui lui permet de ne payer ni intérêt ni capital d'ici-là.

(8) Voir Albrecht Ritschl, accessible sur : http://www.lse.ac.uk/researchAndExpertise/researchImpact/caseStudies/ritschl-germany -hypocrisy-eurozone-debt-crisis.aspx

(9) On ne comprend pas sinon pourquoi la dette publique d'un pays représentant moins de 2% du PIB de la zone euro pose un tel problème. La situation est d'ailleurs très révélatrice des fragilités de la monnaie unique.

(10) K. Rogoff et C. Reinhart (2013) rappellent utilement que, contrairement à une croyance répandue, les pays riches ont historiquement recours aux mêmes recettes que les pays en développement pour gérer leur surendettement : une plus grande tolérance vis-à-vis de l'inflation, le contrôle des capitaux et la répression financière, la restructuration ou la conversion des dettes. Accessible sur : http://www.imf.org/e xternal/pubs/ft/wp/2013/wp13266.pdf

(11) Ce serait loin d'être la première fois, comme le rappelle Michael Waibel qui décrit les nombreux défauts grecs sur la dette publique depuis l'indépendance acquise en1832. Voir « Echoes of History: The International Financial Commission in Greece », in A Debt Restructuring Mechanism for Sovereigns, Christoph Paulus, 2014.

(publié en ligne 15 septembre 2015)

Politique: la singularité française en Europe

Eddy Fougier

Cela fait un petit moment déjà que la vie politique française tend à surprendre et même à dérouter quelque peu les autres pays européens. Le résultat du premier tour des élections régionales en décembre 2015 n'en a été que le dernier exemple en date. Il existe à coup sûr de nombreuses singularités politiques françaises. Certains estiment que ce sont des anachronismes et que le pays doit se « normaliser » au plus vite. D'autres soutiennent que la France est, au contraire, à l'avant-garde en se distinguant ainsi des autres. Force est de constater néanmoins que ces singularités semblent être en grande partie à l'origine des difficultés rencontrées par le pays et notamment de la crise identitaire qu'il vit depuis plusieurs années à partir du moment où elles contribuent largement à empêcher la mise en oeuvre de réformes structurelles, qui pourraient pourtant donner une chance de relancer la croissance économique et éventuellement de réduire le chômage comme cela s'est produit dans la plupart des autres pays européens.

Une France politique souvent à contre-courant

La première singularité politique française réside dans le fait que l'évolution idéologico-politique dans ce pays se situe souvent à rebours de ce qui peut se passer ailleurs en Europe et dans le monde occidental.

Ainsi, dans les années 1970, la France est gouvernée par la droite, tandis que la Grande-Bretagne, l'Allemagne ou les Etats-Unis étaient, eux, respectivement dominés par les travaillistes, les sociaux-démocrates ou les démocrates. En 1981, la France élit un président socialiste, François Mitterrand, qui entend rompre avec le capitalisme, tandis que la Grande-Bretagne et les Etats-Unis connaissent une « révolution conservatrice » avec Margaret Thatcher et Ronald Reagan. Le pays semble néanmoins quelque peu se normaliser politiquement à partir de 1983-1984. Une partie des dirigeants socialistes, avec le président Mitterrand à leur tête, décident de rester dans le Système monétaire européen (SME) et d'appliquer une politique de rigueur en acceptant donc de fait l'économie de marché. La droite, qui arrive au pouvoir en 1986, semble épouser la vision libérale alors dominante dans le monde anglo-saxon. Cette « normalisation » ne dure cependant qu'un temps, d'autant que, durant cette même période, émerge un important courant d'extrême-droite avec le Front national de Jean-Marie Le Pen.

A partir des années 1990, la France se remet, en effet, à être à nouveau à contre-courant des tendances européennes ou occidentales. Alors que la construction européenne passe un nouveau cap (marché unique, Union européenne, perspective d'une monnaie unique), notamment sous l'influence de François Mitterrand et de Jacques Delors, émerge à l'occasion du référendum sur le traité de Maastricht en 1992 un courant politique souverainiste emmené par des personnalités comme Philippe Séguin, Charles Pasqua ou Jean-Pierre Chevènement. On peut observer des « répliques » lors des scrutins européens de 1994 et de 1999 où les mouvements eurosceptiques réalisent autour de 40 % des suffrages. Alors que dans le monde occidental il n'est question que de mondialisation, d'intégration à l'économie mondiale ou de « fin de l'histoire » réémerge en France un important courant contestataire de la gauche anticapitaliste à compter du long mouvement de grève de 1995 et apparaît un courant altermondialiste à partir de 1998 autour du mouvement Attac et de José Bové. Enfin, si en France, la gauche est au pouvoir à la fin de cette décennie comme un peu partout en Europe et aux Etats-Unis, celle-ci tend à se démarquer assez nettement de la tendance globale, qui est alors la « troisième voie » (Third Way) incarnée par des personnalités telles que Bill Clinton, Tony Blair ou Gerhard Schröder.

Les décennies suivantes vont continuer à étonner, voire à déconcerter les Européens avec la qualification pour le second tour de l'élection présidentielle de Jean-Marie Le Pen en 2002, la spectaculaire victoire du « non » au référendum de 2005 sur le traité constitutionnel européen, l'arrestation à New York en 2011 pour agression sexuelle du favori de la présidentielle prévue l'année suivante, Dominique Strauss-Kahn, ou encore la poussée du FN dirigé par Marine Le Pen lors des derniers scrutins, celui-ci arrivant en tête des élections européennes de 2014, ce qui a été une première en France pour une élection nationale, et aux premiers tours des élections départementales et régionales de 2015.

Un régime semi-présidentiel qui se présidentialise

Le président de la République français est la clef de voûte des institutions de la Ve République, selon l'expression de Michel Debré, le « père » de la Constitution de 1958. Cette tendance a été bien entendu renforcée par l'élection du chef de l'Etat au suffrage universel direct à partir de 1965, la pratique des différents présidents qui se sont succédés à l'Elysée et de façon encore plus évidente avec l'instauration récente du quinquennat et l'inversion du calendrier électoral, la présidentielle précédant désormais de peu les élections législatives.

Tableau 1 : Mode d'élection et pouvoirs du chef de l'Etat dans les diffé-rents Etats-membres de l'Union européenne

Chefs de l'Etat élus au suffrage universel direct et exerçant vérita-blement le pouvoir exécutif	Chefs de l'Etat élus au suffrage universel direct, mais sans pou-voir véritable ou avec des pouvoirs peu im-portants	Chefs de l'Etat élus par le parlement, sans pouvoir véri-table ou avec des pouvoirs peu impor-tants	Monarques constitu-tionnels sans véritable pouvoir
Chypre France	Autriche Bulgarie Croatie Estonie* Finlande Irlande Lituanie Pologne Portugal Roumanie Slovaquie Slovénie République tchèque	Allemagne Grèce Hongrie Italie Lettonie Malte	Belgique Danemark Espagne Luxembourg Pays-Bas Royaume-Uni Suède

*Election du chef de l'Etat par un collège électoral au suffrage universel indirect.
Source : d'après l'Observatoire des élections en Europe de la Fondation Robert Schu-man.

Le rôle éminent joué par le président de la République français est néan-moins assez singulier au sein des Etats-membres de l'Union européenne. La France n'est certes par le seul Etat-membre à avoir un régime semi-présidentiel ou à organiser une élection du président de la République au suffrage universel direct (voir Tableau 1). Mais, à l'exception notable mais très singulière du cas chypriote, aucun président de la République d'un autre membre de l'UE, ou plus largement aucun chef de l'exécutif euro-péen, ne dispose d'autant de pouvoirs que le président français. Celui-ci est, en effet, le véritable chef de l'exécutif qui nomme le premier ministre, préside le Conseil des ministres et décide des grandes orientations que le gouvernement est chargé de mettre en oeuvre. Il dispose en outre d'un pouvoir que les autres dirigeants européens n'ont pas en ayant la capacité à engager les forces nucléaires françaises. Enfin, il peut recourir à des pouvoirs exceptionnels en mettant en application l'article 16 de la Constitution dans certaines circonstances. C'est la raison pour laquelle certains parlent d'un véritable « monarque républicain » à son propos.

L'élection majeure en France est donc bien évidemment l'élection présidentielle. L'ensemble de la vie politique française est focalisé sur cette élection. Dans un tel contexte politique, le Parlement se cantonne généralement à être une sorte de chambre d'enregistrement des différentes initiatives gouvernementales, et donc de la politique présidentielle, et les partis politiques sont devenus de simples instances de sélection et de désignation des candidats à l'élection présidentielle, notamment à travers l'instauration d'un système de primaires. Enfin, cette élection est aussi la seule qui intéresse vraiment les Français, comme peuvent en témoigner les taux de participation, qui se situent la plupart du temps aux alentours de 80 %.

Cette présidentialisation présente néanmoins un certain nombre d'inconvénients. La vie politique française obnubilée par l'élection présidentielle tend ainsi à générer une atmosphère générale de campagne électorale permanente. C'est un contexte propice au triomphe de la démocratie d'opinion. La politique menée par le pouvoir apparaît ainsi largement déterminée par les sondages et les indices de popularité de l'exécutif avec en ligne de mire la prochaine présidentielle. Or, les hommes politiques français le savent bien : on ne gagne pas une présidentielle en mettant en oeuvre des réformes souvent impopulaires et douloureuses ou en promettant de le faire. Gagne donc celui qui promet d'agir pour résoudre les problèmes du pays en mettant l'accent sur le volontarisme politique, quitte à nier quelque peu la réalité et ses contraintes. Or, ces promesses ne sont généralement pas suivies d'effet car ce qui permet de gagner une élection se heurte vite à la réalité, notamment européenne, comme on a pu le voir avec François Mitterrand en 1981, Jacques Chirac en 1995 ou bien François Hollande en 2012. Cela explique la déception systématique des électeurs, qui peuvent avoir le sentiment d'avoir été trompés ou trahis, le maintien d'une sorte de « pensée magique » en France assez typique des extrêmes politiques qui nie toute forme de réalité économique et le fait que la « contrainte » européenne soit perçue par une partie des Français comme la source de tous les maux dont souffre le pays.

La présidentialisation de la vie politique française tend par ailleurs à favoriser les hommes politiques susceptibles de gagner cette élection. Or, ce ne sont sans doute pas ceux qui sont les plus à même de bien gérer les affaires du pays, comme le passé a pu nous le montrer. Enfin, cette présidentialisation tend également à renforcer la bipolarisation et les clivages politiques à partir du moment où au premier tour de l'élection présidentielle, il faut que les candidats mobilisent leurs propres soutiens en mettant en exergue ce qui les distingue de leurs adversaires et à partir du moment où au second tour, la plupart du temps, le candidat de droite arrivé en tête affronte le candidat de gauche le mieux placé. Dans un tel contexte, il est quasiment impossible d'envisager une union nationale ou bien une coalition droite-gauche ou une coalition des centres (centre-droit et centre-gauche). Ce système ne favorise donc pas du tout les compromis et la recherche de consensus, ce qui pourrait s'avérer nécessaire par exemple pour entreprendre un certain nombre de réformes structurelles.[1]

Une culture politique toujours aussi conflictuelle

Autre singularité politique nationale, il existe en France une culture politique conflictuelle avec une atmosphère de « guerre civile larvée » comme si l'on ne pouvait s'empêcher de rejouer indéfiniment la Révolution française lors de chaque élection, référendum ou réforme d'envergure, comme ont pu l'illustrer par exemple les mobilisations contre le mariage homosexuel en 2013. Chaque camp tend à voir son adversaire comme un ennemi n'ayant pas vraiment de légitimité à exercer le pouvoir. Les projets politiques portés par chacun des camps opposés paraissent ainsi totalement inconciliables dans une atmosphère de passion politique, d'intransigeance idéologique et de politisation systématique des enjeux et des débats.

En témoigne la vigueur particulière des mouvements protestataires en France. Ainsi, depuis 1988, les suffrages en faveur des candidats d'extrême droite (FN) et d'extrême gauche (partis trotskistes) aux premiers tours des élections présidentielles ne sont plus descendus en dessous de 16 % pour monter jusqu'à près de 30 % le 21 avril 2002 (Tableau 2). On observe d'ailleurs une nette poussée du FN depuis l'arrivée de Marine Le

---

1 C'est ce que déplorait le think tank américain Peterson Institute for International Economics en 2014. Voir Jacob Funk Kirkegaard, « Why France Needs Political Reform », 29 octobre 2014, https://piie.com.

Pen à la tête du parti en 2011 et sa volonté de « dédiaboliser » celui-ci. Il est d'ailleurs le parti de la droite radicale qui, en Europe, recueille le plus grand nombre de suffrages avec plus de 6 millions de voix au premier tour de la présidentielle de 2012, et aux premier et second tours des élections régionales de 2015.

Tableau 2 : Résultat des candidats d'extrême droite et d'extrême gauche aux premiers tours de l'élection présidentielle, en % des suffrages exprimés

Election présidentielle	Extrême droite*	Extrême gauche**	Total des suffrages en faveur des extrêmes
1981	Aucun candidat	2,3%	**2,3%**
1988	14,4%	2,4%	**16,8%**
1995	15,0%	5,3%	**20,3%**
2002	19,2%	10,5%	**29,7%**
2007	10,4%	5,7%	**16,1%**
2012	17,9%	1,8%	**19,7%**

*Candidats du Front national (JM. Le Pen et M. Le Pen) et Bruno Mégret - ** Candidats des partis trotskistes (Lutte ouvrière, Ligue communiste révolutionnaire/Nouveau parti anticapitaliste, Parti des travailleurs/Parti ouvrier indépendant). Source : ministère de l'Intérieur.

Si l'on rajoute aux suffrages en faveur des candidats des extrêmes ceux en faveur des candidats de gauche et de droite que l'on peut qualifier de « souverainistes », on obtient alors une moyenne supérieure à 30 % des suffrages exprimés aux premiers tours des élections présidentielles depuis 1988 (Tableau 3) et d'un tiers des suffrages lors des élections européennes depuis 1989 (Tableau 4). Cette importance électorale de la France protestataire est sans aucun doute sans équivalent dans les autres pays européens, malgré la montée en puissance récente de la droite radicale dans nombre d'entre eux.

Tableau 3 : Résultat des candidats d'extrême droite, d'extrême gauche et des candidats « souverainistes » aux premiers tours de l'élection présidentielle, en % des suffrages exprimés

Election présidentielle	Extrême droite	Extrême gauche	Souverainistes de droite*	Souverainistes de gauche**	Total
1981	-	2,3%	3,0 %	16,4%	**21,7%**
1988	14,4%	2,4%	-	8,9%	**25,7%**

1995	15,0%	5,3%	4,7%	8,6%	**33,6%**
2002	19,2%	10,5%	4,2 %	8,7%	**42,6%**
2007	10,4%	5,7%	3,4%	3,3%	**22,8%**
2012	17,9%	1,8%	1,8 %	11,1 %	**32,6 %**

*Candidats néogaullistes en 1981 (M. Debré et MF. Garaud), P. de Villiers, N. Dupont-Aignan ou les candidats du parti Chasse Pêche Nature et Traditions (CPNT). ** Candidats du PCF ou dissident (P.Juquin en 1988), du PSU (H. Bouchardeau en 1981), JP. Chevènement, J. Bové, JL. Mélenchon. Source : ministère de l'Intérieur.

Tableau 4 : Résultat des candidats d'extrême droite, d'extrême gauche et des candidats «souverainistes» aux élections européennes, en % des suffrages exprimés

Election euro-péennes	Extrême droite	Extrême gauche	Souverainistes de droite*	Souverainistes de gauche	Total
1984	11,0%	3,0%	-	11,2%	**25,2%**
1989	11,7 %	1,4%	4,1%	7,7%	**24,9%**
1994	10,5%	2,3%	16,3%	9,4%	**38,5%**
1999	9,0%	5,2%	21,7%	6,8%	**42,7%**
2004	10,1%	3,3%	10,6%	5,3%	**29,3%**
2009	6,9%	6,1%	6,7%	6,1%	**25,8%**
2014	24,9%	1,6%	6,0%	6,3%	**38,8%**

* Candidats divers droite (autres que l'UMP et les partis centristes) et CPNT. N'ont pas été prises en compte ici les petites listes qui ont réalisé moins de 1 % des suffrages exprimés. Source : ministère de l'Intérieur

Cette culture politique propre à la France apparaît largement incompatible avec un certain nombre de pratiques pourtant courantes dans d'autres pays européens et avec les conditions nécessaires pour la mise en place de réformes d'envergure. Elle est incompatible avec la recherche de compromis et la quête de consensus, qui sont vues en France la plupart du temps comme un aveu de faiblesse, une compromission et une trahison de son camp et de ses idéaux. Elle semble également peu compatible avec les idées de réformisme et de pragmatisme. En France, rares sont les hommes politiques de l'opposition à oser affirmer que telle ou telle décision gouvernementale va dans le bon sens ou à voter certains de ses textes législatifs.

Par ailleurs, le poids électoral des mouvements protestataires ou anti-système aboutit au fait que l'on semble assister en France à une sorte de course vers les extrêmes, où droite et gauche apparaissent largement prisonnières des extrêmes d'un point de vue idéologique, dans un contexte politique où le centre est généralement faible. Cela tend ainsi à distinguer grandement la situation française de ce qui peut se passer dans les démocraties parlementaires européennes.

Une tendance à vouloir sortir de façon systématique les « sortants »

L'histoire politique récente de la France peut donner une fausse impression de stabilité, notamment par rapport aux régimes précédents des IIIe et IVe Républiques. Ainsi, très peu de présidents ont été élus depuis le début des années 1980 avec seulement quatre chefs de l'Etat, dont deux qui ont effectué de très longs mandats après avoir été réélus : François Mitterrand (1981-1995) et Jacques Chirac (1995-2007). C'est à peu près comparable aux trois chanceliers allemands depuis 1982 ou aux six premiers ministres britanniques depuis 1979.

Néanmoins, au-delà de cette stabilité apparente, on peut constater que, depuis les élections législatives de 1978, aucun détenteur effectif du pouvoir en France, à savoir un président de la République en période normale ou éventuellement un premier ministre en période de cohabitation, n'a été en mesure de conserver le pouvoir lorsque celui-ci a été mis en jeu lors d'élections présidentielles ou législatives. Ce fut le cas de Valéry Giscard d'Estaing (président sortant) lors de la présidentielle de 1981, de la majorité socialiste sortante lors des législatives de 1986, de Jacques Chirac (premier ministre sortant en période de cohabitation) lors de la présidentielle de 1988, de la majorité socialiste sortante lors des législatives de 1993, d'Edouard Balladur (premier ministre sortant en période de cohabitation) lors de la présidentielle de 1995, de la majorité de droite sortante lors des législatives de 1997, de Lionel Jospin (premier ministre sortant en période de cohabitation) lors de la présidentielle de 2002, et de Nicolas Sarkozy (président sortant) lors de la présidentielle de 2012. Cette tendance pourrait bien se reproduire en 2017. Il en a été de même dans la période récente pour les élections intermédiaires. Ainsi, à l'exception des élections européennes de 2009, il faut remonter aux élections cantonales de 2001 pour voir la majorité parlementaire gagner une élection intermédiaire.

En définitive, depuis le début des années 1980, il y a eu seulement deux alternances au pouvoir entre la droite et la gauche en Grande-Bretagne (1997, 2010), trois en Allemagne (1982, 1998, 2005) ou quatre aux Etats-

Unis pour ce qui concerne la Maison Blanche (1980, 1992, 2000, 2008). Or, on en a compté pas moins de sept en France (1981, 1986, 1988, 1993, 1997, 2002, 2012), tandis qu'une huitième alternance pourrait se profiler en 2017.

Ce rejet systématique des « sortants » en France s'explique bien évidemment en premier lieu par l'insuffisance de résultats, en particulier sur le front du chômage, la principale préoccupation des Français. Cette situation tend à alimenter un sentiment d'insécurité économique et sociale et plus largement un grand pessimisme sur l'avenir du pays autour d'un sentiment assez souvent partagé de décrochage de l'économie française, notamment par rapport à celle de son voisin allemand, et un fatalisme sur la capacité des responsables politiques à améliorer la situation.

Il est lié également à une crise du leadership politique. Comme on l'a vu, les dirigeants français finissent rapidement par renier leurs promesses électorales qui s'avèrent impossibles à tenir une fois au pouvoir. Ils ne disent pas non plus ce qu'ils font car ils tendent souvent à refuser d'assumer explicitement un certain nombre d'orientations qu'ils ont prises ou bien validées (ouverture économique, évolution de la construction européenne avec notamment la monnaie unique et l'élargissement à l'Est, société multiculturelle) et par conséquent à ne pas préparer les Français aux efforts, voire aux sacrifices, que cela peut impliquer. Ils donnent ainsi l'impression de subir des événements qu'ils ne semblent pas ou plus maîtriser. Ils ont même eu tendance quelquefois à recourir à une instrumentalisation des contraintes extérieures (conjoncture économique internationale, mondialisation, construction européenne) afin de justifier la mise en place de politiques impopulaires ou bien leur impuissance à régler des questions jugées essentielles, telles que le chômage et la montée de la précarité.

Ils n'ont eu de cesse également de repousser la mise en oeuvre d'un certain nombre de réformes structurelles par peur de la sanction de l'opinion, dans la rue et dans l'isoloir. L'ancien conseiller spécial de François Mitterrand à l'Elysée, Jacques Attali, affirme ainsi dans un entretien accordé au Monde le 13 décembre 2015 : « Trente ans que les hommes politiques ne font rien ! Rien ! Ils ne cherchent qu'à garder le pouvoir et évitent toute réforme, par définition impopulaire. [...] Vous vous rappelez l'image du DRH d'Air France escaladant le grillage ? C'est l'image qu'ils ont tous d'eux-mêmes s'ils se prenaient à agir. [...] J'ai entendu tous les présidents – sauf François Mitterrand – me dire : "si je fais ce que tu dis, ils vont me couper la tête". Ils étaient pourtant d'accord sur le diagnostic et les remèdes. [...] "Oui, disent-ils en privé, tu as raison, il faudrait le faire". Et ils ne font rien ! [...] Comment s'étonner alors que les gens trouvent inutile d'aller voter pour des gens qui ne font rien ? »...

Enfin, on peut aussi reprocher aux dirigeants français leur incapacité à tracer les contours d'un « grand dessein » national auquel les Français pourraient adhérer. Ces dernières décennies, les élites politiques se sont montrées, en effet, incapables de définir et de proposer aux Français un projet collectif mobilisateur. Elles se sont donc contentées de projets par défaut bien peu enthousiasmants, comme sortir de la crise sans trop de dommages, s'adapter tant bien que mal aux contraintes de la mondialisation et de l'intégration européenne, tout faire pour sauvegarder le « modèle social » français ou bien « gérer » au mieux le déclin national.

Au bout du compte, on peut estimer que la grave crise que connaît la France depuis des années est liée en grande partie aux défaillances de son système, de sa culture et de son leadership politiques si singuliers en Europe. Comment cette crise peut-elle être dénouée ? La tentation pour certains est celle de la table rase se traduisant par l'arrivée au pouvoir de Marine Le Pen. Il est certain que, dans ce cas, la crise se transformerait en un drame national, ce qui aurait bien évidemment des répercussions terribles pour le reste de l'Europe et pour l'intégration du continent. Mais le pire n'est pas toujours certain car une partie de la société et de la société civile qui ne croît plus en sa classe politique ne se résout pas non plus à se donner à Marine Le Pen. Elle commence d'ailleurs à s'auto-organiser en privilégiant les actions pragmatiques et le dépassement des clivages traditionnels avec même la tentation d'« ubériser » la politique et en particulier la présidentielle de 2017. C'est donc sans doute plus de ce côté-là que la solution à la crise française réside.

(publié en ligne début avril 2016)

Poland's conservative turn of 2015: Where are its real origins?

Roland Benedikter and Ireneusz Pawel Karolewski

The victories of the national-conservative Law and Justice (PiS) party in Poland in both the presidential elections of May 2015 and the parliamentary elections of October 2015 have been controversially debated by journalists and pundits.1 Many observers interpret Poland's shift to the right as a sign of a broader Central and Eastern Europe (CEE) backslide towards a new form of authoritarianism. On 13 January 2016 for the first time in its history since the founding treaty of Rome in 1958, the European Union (EU) initiated a formal investigation against one of its member states, i.e. Poland. The investigation is intended to question whether new laws introduced by the government of the conservative Law and Justice party (*Prawo i Sprawiedliwość*, PiS), in charge since November 2015, are breaking EU democracy rules and whether they are in accordance with the rule of law and fundamental democratic values.

The EU investigation came after Szydło's government in December 2015 passed controversial laws enabling the government to directly appoint the heads of public TV and radio. At the same time, a new law of December 2015 changed the set-up of Poland's Constitutional Court and its rules of decision-making, forcing it, among other things, to make decisions exclusively with a two-third majority. It is argued that this makes it de facto difficult for the court to act at all. These two moves have been seen as disempowerment of the check-and-balance principle based on the independence of institutions vital for democratic pluralism by many observers and parts of the citizenry. The new law on the Constitutional Court was signed by President Andrzej Duda in December 2015 but has been disregarded by the Constitutional Court itself, who in a decision of March 2016 ruled the law to be unconstitutional. As a response, the Szydło government decided not to publish the March ruling of the Constitutional Court, as it took place in a set-up determined by an older law on the Court. Both steps paved the way for an ongoing constitutional crisis in Poland. In addition, the so-called "Venice Commission" of the Council of Europe— i.e. the "European Commission for Democracy through Law" which is the Council of Europe's advisory body on constitutional matters of its member states—, who explored the issue on the invitation of the Polish government, questioned some of the contents of the new law on the Constitutional Court, thus giving the opposition additional arguments against the government.

After Hungary, Poland is the second of the Central and Eastern European countries that raises fears of an authoritarian backslide in the CEE region.2 Both countries were long viewed as role models with regard to their political and economic transformation from communism (or the so-called "real existing socialism" as political purists would have it) to democracies starting in 1989-91 until their accession negotiations with the EU in 1998-2002. Given the controversial events in Poland since November 2015, some outside observers continue to offer reductionist readings of the Polish crisis. For example, Daniel Kelemen and Mitchell Orenstein in their *Foreign Affairs* article "Europe's Autocracy Problem: Polish Democracy's Final Days?" are already counting the days of Polish democracy and see its only rescue in the pressure of the EU on the Polish government to withdraw or modify some of the contested laws. Others, such as Ivan Krastev with his "Plane crash conspiracy theory" in Foreign Policy, or Judy Dempsey with her assertion that Poland's case is crucial for the future of the EU and must therefore be handled "strongly" in *Carnegie Europe*, are pointing toward the same direction.3

Structural causes

In reality, the "conservative turn" can be explained to a large extent by the specific problems of CEE governance. From a realistic point of view, the most important reason for the recent electoral victory of the Polish right is historic and structural, since it is related to the specific pathologies of CEE post-communist governance. Liberal democracy (accompanied by neoliberal capitalism) was introduced in CEE nations at the historical peak of the neoliberal interpretation of governance, democracy, and capitalism during the years 1989-1990. This led on the one hand to positive effects including robust economic growth and an increase of average living standards. On the other hand, the non-transparent privatization processes and lagging reforms of crucial sectors of productivity manifested specific governance pathologies in Poland and other CEE countries.4

In 2016, after 25 years, the CEE version of governance still remains pathological in many ways. It is showing serious limitations in responding to the social needs of the region's transforming societies. Despite positive macroeconomic development, both young people and senior citizens in CEE have lived under existential pressure for many years with governments unable (and partly unwilling) to strengthen the welfare systems and balance growing social inequality.5

As a result, in the past ten years, more than 2.3 million Poles have decided to emigrate to the United Kingdom, Ireland, the Netherlands, and Germany. Today, the majority of Polish pensioners have to live on 400 EUR per month and must pay for their medicine in full. In addition, Polish pensioners are heavily indebted; their accumulated debt burden was roughly equal to 450 million EUR in 2015. The public health system operates at a dismal level due to chronic underfunding and corruption. Consequently, the majority of Polish citizens have to use private medical services, despite the fact that the average Polish household's net financial wealth is $10,919, while the OECD average is close to $67,000.

At the same time, numerous Polish governments after 1989 used state agencies and enterprises for cronyism and politico-economic clientelism, draining financial resources from the state budget that otherwise could have been invested into higher education, research, health, and pension systems. Foreign capital has not only been unable to substitute for many of these structural difficulties and for the chronic problem of the mismanagement of public funds, but also has produced its own problems, such as real-estate bubbles and problematic mortgages, denominated in Swiss francs. While international corporations, banks, and consultancies have mushroomed all over the CEE area, its most important nations Poland, the Czech Republic, Slovakia, and Hungary have become virtual assembly lines for foreign producers that do not hold their Research and Development departments in these nations and in many cases pay their taxes in other EU countries due to lower VAT and better legal certainty. As a result, 70 percent of the entire tax burden in Poland is carried not by European or transnational enterprises, but by small and medium-sized firms of local origin. All this can bring the Polish economy close to the middle income trap, which might become a real life scenario in all CEE countries.[1]

Most Polish political parties since 1989 have become complicit in this imbalanced development, widely independent of their leftist or rightist in-

---

1 Marta Golonka et al. 2015. Middle-Income Trap in V4 Countries? Analysis and Recommendations. The Kosciuszko Institute: Cracow.

clinations, dragging their feet for decades on the necessary reforms of the health care, higher education, labor market, and pension systems. Against this backdrop, in the eyes of many voters who completely adhere to democratic values, Poland's political parties and governments have turned into guards of the numerous pathologies associated with CEE governance.6

Polish and European controversies

The recent electoral victory of the conservative right in Poland should be read against these developments. It was not the fruit of a sudden "conservative turn," sparked by the cunning motives of just a few astute anti-democratic politicians, as some observers want to depict it. The fact is that the necessary *structural* reforms of the Polish governance system have been widely neglected both by the Polish and CEE governments, and by EU institutions and partner countries as well. It is no coincidence that, paradoxically, the conservative governments in Poland and Hungary immediately after coming into power embraced "neo-leftist" redistributive measures, common in Western welfare states such as Germany and France, that were largely omitted by previous governments in the CEE area. With this, to some extent the case of current Poland continues one paradoxical mechanism of the late EU: that "leftist" governments usually cut into the welfare net and the social system to introduce liberalization, competitiveness and efficiency reforms, and "rightist" governments *nolens volens* have to mitigate social differences and inequality in order to retain popular consent and thus remain credible as "people's parties" in societies increasingly split 50:50 between center-left and center-right. An example for the first mechanism was the German social democratic chancellors Schröder's "Agenda 2010" (2005) which is now imitated, with 10 years' delay, by the young prime ministers of Italy (Matteo Renzi) and France (Manuel Valls). Both are representatives of leftist parties and alliances, but de facto have to enact a center-liberal program out of the needs of their countries, sometimes denominating it a contemporary neo-European "Third-Way"-approach.

The Polish PiS is *de facto* one of the examples of the opposite: a conservative party that in many ways pursues a clear "socialist" agenda. The irony built into these contemporary European contradictions is that since Schröder it has been the conviction of many experts and politicians that only leftist governments can implement cuts and "serious" reforms of the social system, because they are the only ones who can convince the lower classes of the necessity to do so, while only rightist governments can convince the economy to concede a better social share to the broader community. The current Polish government seems to be an expression of this irony.

Conclusions

The controversies surrounding the disempowerment of the Polish Constitutional Court and the public media in 2015-16 have to be seen in this complex framework, particularly in the context of the conservative Polish government's conviction that the current governance problems of Poland (and other CEE nations) are so serious—and at the same time so widely ignored by the EU partners—that they require an exceptionally far-reaching governmental capacity to act similarly to a government of "national unity". Only such a much empowered government would be able to break vested interests and remove the all too well-known pathologies of CEE governance. Since the PiS has not forged an alliance of "national unity" with other parties in the parliament nor sought respective consensus through public debate though, critics argue that the government is not legitimized to launch game-changing emergency measures appropriate only to a real, i.e. formalized government of "national unity", since they modify the rules of the system, not only its applications.

The question in this situation is, if the 2016 intervention of the EU against the PiS government could mark the beginning of a new crisis—a crisis in which, to make matters worse, the main role could be played by a European Union itself plagued by the historical threat of breaking apart in different sectors and at different levels. At the same time, the EU-Poland crisis might have even more serious consequences on the specific governance problems of Central Eastern European nations than the North-South tensions during the European sovereign debt crisis had on the questions of the Euro and of Austerity versus Stimulus Policies. This is because the case of Poland relates to the center of the East-West axis of the European integration project, which is still younger and more instable than most other internal relations within the EU. The current EU refugee crisis since 2012 could make things—at least temporarily—even worse, mainly psychologically, e.g. regarding the trust between member states and between them and the EU as a whole. For example, today's calls for more European solidarity by the EU are accompanied by voices of European politicians to cut the European funds to the CEE area—a call which understandably does not exactly enhance the EU approval rate with CEE voters.

Our conclusion is that if the debate between Poland, the EU and the international community about the future of governance and democracy in the CEE area - and in Poland in particular - is to be productive and forward-oriented, it must concentrate to jointly and collaboratively implement balanced and reasoned reforms of the CEE governance systems in positive cooperation and by using best practice examples at the interface between the EU and the CEE, instead of focusing almost exclusively on the effects of the victory of the PiS in Poland alone. That will require a new, sound and sober spirit of dialogue and cooperation between all partners involved that will have to substitute the rhetoric of scandal and polemic that these days abound on all sides. With this, a practical and at the same time open policy approach for the further steps of the debate needs to be designed.

References:

1. Marcinkiewicz, Kamil and Mary Stegmaier. 2016. The Parliamentary Election in Poland, October 2015, Electoral Studies 41: 213-224.

2. Ágh, Attila. 2015. De-Europanization and De-democratization Trends in ECE: From the Potemkin Democracy to the Elected Autocracy in Hungary. Journal of Comparative Politics 8(2): 4-26; Berend, Ivan T. and Bugaric, Bojan. 2015. Unfinished Europe: Transition from Communism to Democracy in Central and Eastern Europe. Journal of Contemporary History 50(4): 768-785.

3. Kelemen Daniel R. and Orenstein Mitchell A. 2016. Europe's Autocracy Problem. Polish Democracy's Final Days? Foreign Affairs, January 7, 2016, http://www.foreignaffairs.com/articles/poland/2016-01-07/europes-autocracy-problem; Krastev, Ivan. 2015.The Plane Crash Conspiracy Theory That Explains Poland. Five years after the country's president and 95 others went down in a forest in Russia, Poland's new leaders are pouring fuel on the cover-up fire, Foreign Policy, December 21, 2015, http://foreignpolicy.com/2015/12/21/when-law-and-justice-wears-a-tinfoil-hat-poland-russia-smolensk-kaczynski; Dempsey, Judith.2016. Why Poland Matters. In: Carnegie Europe, January 4, 2016, http://carnegieeurope.eu/stra tegiceurope/?fa=62389.

4. Bruszt, Laszlo. 1994. Transformative Politics: Social Costs and Social Peace in East Central Europe. In: János Mátyás Kovács (ed.) Transition to Capitalism?: The Communist Legacy in Eastern Europe, New Brunswick: Transaction Publishers, 103-120; O'Neil, Patrick H. 1996. Revolution from Within: Institutional Analysis, Transitions from Authoritarianism, and the Case of Hungary. In: World Politics, 48 (4):579–603; Nölke, Andreas and Arjan Vliegenthart.2009. Enlarging the Varieties of Capitalism: The Emergence of Dependent Market Economies in East Central Europe. In: World Politics 61(4): 670-702.

5. Nesvetailova, Anastasia. 2004. From Transition to Dependent Development: The New Periphery in Global Finance Capitalism. In: Neil Robinson (ed.) Reforging the Weakest Link. Aldershot: Ashgate; Milanovic, Branko. 1993. Social Costs of the Transition to Capitalism: Poland 1990-91, Working Paper WPS 1165, World Bank, Policy Research; Ost David et al. 1994. Is Latin American the Future of Eastern Europe? In: Problems of Communism 41(3):44–57.

6. Cf. Standing, Guy. 1996. Social Protection in Central and Eastern Europe: A Tale of Slipping Anchors and Torn Safety Nets. In: Gøsta Esping-Andersen (ed.). Welfare States in Transition: National Adaptations in Global Economies, London: Sage, 225-255; Orenstein, Mitchell. 1995. Transitional social policy in the Czech Republic and Poland. In: Czech Sociological Review 3(2): 179-196.

(published online early May 2016)

The future of the EU after Brexit: Reform or Further Disintegration?

Helgard Fröhlich

Great Britain has voted: 51.9 per cent voted to leave the EU, while 48.1 per cent were in favour of staying; the voter turnout was 72.2 per cent.[1] The result is clear, even if the majority is not overwhelming. As with the Scottish Referendum regarding independence from the United Kingdom (September 2014), a vote has been cast, but none of the underlying problems have been resolved. On the contrary, the situation is more difficult than before, and EU reform is more necessary than ever! Just as the asymmetric and incomplete devolution of Scotland (and other regions) since 2014 has caused problems and intensified centrifugal forces within the UK, the Brexit referendum has also once again brought deep contradictions to the political surface with full force.

In these turbulent days, one reads that this is a turning point in the history of European integration. If the 23rd of June 2016 is to become a turning point - and does not lead to the disintegration of Europe - an honest and thorough analysis has to follow. Not only is Great Britain in a difficult situation, but the EU as a whole. The United Kingdom is deeply divided over the European question. Still technically a member state, how will a future working relationship with Great Britain take shape? Which new measures will be found according to TEU Article 50? Possible scenarios – Norwegian, Swiss or other models – exist,[2] but the fact is that neither the UK nor the European Commission had a plan B. With regard to the overall situation that led to the referendum and the Brexit crisis, and despite the

---

1 EU referendum. Results in full hhttp://www.bbc.com/news/politics/eu_referendum/results (last access 29.6.2016).
2 The Economist, In graphics: Britain's referendum on EU membership. A background guide to "Brexit" from the European Union, 24.2.2016 , http://www.economist.com/blogs/graphicdetail/2016/02/graphics-britain-s-referendum-eu-membership (last access : 26.6.2016).

package of concessions[3] arranged in February 2016 between Cameron and the EU (which will now not become valid), the basic question on the future of the European Union, the *"quo vadis Europe?"*, remains unanswered. During the referendum debate I, the *"quo vadis"question,* and, in turn, a positive vision for Europe was never addressed by either the *Leave* or the *Remain* supporters. Nevertheless, this question has existed for a long time, especially since the EU has found itself in a state of continuous turmoil due to the financial crisis. The frequent answer, "More Europe", has not only failed to convince the British. It has also failed to persuade other Europeans, as has a series of other questions: Which Europe? (What should it look like?) In which areas do we need more Europe? In which do we need less? How much differentiation can the EU stand/manage and how much does it need?

Despite the current discontent, Great Britain has been and remains an important European partner. It has the second largest national economy in the EU and as such has been an important net contributor. If a continued access to the domestic market is negotiated with the EU, Great Britain – like Norway – will probably have to continue to pay contributions. However, even though the circumstances will have changed, as a nuclear power with a permanent chair on the UN Security Council and as a founding member of NATO, Great Britain will hold its weight within NATO and therefore still exert influence over the EU's Common Foreign and Security Policy in one way or another.

Moreover, the United Kingdom, albeit an island nation, has grown to be an organic part of our European community. In the Second World War it played a key role in fighting for our shared values of *Freedom* and *Liberty,* thus laying the foundation for o peaceful development and European integration. As Angela Merkel quite rightly emphasised in her 2014 speech to the British Parliament, "Yes, it is true and cannot be repeated often enough: the United Kingdom has no need to furnish proof of its commitment to Europe and its basic values."[4] In the current situation, this, too, must be remembered.

We still share those common values, even if we demonstrate a lack of unity in terms of following the rules of the institutional game within the

---

3 http://www.consilium.europa.eu/en/press/press-releases/2016/02/19-euco-conclusio ns/ (last access 25.6.2016).

4 http://www.parliament.uk/documents/addresses-to-parliament/Angela-Merkel-addr ess-20130227.pdf (last access 25.6.2016).

EU framework or in relation to the goals and areas of joint action. And the point that David Cameron made in his Bloomberg speech in 2013 is indeed still valid: This framework must be measured according to the degree it serves its citizens - with or without the UK.[5] This is common sense in the most literal British meaning, and it should be the foundation for all future procedures.

A Reconsideration of the British Question in the Context of EU Reform:
First reflections

Article 50 of the TEU states that the United Kingdom must officially declare its desire to leave the EU, but it does not set a time frame. The institutions of the European Union[6] followed by the Heads of State and government have expressed their regrets at the British decision and their wish to start the negotiations soon saying, "There is a need to organise the withdrawal of the UK from the EU in an orderly fashion."[7] One need not be clairvoyant to predict that the negotiations will be difficult, and not only between the UK and the EU 27. There will also be strong disagreement between the EU 27 themselves before a common negotiating position is reached. "The European Council will adopt guidelines for the negotiations of an agreement with the UK."[8] It is likely to be a turbulent process. There is already disagreement. Should negotiations be hard fought and quick or rather sober-minded and reflective, without excessive time pressure? Both positions reflect varying interests.

The EU 27 have announced that an informal meeting of the heads of state and governments will be held in Bratislava in September, 2016. The

---

5 David Cameron, Bloomberg Speech, 23. Jan. 2013, https://www.gov.uk/governmen t/speeches/eu-speech-at-bloomberg (last access 25.6.2016).
6 Joint statement by Martin Schulz, President of the European Parliament; Donald Tusk, President of the European Council; Mark Rutte, Holder of the Presidency of the Council of the EU; and Jean-Claude Juncker, President of the European Commission, http://europa.eu/rapid/press-release_STATEMENT-16-2329_en.htm (24.6.2016).
7 European Council, 28-29/06/2016, Informal meeting in Brussels, 29 June 2016 – statement. http://www.consilium.europa.eu/en/press/press-releases/2016/06/29-27m s-informal-meeting-statement (last access 3.7.2016).
8 Ibid.

coming weeks will reveal the guidelines to be developed. There is a need for serious contemplation. Which issues need to be considered?

• The Brexit crisis has brought into focus a long standing problem which can no longer be ignored by the political elite: that of the *consent of the British and European* **populations** with regard to European integration. However, analysing the reaction of the people is not simply a matter of identifying anti-EU positions, but also to acknowledge the diversity and diffuseness of the fears: social decline, globalisation and the sense of the loss of homeland. A better explanation of Europe will probably not console the individual citizen. The community's lack of legitimacy must be overcome.

• The question of *EU reform* remains virulent, indicating that there was already an urgent need for reform before the referendum. The question of a mutual *"where to"* for the future of the EU 27 not only remains important, but in the light of the latest shock to the EU with the Brexit vote, it is now even more urgent for the remaining members to forcefully promote the long-announced reform of the EU. Some argue for a complete relaunch,[9] others for further reforms. The most sensible approach would be to discuss the *"where to"* and *"how to go on"* with the Britons as well. What does an *"ever closer union"* mean and how is this objective to be defined after Britain's decision to leave? Which *differentiations* in the European integration process are needed and useful in order to secure lasting and sustainable wealth in a peaceful and sustainable environment for our peoples: gradual integration?; multi-paced integration?; a core Europe? How fundamental should and must the reform be? For several years now, the EU has been in crisis mode. The debate over a reform of the EU must consider the EU crisis in different domains (the euro crisis, the refugee crisis, crisis in citizens' support, and now the Brexit crisis). Again, the "we need more Europe" must urgently be clearly specified to avoid further turmoil and a revival of populist-nationalist sentiments within the EU 27. A courageous approach is needed, despite the fear that the necessary changes to the contract could open up a Pandora's box.

---

9 Sigmar Gabriel, Martin Schulz, Europa neu gründen (24.6.2016), https://www.spd.d e/fileadmin/Dokumente/Sonstiges Papiere_et_al/PK_Europa_Paper.pdf (last access 3.7.2016).

- A self-critical view of the EU on *the debate of the referendum* is essential. The EU 27 have backed off from comments and statements in the last few months for fear this would be perceived as "intervention by Brussels" and counterproductive - and was therefore a correct decision. However, that all the parties involved were probably aware of the fact that the so-called "New Settlement" that resulted from the *renegotiation* between the EU and UK in February 2016 was, in the best case, something that would somehow soften the voices of the Euro-sceptics in Cameron's own party and give British citizens the impression that EU-UK relations had indeed been completely renegotiated and regulated.[10] The EU 28, including Cameron, were hoping that they would, be able to once more *"muddle through"*. Next to commitments to the four fundamental freedoms of the internal market as a matter of principle, one could read that other countries, too, might consider using the emergency brake and reduce social security benefits for EU migrants – one of the previous concessions – in case the agreements come into force. Is this going to strengthen the citizens' trust in the EU? Probably not! A joint effort in allocating the refugees and an agreement on distribution quotas, which are still inadequately regulated, would have probably made a more tangible contribution to a successful joint action.
- The British Brexit debate will remain an issue in domestic politics for a long time to come. Never before has so much attention been paid to European issues. In Great Britain, the populist pro-Brexit campaign focused primarily on *EU migrants* rather than on refugee flows from outside the EU. The Conservatives were not able to keep their election promise to limit net immigration to under 100,000 per year.[11] In this context, the question of social welfare benefits for EU migrants – despite the "emergency brake" measure conceded by the EU in February 2016 to temporarily reduce these benefits – became one of the dominant topics of the Brexit supporters. Beyond this, the discussion was

---

10 European Council, European Council conclusions, 18-19 February 2016 (EUCO 1/16), http://www.consilium.europa.eu/en/press/press-releases/2016/02/19-euco-c onclusions/ (last access 23.6.2016).

11 The 2010 campaign promise to reduce net immigration (immigration minus emigration) to under 100,000 per year heated up the Brexit debate fiercely and became one of the UKIP's main points of argumentation. See: Alan Travis, Net migration to UK soars by 39% to 243,000, The Guardian, 28.8.2014 https://www.theguardia n.com/uk-news/2014/aug/28/uk-net-migration-soars-to-243000-theresa-may (last access 4.7.2016).

defined by emotions ('I want my country back') and tabloid hostility,[12] and both sides linked the consequences of remaining or leaving to horror scenarios devoid of any positive prospects. The flimsiness of the promises and scenarios was made apparent in the days after the referendum. Examples include the repudiation of the promise that all EU contributions could thenceforth be invested in the Public Health Service and Nigel Farage's resignation as head of the UKIP on July 4th. The atmosphere was and remains heated, reaching a negative climax with the murder of the pro-European House of Commons member Jo Cox on June 16th. Ongoing demonstrations after the Brexit vote demonstrate the dissatisfaction of British EU supporters. Subjects like EU labour migrants and, of course, the refugee flows remain on the agenda after the referendum, also in other European countries. At the summit held on June 28-29 - *after* the Brexit vote - the Heads of State had no choice but to appreciate that the flow of refugees in the central Mediterranean area had not decreased.[13]

• How much weight does this referendum hold? Unlike referenda in other European countries, the Brexit poll was only *consultative* and not *binding*. According to British constitutional understanding, this was the only option owing to the basic principle of the "undivided sovereignty"[14] of parliament. Since the vote to leave, doubts regarding the usefulness of referenda in general have been expressed all over Europe. But it is **not** referenda that are to blame! For a meaningful analysis of the situation we should examine the responsibility of those politicians and elites who exploited the Brexit poll to play political power games. The 2011 European Union Act[15] was a reaction to the ratification of the Treaty of Lisbon under a Labour government. In the 2010 election

---

12 See, i.e., The Sun's call to "break free from Brussels" and vote pro Brexit on 14.6.2016. https://www.thesun.co.uk/news/1277920/we-urge-our-readers-to-believ e-in-britain-and-vote-to-leave-the-eu-in-referendum-on-june-23/ (last access 24.6.2016).

13 "...Central Mediterranean route, where flows of predominantly economic migrants remain at the same level as last year". European Council, 28-29/06/2016, www.consilium.europa.eu/en/meetings/european-council/2016/06/28-29 (last access 30.6.2016).

14 Vernon Bogdanor, Footfalls Echoing in the Memory. Britain and Europe: The Historical Perspective, in: International Affairs 81, 4 (2005), 689-701, p. 698.

15 European Union Act 2011, http://www.legislation.gov.uk/ukpga/2011/12/contents (last access 30.6.2016).

campaign, David Cameron promised to make further amendments to the European treaties ('power transfer to Brussels') contingent upon a referendum. Later Cameron tried to appease the critics in his own party, who – facing the success of the UKIP party in regional and European elections – demanded a more Euro-critical position from the Conservative Party leadership. In the end, UKIP and the damaging quarrels within the party, were to be kept in check and contained by the pseudo-concession, "We will renegotiate, and then the people will decide in a referendum". The European Union Referendum Act of 2015[16] foresaw an in-out referendum by 2017 at the latest. So what was actually voted on? *Renegotiate and referendum*[17] was the promise Cameron made to the British in the Bloomberg speech on January 13, 2013. In reality, time constraints alone rendered renegotiation of the EU treaties unrealistic. During the European Council on the 18th and 19th of February 2016, the Heads of State accepted "A new settlement for the UK in the EU."[18] This compromise addressed some aspects of the issues of EU–UK relations, but in no way encompassed (or could possibly have encompassed) all the questions, problems and implications in the sense of a possible realignment. It was, as the British say, "too little, too late" to stem the anti-EU attitude. Nonetheless, the "New Settlement" gave Cameron a basis on which to hold the promised vote as announced. Cameron's tactics- and those of the Conservative Party leadership, were reckless and failed. The Labour Party's drawn-out tactical manoeuvring also proved indecisive and divided Corbyn's commitment to the "Remain and Reform" position[19] in mid-April 2016 came too late and stemmed from a weak opposition. The Liberals had already been punished for their pro-European position in the 2015 elections with a massive drop in votes. . The battle over the Brexit was fiercely fought

---

16 European Union Referendum Act 2015, http://www.legislation.gov.uk/ukpga/2015 /36/contents/enacted (last access 30.6.2016).

17 David Cameron, Bloomberg Speech 23 Jan. 2013, https://www.gov.uk/governmen t/speeches/eu-speech-at-bloomberg (last access 25.6.2016).

18 European Council, *European Council conclusions,* 18-19 February 2016 (EUCO 1/16), http://www.consilium.europa.eu/en/press/press-releases/2016/02/19-euco-c onclusions/ (last access 23.6.2016).

19 Very late, on 14.4.2016, the new Labour Party leader, Jeremy Corbyn, held a speech on Euro politics with a clear appeal to remain in the EU. Jeremy Corbyn, EU Speech, London 14 April 2016, http://www.unitetheunion.org/uploaded/docu ments/JCEU%20speech11-26326.pdf (last access 26.6.2016).

and divided both British society and the political parties. Some of the Conservative party's own ministers and around half of its parliamentary members in the House of Commons supported the Brexit, taking a position against their own Prime Minister.[20] After the vote and Cameron's decision not to re-contest the Party's leadership, Theresa May, Michael Gove, and three other Conservative delegates officially sought to succeed Cameron as PM. Gove advocated a *reform of capitalism* and the Australian immigration system[21] but was defeated by May and Andrea Leadom in the preliminary internal poll. The last word about who will succeed Cameron has not yet been spoken, but the EU-UK negotiations, which will most likely begin in autumn 2016, require one thing more than anything else: reliable, level-headed partners on both sides!

- *The United Kingdom: Now a Divided Kingdom?*! The majority of the electorate in Scotland, Northern Ireland and London voted to remain in the EU. Can the UK withstand this political rift? In *Scotland* 62 per cent of the voters chose to remain in the EU. Every single one of the 42 Scottish regions voted "remain". Nicola Sturgeon declared her resistance to Brexit and brought a second referendum for Scottish independence into play. However, before any such referendum, the provisions of the Scotland Act of 1998 dictate that the foreign affairs of Great Britain , including Scotland's relations with the EU, are regulated solely by the Westminster Parliament. Experts state that Scotland could theoretically refer to Article 29 of the Scotland Act, which regulates the implementation of EU laws to Scottish jurisdiction.[22] It remains uncertain, however, whether Scotland could actually continue to implement EU law if the United Kingdom as a whole is no longer part of the EU, which is why Sturgeon vigorously expressed her desire to negotiate further membership with Brussels directly. It is also a matter of dispute as to whether it would be possible to derive a precedent from the

---

20 See Nicolai von Ondarza, Zwischen den Welten. Großbritannien als Partner für Deutschland in Europa nach dem EU-Referendum (May 2016), https://www.swp-berlin.org/fileadmin/contents/products/aktuell/2016A35_orz.pdf (last access 25.6.2016).

21 Tory leadership: Michael Gove Speech, 1 July 2016 , http://www.bbc.com/news/uk-36684332 (last access 4.7.2016).

22 Scotland Act 1998, http://www.legislation.gov.uk/ukpga/1998/46/contents (last access 4.7.2016).

"Referendum Agreement" that would render London's agreement to a second vote on independence unnecessary. Equally uncertain at the moment is the position of the EU itself. With regard to the previous moves to secede, the EU declared in 2014 that an independent Scotland would not automatically be an EU Member State but would have to apply for membership. The Northern Ireland "remain" vote is complicated as well. The Brexit vote will mean an external border of the EU will pass through the Irish island, and it is already feared that the conflicts pacified with such difficulty by the 1998 Good Friday agreement could erupt once more.

A review of the British and European Question: A Time for Deeper reflection

If an EU reform is to succeed and disintegration and further bursts of nationalist populism are to be prevented, a series of underlying reflections that will bring about long-term solutions need be discussed and put to rest:

- In view of growing aspirations toward renationalisation in the UK and elsewhere and in times of increasing global interdependency, a fundamental *positioning of nation states with* regard to the issue of sovereignty is necessary. The 'semi-detachedness' from Europe of Great Britain was one of many factors that caused confusion among their citizens for a long time - perhaps even dating back to 1973 - regarding the "Brussels and us" relationship. The term "shared sovereignty" needs to be more precisely defined.[23] In Great Britain in particular, but also in other EU countries, the role of nation states in Europe and the broader changing world must be (re-) defined.[24]
- How do political systems function in the "post-democratic "era? Confronted with the division of European society(-ies),we must take more seriously the discomfiture among elements of the population – extend-

---

23 David Charter, Au Revoir, Europe. What if Britain left the EU? London 2012, p. 15 ff.
24 Tim Oliver, Why the EU Referendum Will Not be the End of the Story, The Federal Trust, February 2016, p. 7, 12, http://fedtrust.co.uk/wp-content/uploads/2016/02/Why_the_EU_Referendum_will_not_be_the_end_of_the_story.pdf (last access 3.7.2016). In a similar vein, Roger Liddle, The Europe Dilemma, Britain and the drama of EU integration, London 2014.

ing all the way to right-wing extremist alternatives - vis-à-vis the functionality of national systems, and in particular the European political system. *Democratisation and further constitutionalisation* of the European Union have to be rediscussed.[25] The convention method needs to be revitalised. The EU's executive federalism, which has escalated since the financial crisis, does not meet the needs of a world society based on democracy.[26]

- *"Rediscover our common social model.* Europe is more than a market, a currency or a budget. It was built around a set of shared values."[27] Only those with good future prospects in Europe will advocate European integration. Social standards and active labour market policies - in a phrase, its "output legitimacy" - is how European citizens' evaluate the European project. Europe's high youth-unemployment rates in particular are no longer acceptable. The EU 28 agreed upon the 2020 Strategy, but it has not yet been implemented. Proposals for the 'rediscovery of our common social model' have existed for a long time, and now - thanks to the Brexit - they have been reinvigorated.[28]

- What could a *symmetric devolution* and the resulting federalisation of the United Kingdom look like? - where the English, Scottish, Welsh and Northern Irish coexist in a larger national state?[29] Just recently, Andrew Blick advocated "a dramatic change in the way the UK is governed", by which he meant a systematic federalisation fixed in a "writ-

---

25 Sigmar Gabriel and Martin Schulz demanded more democratic and comprehensive actions from the EU and again put a European government and a second chamber of the European Parliament on the agenda. Sigmar Gabriel, Martin Schulz, Europa neu gründen (24.6.2016), https://www.spd.de/fileadmin/Dokumente/Sonstiges__P apiere_et_al_/PK_Europa_Paper.pdf (last access 3.7.2016).

26 According to Jürgen Habermas, Zur Verfassung Europas. Ein Essay, Berlin 2011, p. 8, 40.

27 Henrik Enderlein, Jean Pisani-Ferry, Reforms and Investment and Growth: An Agenda for France, Germany and Europe. Report to the French Minister for the Economy, Industry and Digital Affairs and to the German Federal Minister for Economic Affairs and Energy. 2014, http://www.strategie.gouv.fr/sites/strategie.go uv.fr/files/atoms/files/rapport_henderlein_pisani_en_final-1.pdf (last access 26.6.2016).

28 Sigmar Gabriel, Martin Schulz, Europa neu gründen (24.6.2016), https://www.spd. de/fileadmin/Dokumente/Sonstiges__Papiere_et_al_/PK_Europa_Paper.pdf (last access 3.7.2016).

29 In a similar way, this question comes up for other countries as well. Among them are Spain, where Catalonia is seeking a referendum on independence.

ten constitution".[30] The "devolution" is as yet incomplete, but it will be essential for the survival of the United Kingdom.

- Great Britain's political system and culture have evolved over centuries into a flexible tension *between continuity and change* of which the British are proud. A great deal has been written on the opt-outs and British exceptionalism.[31] Less has been reported on Britain's specific and constructive contribution to European integration, for example its contribution to the development of the subsidiarity principle. Only when taken together can a complete picture be assembled. According to an article in the Economist in February 2016, "Thanks partly to British political clout, the EU now has less wasteful agricultural and fisheries policies, a budget to which Britain is a middling net contributor, a liberal single market, a commitment to freer trade and 28 members. Like any club, it needs reform. But the worst way to effect change is to loiter by the exit."[32]

The relationship between national characteristics within the framework of our common history needs further reflection and must be given fundamental consideration in any debate on reform. Multiple identities will also be a constant feature of a reformed EU and of all its Member States! "United in diversity"– should remain a principle pillar of a reformed EU, regardless of how many members it has.

(published online early July 2016)

---

30 Andrew Blick, Federalism: the UK's Future? The Federal Trust for education research, April 2016, p. 29.
31 Timothy Garton Ash, Is Britain European? In: International Affairs 77, 1 (2001), p. 7.
32 The Economist, In graphics: Britain's referendum on EU membership. A background guide to "Brexit" from the European Union, 24.2.2016, http://www.econo mist.com/blogs/graphicdetail/2016/02/graphics-britain-s-referendum-eu-members hip (last access 16.6.2016). Similar arguments in: Robert Cooper, Britain and Europe, in: International Affairs 88, 6 (2012), 1195 ff.

Why I don't think Brexit is going to happen (or, at least not the way the British thought it would)

Sebastian Zeitzmann

Only losers left behind?

It has only been a few weeks since the June 23rd referendum in the United Kingdom which resulted in a narrow majority of participants supporting the Brexit camp. Since then, academic argument1, the media and the general public forum have been dominated by questions about what will happen next and how the British departure from the European Union can be accomplished in practice. Perhaps this debate should also be examining whether or not Brexit is actually going to happen and, assuming this is the case, whether this will be a true departure from EU integration or rather a bogus exit whereby the status quo does not significantly change. Indeed, such a bogus exit would mean in practice that key aspects of British integration into the EU would remain in place, whilst at the same time the situation of the UK would drastically deteriorate in terms of its institutional involvement and the price to be paid in exchange for future British access to the EU single market. Needless to say, the bogus exit option would especially bring little change to those aspects identified by the Brexit supporters as main obstacles for a future EU membership: first, the alleged loss of sovereignty, second, the already mentioned contribution to the EU budget, money allegedly better spent on domestic issues such as the National Health Service, and, third, the migration into the UK from other EU Member States.

It remains unclear who would really benefit from a Brexit apart from those nationalists and populists throughout Europe who continually campaign against any kind of EU integration, espousing the antiquated idea and fake ideal of the national State and seeking easy answers to complex questions, especially the argument that after regaining "full sovereignty" or "independence" from the EU, a golden future would lie ahead for all those States currently held in the paralysing and deadly stranglehold of the European Union. This handful of die-hards would benefit politically whilst at the same time personally suffer the negative consequences of the ideas they propagate in the same way that ordinary people will be affected. Nigel Farage, truly British by name and nature, married, as he is, to a German woman, driving a Swedish car and being on the payroll of a French- and Belgium-based institution, serves as an excellent example here.

Apart from these few winners, Brexit seems to leave only losers behind. Because of this, a Brexit appears, though not impossible, unlikely. In the following paper, I will present reasons for this, focussing on the most important ones and on the UK only and recommend further measures to be taken both by the British government, the European Union, and its 27 other Member States in order to productively move ahead.

Economic implications of Brexit on the UK

It is obvious that a British departure from the European Union would impact negatively on the EU-27 single market and the market economies of the remaining Member States. Even so, this in itself may not serve as a basis for avoiding Brexit. What may well prove decisive, however, are the economic implications for the UK that the electorate was warned about prior to the public referendum, many of which seem realistic.[2]

First and foremost, the British might lose access to the single market, an option even Nigel Farage has ruled out. It is, however, not exclusively up to the British to decide about their future involvement as regards the single market but mainly a decision of the EU-27. There are four options imaginable: the Norwegian, Swiss, Turkish/Korean and WTO models. The latter is highly unlikely, given it would base EU-British trade relations exclusively on WTO rules, allowing for tariffs to be set up between them, and consequently excluding unhindered access to the single market. This would damage UK trade with the EU in terms of goods as well as services, and further exacerbate economic consequences for the UK. Over time, additional non-tariff barriers could emerge to damage trade in services in particular. The WTO model would, however, also exclude free movement of citizens and hence meet one of the main objectives of the Brexit camp. This particular objective could also be achieved by agreeing on the Turkish/Korean model, i.e. the establishment of a customs union between the EU and UK or a free trade agreement respectively. Whether the EU would agree to such models in the British case is questionable, though, since this would mean nothing less than allowing the British to cherry-pick by giving British goods unhindered access to the single market whilst excluding any free movement. It is also questionable whether a customs union or free trade agreement would serve British needs: an important part of the British economy is service-based, especially in the banking and financial services sector. The somewhat loose forms of economic integration such as those in question in the Turkish or Korean model would focus exclusively on opening markets for the trade in goods but would not apply to services. Using these approaches would not invalidate one of the big British fears, the City of London losing access to the EU single market. Consequently, the models preferred in the UK and propagated by the Brexit camp, are the Norwegian and Swiss3 examples. Switzerland is very closely linked to the EU with around 120 bilateral agreements providing for, i.a., almost full access to the single market and even participation in the Schengen area of borderless travel. However, to a great extent, these numerous agreements take into account particular Swiss interests and motivations. This may sound tempting for the British (though less attractive to the EU), but one must not forget that despite internal opposition, even Switzerland has agreed to labour migration and also contributes to the budget of the European Union. For exactly this reason, the Norwegian model will not really match British interests either: Norway, alongside fellow EFTA members Iceland and Liechtenstein, is extremely closely linked to the EU via the European Economic Area (EEA). The three countries have almost full access to the single market, but this also includes the free movement of workers. They also contribute to the EU budget, Norway with even a higher per capita contribution than the UK currently has. What is more, in terms of their relation to the EU, the three EFTA EEA States are merely "law-takers" or -shapers rather than lawmakers: about 2/3 of the acquis communautaire apply to those States (law-taking). They do not, however, participate in the legislative processes of the EU (law-making) but are instead limited to providing legally non-binding input which may or may well not be taken into account (law-shaping). I cannot imagine the British agreeing to the kind of regime which limits them to the role of spectator in EU decision-making whilst being obliged to apply and implement EU secondary law which may well not always meet British interests. In any practical sense, it makes no difference whether or not the UK becomes an EFTA member. The EFTA has already indicated it would welcome back their founding member, but Britain's bargaining power vis-à-vis the EU-27 would not be strengthened by an EFTA membership.

I doubt whether an unprecedented "British model", with or without EFTA membership, possibly based on a large number of Swiss-style bilaterals and providing for single market access for both British goods and services, but at the same time excluding free movement of persons, would be acceptable at all to the EU-27. Leading EU figures and politicians of the 27 Member States have ruled out any such option and if such an option were to be discussed seriously, this might well serve as an incentive for further EU States to bow out of the European Union.

Having said this, it becomes obvious there is no option acceptable to the EU-27 that will fully meet British interests. Given that every single EU Member State will have to assent to any new regime, it rather seems that the UK will have to back down dramatically, resulting in the scenario mentioned above: in effect, nothing much is likely to change. The only difference is that the British will have practically no impact on further EU secondary law which will nonetheless to a large extent apply in the UK – consequently, the British will still have to accept EU made rules and won't be able to regain control on a domestic level – and the UK will most likely end up with an even higher contribution to the EU budget, since the survival of the British rebate seems extremely unlikely post Brexit.

Apart from those mentioned above, numerous other negative effects of a possible Brexit on the British economy already began to emerge months ahead of the referendum and have now materialised since June 24th, the day of the result: a decrease in foreign investment in the UK, a drastic devaluation of the British pound compared to any major currency, severe losses on the stock market and threats of withdrawal from currently UK-based companies or British subsidiaries of multinationals. This has resulted in a predicted fall in British GDP, lower tax revenues, and an expected rise in unemployment. Accordingly, major credit rating agency S&P cut the UK's rating by two steps only days after the referendum. By now, market analysts expect the UK was to slide into recession soon due to the vote. Economic hardship might result in budget gaps/deficits which again would result in cuts to social benefits and public health and educational expenditure whilst at the same time domestic taxes might have to be increased. Parallel to this, loans from the European Investment Bank to the UK are at risk: the UK alone has so far received more than 40 times the amount of loans given to the four EFTA States put together. As regards external relations, the UK would have to negotiate and conclude new free trade agreements with its current partners which might result in less preferential terms and conditions compared to the status quo, given the loss of bargaining power of a UK outside the EU.

Political implications of Brexit on the UK

In recent years, the political landscape in the UK has already experienced change and could only partially be preserved by the distinct British first past the post voting system. However, the need for a coalition government for the first time in 70 years, made up of Conservatives and Liberal Democrats between 2010 and 2015, the rise of UKIP and regional parties, especially in Scotland, or the referendum for Scottish independence (from the UK) in 2014 provide clear evidence of a change in the political climate. The events in June and July 2016, however, are particularly significant and could be considered a breaking point in modern British politics. We have experienced the political fall of a prime minister stepping down, sweeping away most of his cabinet in a rather chaotic procedure and against the clearly verbalised will of his opponents in his own, internally torn party. We see the major opposition party in a state of paralysis. We have experienced the main heads of the Brexit camp retiring, now appearing clueless as to how to move ahead. There is a House of Commons that will have to react to the outcome of a referendum, an outcome which is not in line with the large majority of parliamentarians. We were witness to a shameless referendum campaign dominated by false arguments and horror scenarios from both sides, culminating in the murder of a pro-European MP. In other words: the oldest of all modern democracies and the majority of its leading politicians have failed on the Brexit question, leaving many frustrated. The discussion has also shown a drastically torn and less united kingdom: whereas England and Wales, apart from London and some bigger cities, voted against a future EU membership, north of the Hadrian's Wall and in Northern Ireland, a huge majority were in favour of remaining inside the Club of 28. Not a single region here returned a majority vote for Brexit. It is exactly this division that poses the biggest political threat to today's United Kingdom: its separation into "Leavia" and "Remainia" which might ultimately result in a breakup of the Kingdom.[1] The "UK of Four" has only been in existence in its current form since 1927, the year of Northern Ireland's integration into the Union. Scotland has been part of the United Kingdom since 1707, whereas the union of England and Wales has existed since 1536. The fragility of the UK of Four

---

1 See further Sabine Riedel, Ein Brexit ohne Schotten und Nordiren? Großbritannien droht der Staatszerfall – Hintergründe und Auswege, https://www.swp-berlin.org/fil eadmin/contents/products/aktuell/2016A54_rds.pdf (last access: 07.8.2016).

was already evident in 2014 when a referendum on Scottish independence was held, resulting in 55% of the electorate voting in favour of remaining part of the UK and, consequently, the European Union. Staying inside the EU was one of the arguments of the winning camp of 2014 for opting against secession from the UK. After a Brexit, staying inside the EU or being a member of it will only be possible for Scotland and North Ireland as independent States. Therefore, it is no surprise that especially in Scotland, a movement for a second referendum on UK membership is gaining momentum. According to the Scottish First Minister, Nicola Sturgeon, there is a high probability of such a referendum taking place by the end of 2018. First polls have shown a clear majority for a Scottish secession from the UK in order to safeguard future membership in the EU. The situation may look a bit different in Northern Ireland, but even here, separation from the UK cannot be ultimately ruled out these days. Moreover, it is interesting to note that in Gibraltar 96% of the electorate voted in favour of remaining inside the European Union. Were all those territories, which enjoy certain autonomy within the United Kingdom, to leave the country in favour of independence, the UK would return to the geographical size it had between 1536 and 1707, most probably resulting in a loss of global political power. The consequences of such a development cannot even be foreseen at this time. Certainly, the UK will remain an important player on the international scene, not least because of its permanent seat in the UN Security Council, its position as a nuclear power and NATO member. However, a state facing such dramatic internal political changes will most likely carry less weight in international relations. There could (also) possibly be a huge impact on the Commonwealth of Nations if its leading nation were to suffer politically in the way outlined above.

The British are aware of those risks. Theresa May, new Prime Minister of the UK since July 2016, has already made clear that triggering the exit negotiations will only happen once talks with Scotland on its future have been held, which will likely delay the Brexit process significantly.

Another challenge for the UK are its traditionally close relations with the Republic of Ireland. Both States have abandoned border controls between them, the reason for Ireland's non-participation in the Schengen area. After a Brexit, such border controls would have to be re-established to effectively control migration from the EU member Ireland into the UK. The advantage of this is the removal of the main obstacle for Ireland joining Schengen. The problem that a border closure might bring is a possible re-eruption of the Northern Irish conflicts that were pacified in 1998 by the Good Friday Agreement.

Also, political relations with the vast majority of EU Member States will, at least temporarily, deteriorate. Current generations of EU leaders and politicians might not be willing to fully return to the political status quo ante once the British have left the rest of the Union.

Neither must one forget that particular aspects of EU political integration are of utmost importance to the UK, i.a. the European Arrest Warrant or the joint fight against international crime and terrorism. The UK's further inclusion in common EU action in these areas would be at risk, should the UK depart from the Union.4

Societal implications of Brexit on the UK

Not only will the UK as a state be severely affected by its departure from the EU. British citizens will also have to face a number of consequences which they might not have been aware of when participating in the referendum. Cuts to public spending due to economic hardship, directly affecting citizens, have already been mentioned above. They will affect every single citizen residing in the UK.

What is worse, though a smaller number of persons will be affected, are the effects on EU citizens from other Member States residing in the United Kingdom and British citizens resident in other EU Member States. Whereas the latter adds up to 1.2 million, 2.1 million EU citizens without British citizenship currently live in the UK. Whatever their motivation for moving to the British islands, they might face a forced return to their home countries or any other EU State after a Brexit. Many of those who have been in the UK since the 1970s are well integrated into British society and form a vital part of local, regional and domestic economies. Their forced exit from the UK would likely result in a lack of workers needed for further economic growth. Some regions would lose important since skilled parts of their population, resulting in the need to adapt to a difficult and problematic situation, especially where EU migrants are needed for particular commercial sectors. Various studies have shown that EU migration into the UK has resulted in economic advantages which will clearly be reversed should EU foreigners be forced to leave.

All those British citizens temporarily or permanently residing in an EU country abroad have justified reasons to worry. Post Brexit, they would lose their Union citizenship and all those advantages and rights derived from it, especially free movement and non-discrimination on grounds of nationality. Students, workers, and pensioners would face a severe change in their lives: if they did not fulfil the criteria for citizenship in their host country they might have to return to the UK. In the future, in the worst case scenario, they and their fellow citizens might even have to apply for a visa in order to enter EU Member States, though this is unlikely.

A long, cumbersome, and frustrating Brexit process

Never before has an EU Member State left the Union. Under EU constitutional law, this has only been possible since Article 50 of the EU Treaty, providing for such an exit, was introduced into the legal framework with the Treaty of Lisbon in 2009. For this reason, it is less clear how the exit procedure will take place in practice compared to the accession of new States.5 What makes the British situation worse is the fact that neither the UK government nor the European Commission had a plan B in the case of a negative referendum outcome.

One point must be clearly made: at this point, the exit mechanism has not even been triggered yet. To do so requires a respective notification to the European Council. The referendum result itself does not serve this purpose. What is more, it is not even legally binding, neither internally nor under public international law! That means the new British government of Theresa May could also just ignore the result. Such a move would, however, trigger well-founded protests and may result in the further radicalisation of those outside the traditional party system and opposing EU membership. The British government should instead call for a second referendum, based on post referendum disillusionment and on an honest campaign. Since Britons seem to have realised by now what kind of implications a Brexit move could have on all of them, I am confident they will have changed their minds by the time a second referendum is held.6 Such second referenda are nothing new. We have already experienced them in Denmark or Ireland on the Treaties of Maastricht and Lisbon, respectively. I do believe there is indeed reason enough to call for such a second referendum, since certain aspects have changed since June: the referendum result was pretty close, Britons have realised that many of their main objectives for an out vote can hardly be achieved, as described above, and that they have been strategically lied to by the Brexit camp. Furthermore, the

EU has made clear the dividing lines concerning negotiations and possible consequences, there is a new UK government whilst Brexit main campaigners Boris Johnson, Michael Gove and Nigel Farage have resigned, and the first negative consequences for the country have become visible. An alternative to a second referendum could be snap elections. Were those parties campaigning for future EU membership to win these, the outcome of these elections could be regarded as de facto second referendum on the Brexit question.

If, however, no such referendum or snap elections were to be held, the British government will, at some point, have to initiate the proceedings (whether this needs confirmation by the House of Commons or whether Parliament could even block initiation is still unclear) and the two year deadline will start running. This will be the time frame for negotiating the divorce on many technical and practical aspects, including the huge body of acquis communautaire. However, negotiations regarding the future relationship are unlikely to take place at the same time, especially with regard to trade and economic integration. Throughout those negotiations, with Michel Barnier as chief EU negotiator, a period of uncertainty would determine EU-British relations. Should no agreement be reached within two years and unanimity in the European Council on an extension of the deadline were to prove impossible, the UK would have to leave the EU with many questions unanswered, many issues unsolved and, in the worst case, without any relations to the EU apart from those under public international law, e.g. WTO rules. Such a messy divorce will cause massive harm to the UK, especially to its economy.

But even if, probably after a number of years, an agreement was on the table, the result might be fully disillusioning for the British citizens. The European Union and its Member States will not wish to give too many incentives for other States to leave the EU by being a gentle negotiator and meeting many of the British requests. I rather expect a very tough stance – at this point in time, the EU has an advantage over the UK. However, concluding such an agreement might make sense: it will very clearly show to the British population what is at stake and how unrealistic their expectations in the run-up to such an agreement will have been. This would be the right time to call for a referendum on whether the UK should indeed leave the EU according to the conditions laid down in the agreement. I would expect a huge majority to vote against such an agreement at that point, i.e. a vote for staying inside the Union. Based on this result, the House of Commons will not ratify the agreement which, lacking ratification in the

UK, would not come into force and the EU would not end up without one of its most important Member States. At this point, however, it will be time for a reform of the EU at the very latest, taking into account the position of the Britons and citizens in the other 27 Member States.7

Conclusion

A British departure from the European Union will definitely cause harm to the EU and its members. Most likely, the damage to the United Kingdom economically, politically and socially will be even greater. The next months will be crucial for future development: will the British government trigger the Article 50 mechanism and, if so, when is this going to happen? Most important will be to establish a clear negotiation mandate for both the British and the EU sides. I doubt the British mandate, adopted by a widely pro-European House of Commons, will be aiming towards total separation from the European Union. I expect the EU mandate to be tough, however. It will show that the EU won't be willing to make concessions to the UK and that it will be up to the latter to accept a number of concessions in order to secure an acceptable, yet feasible, deal. With that knowledge, the British government, if snap elections have not taken place anyway, should call for a second referendum, clearly explaining to the people that even outside of the European Union, nothing much will change for the United Kingdom if they still want to benefit from some of the most important advantages of the EU – However, the ability to systematically influence, shape or veto Brussels legislation will no longer exist. If, nonetheless, negotiations between the two sides were opened and not successfully finished after two years, which is likely, the UK faces the real risk of being literally kicked out of the EU if just one single EU State were to refuse a deadline extension. Such an end to Union membership will probably push the UK into a deep crisis, especially in terms of its economy. Obviously, it could always apply for re-accession to the EU under the application of Article 49 of the EU Treaty. However, I strongly doubt that in re-accession negotiations, the EU will be happy to grant the UK all the opt-outs of important policy areas such as Schengen or the Euro that it currently enjoys. And that is what is also at stake when talking about Brexit – the UK would lose its particular role in the EU. I am afraid it would be a loss that could never be regained.

(published online early August 2016)

Europe and the world around

Éléments pour un Partenariat oriental Plus - une nouvelle formule d'association pour la Moldavie, la Géorgie et l'Ukraine

Katrin Böttger et Cristian Ghinea

La politique européenne de voisinage est sous surveillance depuis le début de la crise ukrainienne en septembre 2013. Afin de surmonter le fait que ses objectifs de prospérité, de stabilité et de sécurité sont loin d'être atteints, la Commission européenne a lancé un processus de consultation qui a pris fin en juin 2015. Pendant ce processus a eu lieu le sommet du Partenariat oriental à Riga les 21 et 22 mai 2015. C'était le deuxième (après le sommet de Vilnius en novembre 2013) à apporter plus de critiques que d'engagement et également à ne pas avoir réussi à répondre aux attentes plus qu'optimistes. Ce document préconise que, bien que le Partenariat oriental (Eastern Partnership = EaP) soit un succès, il a malgré tout atteint ses limites dans sa forme actuelle. Un remodelage s'avère donc nécessaire.

L'EaP a été créé sur la base d'une offre spéciale de l'UE à ses voisins de l'Est. La différence entre ces voisins et ceux d'Afrique du Nord et du Moyen-Orient était un désir supposé de relations toujours plus étroites avec l'UE, allant même jusqu'à l'adhésion pour certains d'entre eux.

Six ans après le lancement de l'EaP, trois des six pays ont signé et commencé à implémenter les accords d'association (AA) avec l'UE. Nous soutenons que ces documents sont plus importants en réalité que le débat public sur l'EaP ne le laisse croire. Nous soutenons également que ces trois accords créent, de fait, une nouvelle catégorie de pays associés. L'UE devrait reconnaître cette nouvelle formule d'association en tant que telle, signifiant que, d'une part, l'UE est prête à investir massivement dans la réforme de ces sociétés, mais que d'autre part, elle n'est pas encore prête à leur offrir une perspective d'adhésion, même si cette pensée a gagné du terrain depuis 2009.

Les débats sur l'EaP ont tendance à se concentrer actuellement sur la deuxième partie de la phrase précédente (la perspective d'adhésion) et d'ignorer ou de minimiser l'importance de la première partie (réformer et changer ces pays). C'est regrettable. La perspective d'adhésion est devenue une obsession pour les élites politiques, mais elle changera peu de choses en pratique. L'UE est en crise et centrée sur elle-même ; cela restera le cas pour les 10 prochaines années. Aucune nouvelle adhésion n'est prévue, les pays EaP ne perdent donc rien concrètement. Ce n'est pas la perspective d'adhésion qui est la plus grande préoccupation des pays de l'EaP, mais les réformes. Les deux auteurs de ce document ont des visions différentes pour ce qui est d'offrir ou non une perspective d'adhésion à ce moment précis ou pas, mais nous sommes d'accord pour dire que sa valeur réelle est exagérée.

Ces pays devraient se concentrer sur les réformes, et les preneurs de décisions au sein de l'UE en tiendront compte. Nous acceptons la valeur d'une perspective d'adhésion dans les débats internes dans chacun des pays de l'EaP, mais nous leur recommandons de concentrer le débat sur les vrais changements et les réformes déjà acceptés dans les AA.

Ces observations sont valables pour les trois pays EaP à avoir signé les AA.

Les trois autres ont des positions complètement différentes : la Biélorussie joue sa carte géopolitique sans libéralisation interne, l'Azerbaïdjan s'enfonce dans l'antilibéralisme et ne montre aucun intérêt pour une association, alors que l'Arménie essaye de combiner l'adhésion à l'Union économique eurasiatique à une nouvelle sorte d'accord (accord d'association Moins) avec l'UE. Dans ce contexte, le format initial UE + 6 de l'EaP ne fonctionne pas.

Le sommet de Riga n'était pas un échec, car aucun résultat réel et accessible n'aurait pu répondre aux positions très différentes des six pays. Riga devrait être le dernier sommet à essayer de les mettre tous dans le même moule. Un format UE + 3 + 1 +1 + 1 est bien plus plausible avec une formule d'association Partenariat oriental Plus.

Pour adopter une approche proactive, l'Union européenne devrait redéfinir son Partenariat oriental afin d'adapter son propre intérêt pour une intégration plus profonde de son voisinage immédiat et pour offrir à ces voisins le plus d'aide possible au cours de leurs processus de transformation.

Ce faisant, il ne faudrait pas oublier que le Partenariat oriental n'est pas un échec lorsqu'on considère le développement des relations avec les trois pays mentionnés ci-dessus depuis sa création en 2009. Les accords d'association (AA), ainsi que les zones de libre-échange approfondi et complet (ZLÉAC), les préparent à une intégration plus profonde à l'Union Européenne.

Dans sa redéfinition, le Partenariat oriental devrait conserver son instrument multilatéral et le couronner avec le Partenariat oriental Plus mentionné ci-dessus, qui se concentre sur le soutien de la Moldavie, de la Géorgie et de l'Ukraine dans les processus d'implémentation de leurs AA/ZLÉAC avec une nouvelle formule d'association.

Bien que la ratification des AA/ZLÉAC soit un pas important pour les relations de ces trois pays avec l'UE, c'est seulement le début d'un processus d'implémentation long et ardu qui changera fondamentalement leurs structures légales et administratives. Après tout, les accords d'association sont des documents juridiquement contraignants ressemblant énormément aux accords européens que la CE avait signés avec les pays Visegrad dans les années 1990, et tout particulièrement aux accords de stabilisation et d'association que l'UE avait signés avec les pays des Balkans occidentaux, en tant qu'étape pour leur processus d'adhésion. En implémentant les accords d'association, la Moldavie, la Géorgie et l'Ukraine adopteront jusqu'à 80% des acquis de l'UE, ce qui les mettra sur une voie qui pourra éventuellement mener à une adhésion puisqu'elle les amène au processus d'accès.

Plutôt que d'insister sur une perspective d'adhésion immédiate, les gouvernements de ces pays devraient se concentrer sur l'implémentation de ces réformes qui les prépareront non seulement à une intégration plus profonde potentielle au sein de l'UE, mais qui augmenteront également leurs standards dans tous les domaines politiques. Comme le montrent certains exemples des Balkans occidentaux (Bosnie-et-Herzégovine, Macédoine) et la Turquie, les attentes d'une adhésion ne devraient plus être considérées comme une condition suffisante pour déclencher un processus de transformation réussi. L'enthousiasme public pour une perspective d'adhésion pourrait disparaître rapidement pour faire place au désappointement une fois le pays engagé dans le long et difficile chemin menant à l'adhésion. La concentration sur une perspective à long terme pourrait même encourager le manque d'attention envers des réformes à court terme et des avantages pour les citoyens moyens. Les Balkans occidentaux montrent que cela peut apporter une autre sorte de fatigue d'adhésion, venant cette fois de l'autre camp.

C'est pourquoi les gouvernements de ces trois pays devraient prendre le manque de perspective d'adhésion comme une option « En attente », ni « Oui », ni « Non », et devraient plutôt tout mettre en œuvre pour implémenter les accords d'association.

Ils devraient même expliquer à leurs citoyens la vérité cachée derrière l'option « En attente » ; l'UE, via les AA, investit en réformant ces pays et en apportant à leurs citoyens des biens publics solides (des institutions fonctionnelles avec moins de corruption, l'accès aux marchés de l'UE, des standards de produits plus élevés). Leurs explications ne devraient pas se concentrer sur la perspective européenne à long terme, mais sur l'européisation tangible à court terme grâce aux AA.

Bien sûr, il faudrait que les gouvernements nationaux soient capables d'implémenter les AA et de livrer avec succès les biens publics. Comme le montre l'exemple de la Moldavie (le pays le plus avancé de l'EaP), les politiciens favorables à l'UE sont souvent incompétents et corrompus, ce qui oblige les citoyens pro-UE à trouver de nouveaux champions pour leur cause après chaque tour d'élections.

Un Partenariat oriental Plus devrait aspirer à soutenir le processus d'implémentation des accords en termes pratiques et financiers, et ce, à un niveau bilatéral et multilatéral.

Éléments bilatéraux possibles d'une nouvelle formule d'association :

- Des rapports de progression annuels (plus poussés que les rapports de progression PEV) qui mesurent clairement la progression du pays sur la base des AA et ZLÉAC et qui donnent des conseils concrets sur les prochaines étapes, similairement à la manière dont les plans de libéralisation des visas sont implémentés ;
- Des fonds IEVP spéciaux utilisés pour soutenir l'implémentation des AA/ZLÉAC dans les divers domaines ;
- Les mêmes fonds pour le dialogue interculturel prévu entre les États membres et la société civile et les institutions culturelles des pays du Partenariat oriental ;
- La possibilité pour les pays orientaux associés de participer à tous les programmes de coopération à l'échelle de l'UE sur le principe « Optin ». Le programme Horizon 2020 est un bon exemple. La Moldavie a signé son association à Horizon en juillet 2014 avec les pays des Balkans occidentaux, et l'Ukraine s'y est ajoutée en mars 2015. C'est un bon précédent et d'autres programmes devraient être ouverts à la formule Partenariat oriental Plus (le programme LEADER pour le développement rural serait un autre bon début).

Éléments multilatéraux possibles pour une nouvelle formule d'association :

- Des rapports comparatifs annuels, donnant des exemples des meilleures pratiques des trois pays, avec des étapes concrètes à suivre et des informations de contacts des agents publics responsables de ce succès ;

- Des fonds IEVP spéciaux utilisés pour permettre l'échange des agents publics dans les administrations responsables de l'implémentation des AA/ZLÉAC (dans le cas de l'Ukraine, le Bureau gouvernemental pour l'intégration européenne (Government Office for European Integration – GOEI)) ;
- Des groupes de travail composés de la Moldavie, de la Géorgie et de l'Ukraine, ainsi que de la Commission européenne et des représentants des États membres les plus récents de l'UE pour échanger les meilleures pratiques sur des sujets relatifs à la ZLÉAC ;
- Des groupes de travail pour les diverses institutions civiles prévues par les AA/ZLÉAC des trois pays.

Dans le cadre du Partenariat oriental Plus, des réunions supplémentaires distinctes peuvent être prévues lors des sommets du Partenariat oriental, au cours desquelles des déclarations pourront être formulées sans qu'elles ne conviennent forcément aux trois autres pays du Partenariat oriental, l'Arménie, l'Azerbaïdjan et la Biélorussie. Il serait par contre possible à ces trois pays de rejoindre individuellement le groupe selon leur avancée à un niveau similaire d'intégration à l'Union européenne. Les pays 1+1+1 devraient se voir apporter une attention particulière afin qu'un tel changement soit vu comme un encouragement plutôt que comme un abandon ; ils pourront toujours joindre la formule EaP Plus dès que les réformes et la politique le permettront.

Pour le moment, ces trois pays ne sont pas seulement dans une situation très différente de la Géorgie, la Moldavie et l'Ukraine, mais leurs intérêts et leurs relations avec l'UE ne sont également pas comparables entre eux. L'Arménie cherche une formule pour obtenir un accord comprenant une zone de libre-échange avec l'UE qui soit compatible avec l'Union économique eurasiatique. Par conséquent, l'Arménie pourrait être un modèle pour la Biélorussie, mais seulement sur le long terme. L'Azerbaïdjan est différent et seulement intéressé par un accord avec l'UE, mais sans ZLÉAC.

Au-delà de la nouvelle formule d'adhésion, un Partenariat oriental réformé devra également œuvrer de manière proactive à la réconciliation avec l'Union économique eurasiatique, pas seulement dans le cadre de l'Arménie, mais encore au-delà. Cela permettrait à tous les pays de l'EaP de continuer leurs relations commerciales également avec la Russie. Afin d'y arriver, des groupes de travail devraient être établis à de nombreux niveaux :

- Entre les agents civils de la Commission européenne et la Commission économique eurasiatique;
- Entre les pays du Partenariat oriental et les États membres de l'Union économique eurasiatique.
- Ce processus de réconciliation pourrait être accompagné de forums de dialogue trilatéraux de la société civile (par ex. UE-Ukraine-Russie).

(publié en ligne début octobre 2015)

Revisiting European humanitarian aid: From noble intentions to implementation difficulties

Dagmar Röttsches

The European humanitarian undertaking in the context of a staggering European project

No matter which aspect of European integration one would like to refer to nowadays, it is most likely crisis prone: The European Union has recently undergone - and is still undergoing – a deep economic and financial crisis. Furthermore, it is confronted with serious attempts to question European values originating from new and old member states alike. Fierce bargaining and utilitarian politics have now replaced[1] old win-win perspectives on European integration.

The most recent episode illustrating a divided and standstill Europe was this year's refugee crisis. While the European Union is considered to be an important player in the international disaster relief regime, many observers stated it did comparatively little to alleviate the suffering in the Syrian refugee crisis.[2] At first sight, even EU documents seem to confirm this criticism, so does the Humanitarian Implementation Plan on the Syria Crisis where "dire financial constraints"[3] for the EU's humanitarian aid work and its difficulties for conducting a "whole-of-Syria"[4] needs analysis are mentioned. But the external criticism relates to various aspects of the EU's activities concerning the Syrian refugee crisis at a time, hence, it is crucial to have a more detailed look in order to avoid a glossing over different EU actors and policies. Furthermore, the usual media focus on member states' bickering turns a blind eye to the silence of most successful humanitarian assistance where needs assessment analysis is conducted far away from public attention.

This Policy Paper aims at assessing the EU's recent role as an actor in the international humanitarian relief regime, mainly focusing on internal and external challenges and the EU's way of coping with them. An analysis of the EU's role as a humanitarian assistance provider is a topical and interesting undertaking for several reasons. The question of performance is particularly interesting because it is an area where input legitimacy is of

minor importance and at the same time, it would be too superficial to analyse its effectiveness on the basis of general media reports. What is more,
humanitarian assistance as a policy seems to be at the very heart of the
idea of a normative power Europe and some authors now claim that recent
events belie a true European commitment. Precisely for this reason, authors see the pressure for the EU to act and display leadership.[5] Furthermore, the performance question has gained importance in the field of humanitarian assistance: Good intentions are no longer enough. Last but not
least, it might be surprising given the circumstances, but some positive
signs or improvements have recently come to the surface when it comes to
the EU's performance in this area, bucking the trend of a rather negative
view on European policies. The assessment of the EU's role has two parts:
Firstly, there is a focus on the EU's approach to humanitarian assistance
concerning its content and its definition as well as its historical evolution.[6]
Secondly, a look on two recent EU efforts to deal with humanitarian crises
will result in a juxtaposition of rhetorical commitment and practice.

The way from a broad approach to a narrow one

Struggling to deliver a comprehensive and adequate response to the humanitarian crisis in Iraq after the first Gulf War and the conflict in former
Yugoslavia in the beginning of the 1990s, EU member states realized the
need for change. They created a body responsible for the management of
European humanitarian aid, the European Commission Humanitarian Aid
Office ECHO[7], in order to enhance its effectiveness and its credibility.[8] In
addition to this rather pragmatic motivation, symbolic politics and its potential to strengthen the EU's image as a soft power did play their part,
too.[9]

Humanitarian aid comprised all relief aid delivered to victims of natural
disasters or armed conflict outside the EU. Throughout the 1990s, the
EU's interpretation of relief aid was quite broad and included not only
emergency relief aid such as medical care, food and shelter, but also the
rebuilding of infrastructure, financing social integration projects, water
and sanitation operations as well as disaster preparedness and prevention.
[10] These early activities displayed a development component with several
dimensions such as for example the Commission Communication on
Linking Relief, Rehabilitation and Development from 2001. Finally, some
authors state that the very broad approach originated from an effort to

compensate for the absence of a real common foreign and security policy.
[11] Keeping this in mind, it is of no surprise that the 1990s EU humanitarian aid was often considered to be too biased. Authors often refer to the Kosovo conflict in 1999 or Afghanistan in 2002.[12] In 1999 and 2000, ECHO underwent an internal evaluation that triggered an important shift towards a strengthened commitment to needs-based humanitarian aid. According to the needs approach, countries or regions most in need of assistance are identified based on national indicators that take into account the situational context. The global needs assessment consists of a vulnerability and crisis index, these two indexes indicate the EU's priority for the delivery of humanitarian aid.[13] What is more, there is an index for forgotten emergencies which are defined as a situation where humanitarian needs largely exceed funding and hardly any other international donors are contributing. With these new selection criteria in place since the early 2000s, ECHO started a narrow interpretation of humanitarian aid, focusing on primary emergency aid with strict standards for financial and administrative procedures for those NGOs it works with in Framework Partnership Agreements. With this new more clear-cut approach, the European Commission earned recognition as a well performing humanitarian aids provider. For example, according to DARA - an independent non-profit organisation that specializes in evaluating humanitarian donor's performance with the Humanitarian Response Index – the European Commission scores well.[14]

This approach is made more visible with the European Consensus on Humanitarian Aid from 2007. The Consensus, signed by member states, the European Commission, the Council and the European Parliament in December 2007, is the first comprehensive EU document on European humanitarian aid.[15] The European Commission and the European Parliament aimed at enhancing member states' as well as external actors' awareness of a specific European understanding of humanitarian aid and strengthening member states' commitment to it. The Consensus reinforces the commitment to impartiality, neutrality, independence and humanity and it talks about how to implement this vision into practice. It also states that under no circumstances should humanitarian aid be considered as a crisis management tool. Before the Lisbon Treaty, there was no official treaty basis for a common European policy on humanitarian aid. Money spent for humanitarian aid came from the European Development Fund, the EU budget and the Emergency Aid Reserve. In the 1990s, the EU spent between 0.6 and 0.8 billion Euros on average per year for humanitarian aid.[16] The numbers have risen significantly in recent years despite the European economic and financial crisis. For the year 2014, ECHO indicates 1.273 billion Euro spent on humanitarian aid.[17]

Article 214 of the Lisbon Treaty lays the groundwork for EU humanitarian aid. It highlights the independent status of humanitarian assistance as a European autonomous external policy. European relief work is therefore to be located far away from any political, economic or military issues. Its independent status is obvious in the maintenance of ECHO's responsibility for humanitarian assistance. Nevertheless there are some doubts about its independent status because of the EEA's eventual role[18] and the "Comprehensive Approach".[19] The latter concerns a European Commission and EEA effort to array all policy fields in order to improve the EU's crisis management. Up to now, many NGOs remain highly skeptical about it because they think the risk of compromising the humanitarian principles is high.[20]

The most recent issues concerning humanitarian aid are the debate about resilience and the children for peace initiative. Resilience means "the ability of an individual, a household, a community, a country or a region to withstand, to adapt, and to quickly recover from stresses and shocks".[21] The EU Commissioner for Humanitarian Aid and Crisis Management, Christos Stylanides, gave it a prominent standing in his hearing in the European Parliament in October 2014.[22] The NGO community has misgivings about the resilience concept, claiming it undermines the needs-based approach of humanitarian aid.[23] Despite its rather narrow definition of humanitarian aid, the European Union set a new priority in its humanitarian aid work with the children for peace initiative that started in 2012. It funds NGO and UN projects aiming at providing education to children in conflict zones or children who have fled conflict zones.

Recent European humanitarian aid efforts: the Ebola crisis in West Africa and the Syrian crisis

The Ebola outbreak in Guinea, Sierra Leone and Liberia in 2014 represented a particular challenge for humanitarian assistance because of its extensive demand for humanitarian aid and civil protection measures at a time. ECHO provided funds for medical and emergency supplies. According to an ECHO fact sheet, the EU spent 1.8 billion in 2014 and 2015 for humanitarian aid in the Ebola crisis.[24] For the time period January-July

2015, in its donors' profile data base, the OCHA Financial Tracking Service indicates 0.997180 billion of funding originating from the European Commission.[25] It also funded a medical research programme dealing with vaccine treatment, diagnostic tests and treatment.[26] Furthermore, it sent humanitarian experts for monitoring and liaising with local authorities to the region. In comparison with other international humanitarian aid donors such as the US, the European Union reacted relatively quickly to respond to the crisis.[27] For a very long time, MSF (Medecins Sans Frontières) was the only organization lobbying for more global attention to the seriousness of the crisis.[28] ECHO allocated extra financing to MSF.[29] The European Parliament adopted several resolutions complaining about the international response and asking for a quicker and more solid European response.[30] Alongside traditional ECHO aid, the Civil Protection Mechanism was activated. It provided for a better coordination of all civil protection measures related to the fight against Ebola in the West African region. In September 2014, the European Response Coordination Center (ERCC), the Commission's operational arm for Civil Protection, played an important role in setting up an international evacuation mechanism for professional health personnel to specialized European hospitals.[31]

When it comes to the Syrian refugee crisis, one has to distinguish between two different areas: First of all, humanitarian aid delivered to victims in Syria or neighbouring countries outside the European Union. And secondly, humanitarian aid and the treatment of refugees once they have reached a EU member state. ECHO tasks are mainly about the former, but a member state that needs help because of the increased flow of refugees in its country can ask for other member states' assistance in the framework of the civil protection mechanism. Therefore, this section will deliberately exclude the more controversial part, the one about the EU's treatment of Syrian refugees having entered the European Union.

In June 2013, the High Representative and the European Commission declared a comprehensive EU approach to the Syrian crisis. This comprised different topics such as humanitarian and a European contribution to a political solution of the conflict.[32]

According to a November 2015 factsheet, the European Commission has spent 4.4 billion euros on humanitarian aid for refugees in Syria and in its neighbouring countries.[33] Almost half of the money was spent on emergency relief aid for victims in Syria, including medical aid, the provision of food, child protection programmes, WASH (Water, Sanitation, Hygiene) and vaccination programmes for children. Based on a comprehensive needs assessment, the EU reinforced its assistance in Jordan, Lebanon and Turkey. In the framework of the Children for Peace initiative, it provided 7000 Syrian refugee children in Turkey with education programmes. [34] Nevertheless many say that help for these countries came too late and was not sufficient. In particular, this is the case for Turkey.[35] It is said to have spent 7.6 billion US dollar on humanitarian assistance for Syrian refugees since 2011.[36] In October 2015, the EU announced its willingness to step up its assistance for Turkey. Funds for humanitarian aid in Turkey included provisions from the Pre-Accession Instrument.

Previously mentioned criticism on the EU's humanitarian aid concerning Syria (footnote 2) that relates to humanitarian aid in Syria or its neighbourhood, argue that the EU is far from doing a good job in helping those countries neighbouring Syria facing the challenge of taking care of a very high amount of refugees.[37] In December 2014, the EU created the Madad Fund, also called The Regional Trust Fund in response to the Syrian crisis, that is aimed at helping Syria's direct neighbourhood to improve the living conditions for refugees. Its nature is unique in so far as it is more flexible than the standard grant application procedures NGOs have to go through if they want to become an ECHO partner and receive ECHO funds.[38] For the time being, the Madad Fund comprises 350 million euros originating from the EU budget as well as from member states.[39]

Conclusion

So far, the EU's humanitarian assistance for Syrian refugees in Syria and Syria's neighbouring countries can be described as quite slow and underperforming with a late rise in awareness by the end of 2014. In particular, the reluctance to help Turkey before 2015 is striking. While 2015 stands for a more serious and more solid, truly needs based assessment for humanitarian aid to Syrian refugees in Syria's neighbouring countries, the comprehensive approach obviously questions a truly independent humanitarian aid that is solely based on humanitarian principles.

It is obvious that the EU's activities do not liveup to the Consensus' vision of humanitarian aid. Nevertheless there is a positive development with the Madad Fund that shows that ECHO is capable to adapt and to deliver humanitarian aid corresponding to the particular needs of the region.

The Ebola crisis is also representative for a slow startfor European humanitarian aid with the exception of the extra money for MSF in March

2014. But later on, it is thanks to EU's meticulous needs assessment that an international evacuation system for international health personnel was established. This role could be played because of earlier internal reforms towards a more integrated approach of humanitarian aid and civil protection issues.

The Consensus was widely appreciated for its content. Therefore, it is unfortunate that new concepts such as resilience and the comprehensive approach blur this straightforward approach from the early 2000s and shed doubts on its coherence. The EU's key documents about its commitment to humanitarian aid mainly mirror the principles and norms one can find in the international disaster management regime.[40] To describe the EU as a "norm shaper" in this regime seems too daring, particularly because of its time span for reaction.[41] A "norm follower" for most of the time would definitely be the best matching categorization. Nevertheless, at some points, it might be adequate, for example in the case of the children for peace initiative.[42]

* Dagmar Röttsches is programme director for an undergraduate law and political science programme at the Catholic Institute of Toulouse

Sources:

1 Josef Janning, European Council of Foreign Relations (2015), More Union for the European Union, 17 September 2015, ttp://www.ecfr.eu/article/commentary_more_union_for_the_eu4023, (last access 20 December 2015).

2 Andreas Liljeheden (2014), Refugee Crisis Divides EU Countries, 24 September 2015, http://euranetplus-inside.eu/refugee-crisis-divide-eu-countries/ (last access December 2015). Nando Sigona writes: "Less wealthy countries are doing much more than the EU's member states to provide shelter and protection to refugees fleeing persecution in places like Syria, and previously Libya." Nando Sigona (2015), The death of migrants in the Mediterranean is a truly 'European' tragedy, http://blogs.lse.ac.uk/europpblog/2013/10/14/the-death-of-migrants-in-the-mediterranean-is-a-truly-european-tragedy/, (last access 21 December 2015).

3 ECHO (2014), Humanitarian Implementation Plan Syria Crisis ECHO/SYR/BUD/2015/91000, last update 28/10/2014, http://reliefweb.int/report/syrian-arab-republic/humanitarian-implementation-plan-hip-syria-crisis-echosyrbud201591000, (last access 20 June 2015). There are different versions of this document. I refer here to the document's first version of October 2014.

4 ECHO (2014), Humanitarian Implementation Plan Syria Crisis, ibid..

5 Nando Sigona, op.cit..

6 Unfortunately, there is not enough space to elaborate on all aspects of the EU's role in the humanitarian field, for example within the framework of the EU actorness approach. For a more detailed analysis, see Erik Brattberg and Mark Rhinhard (2012), The EU and the US as international actors in disaster relief, College of Europe, Bruges Political Research Papers, https://www.coleurope.eu-/study/european-political-and-administrative-studies/research-activities/bruges-political-research, (last access 20 November 2015).

7 ECHO stands for DG ECHO and civil protection because the civil protection portfolio was attached to ECHO in 2010. The author will refer in this article to ECHO and implies both services with this term.

8 Versluys underlines that humanitarian aid was part of the European Communities' activities since the Yaounde II Convention in 1969. Nevertheless, up until 1992, there was no single entity in charge for humanitarian aid. Helen Versluys (2008), European Union Humanitarian Aid: Lifesaver or Political Tool?, in: Jan Orbie: Europe's Global Role. External Policies of the European Union, Farnham: ashgate, p. 91.

9 Versluys, ibid., p. 91.

10 Versluys, ibid., p. 102.

11 Versluys quotes a former ECHO staff who refers to the creation of ECHO as the "good conscience" of Europe. Versluys, ibid., p. 101.

12 See for example Michael Barnett and Jack Snyder (2008), The Grand Strategies of Humanitarianism, in: Thomas Weiss and Michael Barnett: Humanitarianism in Question, Politics, Power and Ethics, London: Cornell University Press, p. 159. They observe biased humanitarian aid as general phenomenon in the Kosovo crisis. Concerning Afghanistan, Khaliq describes a worsening of the humanitarian situation with the outbreak of hostilities in October 2001, mentions the immense increase of humanitarian assistance delivered and says one should keep in mind that the humanitarian situation "had not worsened eighteen-fold". Uran Khaliq (2008), The Ethical Dimensions of the Foreign Policy of the European Union. A Legal Appraisal, Cambridge: Cambridge University Press, p. 431. Khaliq also mentions that ECHO funds were used earlier in order to "isolate the Taliban." Khaliq, ibid., p. 441.

13 For more details on the indexes and their subcategories, see the ECHO website that explains the indicators to NGOs demanding funding: http://eu-unfafa.dgecho-partners-helpdesk.eu/financing_decisions/dgecho_strategy/gna 14 For 2011, it ranked 7th in the HRI. See http://daraint.org/humanitarian-response-index/humanitarian-response-index-2011/ (last access 26 December, 2015).

15 European Commission (2007), The European Consensus on Humanitarian Aid, http://ec.europa.eu/echo/who/humanitarian- aid-and-civil-protection/european-consensus_en (last access 20 December 2015).

16 Versluys, op.cit., p. 95.

17 ECHO (2015), 2014 annual report, 21 August 2015, http://ec.europa.eu/echo/who/accountability/annual-reports_en, (last access 22 November 2015). One has to keep in mind that Europe-Aid also spends money on humanitarian aid. Therefore, the actual figure must be higher.

18 Officially, the EEA will not be in charge of humanitarian tasks because ECHO kept its mandate. But certain authors are skeptical about this point. Jan Orbie, Peter Van Elsuwege and Fabienne Bossuyt (2014), Humanitarian Aid as an Integral Part of the European Union's External Action: The Challenge of Reconciling Coherence and Independence, Journal of Contingencies and Crisis Management 22, no 3, p. 158 – 165, p. 161.

19 European Commission (2013), Joint Communication to the European Parliament and the Council: The EU's comprehensive approach to external conflicts and crisis, 11 December 2013, http://eur-lex.europa.eu/legal-content/EN/TXT/?uri=CELEX-: 52013JC0030, (last access 26 December 2015).

20 Charlotte Dany (2015), Politicization of Humanitarian Aid and the European Union, European Foreign Affairs Review 20, no 3, p.419-438, p. 431.

21 European Commission (2012), EU approach to resilience: Learning from Food Crisis, 3 October 2012, http://europa.eu/rapid/press-release_MEMO-12-733_en.htm?locale=FR, (last access 20 December 2015).

22 Euractiv video from the Commissioner Designate Hearing at the European Parliament, Each Euro invested in resilience saves 7 euro in emergency aid, 1 October 2014, http://www.euractiv.com/video/stylianides-each-euro-invested-resilience-saves-eu7-emergency-aid-308845, (last access 20 December 2015).

23 Charlotte Dany quotes an author from the Overseas Development Institute. Charlotte Dany, op. cit., p. 434.

24 ECHO (2015), Factsheet 2015, Emergency Response Coordination Centre, http://ec.europa.eu/echo/factsheets_en, (last access 26December 2015).

25 OCHA Financial Tracking Service, Donor Profile European Commission in 2015, www.reliefweb.int/fls , (last access 4 December 2015).

26 ECHO (2014), Factsheet December 2014, EU Response to the Ebola epidemic in West Africa, http://ec.europa.eu/echo/factsheets_en, (last access 18 December 2015).

27 Taking into account the very slow overall international response, this can only be observed in comparative and not in an absolute context. See Andrew Higgins (2014), European Leaders Scramble to Upgrade Response to Ebola Crisis, New York Times, 8 October 2014. Higgins writes: "(…) Europe moved quickly to battle a disease….(…). " and "For many months, the struggle against Ebola was a largely African and European effort". http://www.nytimes.com/2014/10/09/world/european-leaders-scramble-to-upgrade-response-to-ebola-crisis.html?_r=0, (last access 17 November 2015).

28 It was the only INGO present in West Africa in March 2014, it rang the alarm bell and led the international effort to fight Ebola. See for example: Erika Check Hayden (2015), Ebola Outbreak thrusts MSF into new roles, 3 June 2015, http://www.nature.com/news/ebola-outbreak-thrusts-msf-into-new-roles-1.17690, (last access 4 December 2015).

29 Higgins, op.cit..

30 See for example: European Parliament (2013), European Parliament resolution on the situation in Syria, 12 September 2013, http://www.europarl.europa.eu/sides/ getDoc.do?pubRef=-%2f%2fEP%2f%2 fTEXT%2bTA%2bP7- TA-2013-0414%2b0%2bDOC%2bXML%2bV0%2f%2fEN&language=EN, (last access 26 December 2015). It identified the need for a more serious effort relating to the operational capacity needed in order to combat the disease.

31 Florika Fink-Hooijer (2015), Civil protection and humanitarian aid in the Ebola response: lessons for the humanitarian system from the EU experience, http://odih-pn.org/magazine/civil-protection-and-humanitarian-aid-in-the-ebola-response-lessons-for-the-humanitarian-system-from-the-eu-experience/, (last access 14 December 2015). 32 Jan Orbie et al., op.cit., p. 162. Orbie et al. highlight that both the demand for more sanctions and more humanitarian aid to Syria were made at the same council session by EU ministers of Foreign Affairs.

33 ECHO (2015), Factsheet Syria Crisis, November 2015, www.bit.ly/echo-fs. It also gave 70 million euros in emergency funding to member states that were heavily affected by the crisis. Jeff Tyson (2015), Short on Cash, EU Commission eyes private sector engagement in humanitarian action, 1 October 2015, https://www.devex.com/ news/short-on-cash-eu-commission-eyes-private-sector-engagement-in-humanitari-an-action-87016, (last access 25 November 2015).

34 ECHO (2015), Factsheet, ibid.. 35 Pinar Elman (2015), From Blame Game to Co-operation: EU-Turkey Response to the Syrian Refugee Crisis, Policy Paper Polish Institute of International Affairs 136, no 34, October 2015 http://www.isn.ethz.ch/ Digital-Library/Publications/Detail/?lng=en&ots627=0c54e3b3-1e9c-be1e-2c24-a6a8c7060233&id=194447, (last access 27 December 2015).

36 Pinar Elman, ibid..

37 See for example a guardian article that talks about Robert Fadel, a Lebanese MP, blaming the EU. No author indicated (2015), Refugee crisis: EU urged to focus funds on displaced Syrians in Middle East, 13 November 2015, http:// www.theguardian.com/global-development/datablog/2015/nov/13/refugee-crisis-eu-european-union-urged-focus-funds-displaced-syrians-middle-east, (access December 25, 2015).

38 Manola de Vos (2015), Want to Help Syrian Refugees? Start Working with the EU's Madad Fund, 18 September 2015, devex, https://www.devex.com/news/want-to-help-syrian-refugees-start-working-with-the-eu-s-madad-fund-86921, (last access 25 November 2015).

39 See European Commission (2015) , EU Regional Trust Fund in Response to the Syrian Crisis, http://ec.europa.eu/enlargement/neighbourhood/countries/syria/ madad/index_en.htm, (last access 26 December 2015).

40 Brattberg and Rhinhard (2012), op. cit., p. 14.

41 Brattberg and Rhinhard see the EU's role in a more optimistic light and refer to the EU as a leader in the field because of the amount of money being spent by the EU (no other international actors spends as much) and because of its leading role for the Good Humanitarian Donorship Initiative. Brattberg and Rhinhard (2012), ibid., p. 13.

42 A recent article mentions the EU's potential to play a leading role in this area. Manola de Vos (2015), The EU, a rising champion ofeducation in emergencies?, 20 July 2015, https://www.devex.com-/news/the-eu-a-rising-champion-of-education-in-emergen-

(published online December 2015)

Readmission agreements of the European Union - A policy instrument with lacking incentives

Franziska Wild

Introduction

In 2015, the European Union faced a new dimension in terms of the number and variety of origin of people seeking asylum in member states of the European Union (EU). Until September 2015, Eurostat registered over 645,015 first-time asylum seekers in the territory of the EU.[1] The European external migration policy once again faced critics and pressure arising from events in 2015 in the Mediterranean Sea and other 'hotspots' of migration routes, such as Greece and the Balkan states. Following the European Agenda on Migration, proposed by the European Commission under its president Jean-Claude Juncker in May 2015, documents, plans and policies have been discussed and set up. While in 2015 political debates mainly focused on the distribution of asylum seekers and the securitization of the Union's external borders, the events in Cologne on New Year's Eve 2016 resulted in an effective European return policy being stressed. And the record is not a positive one. In 2014, less than 40 percent of the decisions issuing a departure of irregular staying migrants were exercised.[2] In particular, African states often challenge the European migration policy, disregarding for example the obligation to readmit own nationals.[3]

Negotiating European Union Readmission agreements with third states

Aware of this problem, the European Commission published the EU Action Plan on Return in September 2015. It highlights the return of people who do not have the right to stay in Europe as an "essential part"[4] of a functioning EU migration and asylum system. In its communication, the European Commission therefore aims to 1) increase the effectiveness of the EU system to return irregular migrants and 2) enhance cooperation on readmission with countries of origin and transit. The idea behind this communication: where there is a functioning system of systematic return, many people might be kept from risking their lives if they know they will be forced to return.

Readmission pertains to the removal of "any person who does not, or no longer, fulfil[s] the conditions of entry to, presence in or residence".[5] Since the treaty of Amsterdam has provided competences in this policy field, the EU aims to strengthen its cooperation with countries of origin and transit in readmission agreements.[6] Today, the competence to conclude such agreement on the level of the European Union is integrated in Article 79 (3) of the TFEU.

These readmission agreements on European level do not only rephrase agreements already concluded on bilateral level between a member state and a non-member-state.[7] In contrast to most agreements on state-level, EU readmission agreements also require the readmission of third state members, who transited through the contracting non-member state. It is this 'third national clause' which constitutes "[o]ne of the main stumbling blocks in the negotiation of readmission agreements".[8] It involves a set of high social, political and economic costs for the non-member state.

Resonance of national policy objectives in the negotiations

The negotiations on readmission agreements with non-European countries have hence recently become more and more difficult. On the one hand, when the EU entered into negotiations with Turkey and Morocco, with both countries showing resistance to sign such agreements for a long time. [9] On the other hand, it has become practicse to embed readmission agreements in a broader framework of negotiations on migration and mobility. In negotiations with third states, having no prospect of accession, this allows the achievement of EU interests in migration policy as well as the promotion of "deal-sweeteners".[10] Visa facilitation has become one of the main incentives when it comes to negotiations on readmission agreements. [11] Financial assistance for implementing an agreement can be seen as another incentive. [12]

Until today, over 17 readmission agreements have been concluded and the EU is in negotiation with another five states.[13] The different outcomes, periods of negotiation and levels of integration show the importance of third state preferences in the negotiations on this policy instrument, as by nature, readmission agreements are seen as an agreement on the one hand

and incentive-based policy instruments on the other hand.[14] The position of a third state in negotiations with the EU is influenced by different factors: the first group consists of the geographical and political closeness to the EU, the salience of emigration in general and migration towards countries of the European Union in particular.[15] While this group of variables is being considered as independent from the negotiations at stake, a second group of variables is characterized by the negotiation-framework. Notably the credibility of threats and promises and the domestic adoption costs for the third state are determined by the incentives made by the European Union during the negotiations and can be influenced by the Union itself.

To be able to cooperate on the readmission of its own and third country nationals, the EU provides incentives in the form of other agreements, such as visa facilitation or visa liberation agreements. A mobility partnership (MP) can be seen as an 'umbrella', or framework, covering different types of projects and agreements. It comprises a broad range of instruments and programmes on issues like development aid, temporary visa facilitation, circular migration programmes and the fight against irregular migration, including the readmission of irregular migrants.[16]

Readmission agreements African countries – hard bargainers challenge the policy instrument

On regional level, the Cotonou agreement between the EU and the ACP-countries contains in Article 13(5)(c) a readmission phrase and an obligation to readmit their nationals. Further negotiations on more detailed readmission agreements are settled in the same article. In subsequent revisions the EU was, without success, particularly interested in further developing this article and making it automatically binding and self-executing.[17] Recently the EU put the topic 'return' on the agenda of the EU-African Valletta Summit in Malta in November 2015, reaffirming the importance of cooperation on readmission and return.[18] With Cape Verde, only one African state signed a EU readmission agreement until today. The archipelago can however be considered a particular case, depending strongly on trade with EU member states and seeing itself as a country with its feed in Africa, but with its head in Europe.[19] With its agreements on labour migration with several EU member states[20] and a Special Partnership signed in 2007, main premises have been settled before the negotiations on a readmission agreement.

The EU shows great interest in readmission agreements with principal transit states in (North) Africa, such as Morocco and Algeria. But the negotiations become more difficult with third states, which are aware of their bargaining power and which cannot be entice with the 'carrot' of potential membership.[21] As "hard bargainers",[22] these states refused to sign a readmission agreement with the EU for over ten years. Moreover, a signature on a mobility partnership does not lead immediately towards the two flagship agreements on readmission and visa facilitation, as has been shown in the negotiations with Morocco. In over ten years of negotiations, Morocco challenged the instrument of European readmission and was only willing to cooperate, once a package deal with visa facilitation was finally agreed upon.[23]

The lacking credibility of EU promises

Coherence in external and migration policy of the EU is one of the most influencing factors for the perception of credibility of promises.[24] The EU's external migration policy is characterized by its multidimensionality. Each of the dimensions requires different legal bases and integration methods. As a result, pluralistic decision-making levels and different objectives appear.

However recommended by the European Commission, a majority of member states do not apply readmission agreements on the European level for all of their returns but adapt national agreements and administrative procedures.[25] Beside official readmission agreements, some member states fell back on a roader framework of non-official or non-standard agreements and cooperation on a bilateral basis (for instance police agreements or economic partnerships including a readmission phrase).[26] Such informal bilateral agreements provide a flexible response to the different assumptions of such an agreement and can be easily renegotiated.[27] Dealing with readmission through channels such as a memoranda of understanding or exchange letters, provides the governments with broader room for manoeuvre. However, falling out of parliamentary and juridical control, they undermine the credibility of the European readmission policy.[28] In 2014, the EU member states held more than 300 bilateral contracts with over 85 third-party countries.[29]

Moreover, mobility partnerships are constructed as legally non-binding declarations between the Commission, interested member states of the

European Union and a third state.[30] Participation on the side of the EU member states in such a declaration is voluntary. This had led to a divergent involvement of each member state, with France taking part in all mobility partnerships and Austria, Finland, Ireland and Malta not participating in any declaration.[31] On the one hand, a member state decision to sign the partnership can be seen as well considered. On the other hand however the lack of a common position of the member states also sends also a message of non-coordination on European level towards potential partner states and therefore risks undermining the credibility of negotiations. Accordingly, as has been showed by Sarah Wolff in her work on the negotiations of readmission agreements with Turkey and Morocco, the lack of a common position of EU member states during the negotiations lead to a distrust on the credibility of EU promises on the Turkish side.[32] Changes in the set of promises, can also lead to distrust. In the negotiations with Cape Verde, visa liberalization was demanded in return to the readmission of third state nationals. Even though Cape Verde succeeded in implementing visa liberalization in the first draft, with additional negotiation rounds, the offer has been replaced by the one of visa facilitation.[33] Such changes in the European bargaining position cause uncertainty and lack of credibility and can endanger the conclusion of other agreements.

Recommendations

1. The European Commission has put emphasis on visa facilitation as a tangible incentive. However, mixing-up of agreements on readmission and those on visa facilitation also implies the risk of losing the possibility to negotiate on readmission agreements without the incentive of visa facilitation. This has been shown vividly during the negotiations on a readmission agreement with Turkey.[34] Therefore, a framework partnership should consist of exchangeable tools, adapting adequate and specific incentives for each third country.
2. The negotiations on readmission agreements showed, that most third-countries are unwilling to accept the 'third national clause'. As readmission agreements with a third national clause represent high domestic costs for a third state, the need for third national clauses should be evaluated. Confronted with a high number of irregular migrants from countries without readmission agreements with the EU, the focus should lie on the conclusion of such agreements. Sending back irregu-

lar migrants to transit states is a short-sighted and insufficient application of readmission. In the third Quarter of 2015, over 16,200 people have been registered as repeat applicants and sent back to transit states, where they often suffer as much as in their home countries, which does not serve as an adequate solution.

3. After they entered into force, the actions taken on mobility partnerships with third countries such as Cape Verde showed a clear imbalance between legal labour migration and the fight against irregular migration. In terms of credibility of promises this figures as a clear obstacle. The EU should therefore increase its actions on labour migration. Furthermore, in educational seminars and study trips should be facilitated as has been done in opening the Erasmus Plus programme for more partner countries.

Conclusions

Recent negotiations with non-member states on EU readmission agreements have shown a need to restructure this policy tool. With its Action Plan on Return, the European Commission tries to address the main challenging points. However, a main obstacle in the negotiations of readmission, a common policy on migration of the EU member states, remains problematic. Without a common position in its external migration policy, the EU instruments lack of credibility, and a conclusion of agreements on sensitive matters as readmission agreements becomes less likeable.

Sources:

1. Eurostat (2015), Pressemitteilung 217/2015: Asyl in den EU-Mitgliedstaaten: Über 410 000 erstmalige Asylbewerber im dritten Quartal 2015 registriert, p. 2.
2. European Commission (2015), Towards an effective return policy, available at: http://ec.europa.eu/dgs/home-affairs/what-we-do/policies/european-agenda-migration/background-information/docs/effective_return_policy_en.pdf, last accessed 02.01.2016, p. 1.
3. The success-rate of returns to African countries was about percent in 2014. European Commission (2015), EU Agenda on Return, COM(2015) 453 final, p. 10.
4. European Commission (2015), COM(2015) 453 final, p. 2.
5. European Commission (2002), Green Paper on a community return policy on illegal residents, COM(2002) 175 final, p. 26.

6. Trauner, Florian/Deimel, Stephanie (2013), The Impact of EU Migration Policies on African Countries: The Case of Mali, International Migration, Vol. 51, No. 4, pp. 20–32, p. 20.

7. Wunderlich, Daniel (2013), Towards Coherence of EU External Migration Policy? Implementing a Complex Policy, International Migration, Vol. 51, No. 6, pp. 26–40, p. 29.

8. European Commission (2015), COM(2015) 453 final, p. 11.

9. Wolff, Sarah (2014), The Politics of Negotiating EU Readmission Agreements: Insights from Morocco and Turkey, European Journal of Migration and Law, Vol. 16, No. 1, pp. 69–95.

10. Boswell, Christina/Geddes, Andrew (2011), Migration and Mobility in the European Union, The European Union Series, Basingstoke, Palgrave Macmillan, p. 31.

11. European Commission (2011), Evaluation of EU Readmission Agreements, COM(2011) 76 final, p. 8.

12. European Commission (2011), COM(2011) 76 final, p. 8.

13. Directorate General 'Migration and Home Affairs' of the European Commission (2015): Return and Readmission, available under: http://ec.europa.eu/dgs/home-affairs/what-we-do/policies/irregular-migration-return-policy/return-readmission/index_en.h tm, last access: 08.01.2016.

14. Wolff, Sandra. (2014), p. 70.

15. See therefore: Cassarino, Jean-Pierre (2014), A Reappraisal of the EU's Expanding Readmission System, The International Spectator: Italian Journal of International Affairs, Vol. 49, No. 4, pp. 130–145, p. 135.

16. Maroukis, Tanos/Triandafyllidou, Anna (2013), Mobility Partnerships, Think Global-Act European (TGAE), Policy Paper 76, p. 1.

17. Koeb, Eleonora, Hohmeister, Henrike (2010), The revision of Article 13 on Migration of the Cotonou Partnership Agreement: What's at stake for the ACP?, European Centre for Development Policy Management, p. 7.

18. Council of the European Union (2015), Valletta Summit, 11.-12. November 2015: Political Declaration, p. 2.

19. "País com os pés em Africa mas a cabeça na Europa", own translation, see therefore : Costa, Suzano (2014), A Política Externa Cabo-verdiana num Mundo Multipolar: entre a ambivalência prática e a retórica discursiva? In: Costa, S., Delgado, J.-p., Varela, O. (eds.), As Relações Externas de Cabo Verde: (Re) Leituras Contemporâneas, Praia, Edições ISCJS, pp. 162–211, p. 194.

20. A bilateral labour migration agreement with Portugal in 1976 and 1997, a treaty of surveillance with Spain in 2008 and labour migration agreements with France and Spain. Further a development agreement with the Netherlands has been signed in 2004. See therefore: Reslow, Natasja (2012), EU Migration Cooperation with Cape Verde, Migration Policy Brief, Maastricht.

21. Boswell, Christina/Geddes, Andrew (2011), p. 133

22. Wolff, Sandra (2014), p. 70.

23. Wolff, Sarah (2014), p. 78

24. Wunderlich, Daniel (2013), pp. 26-27.

25. European Commission (2011), COM(2011) 76 final, Brussels, p. 4.

26. Cassarino, Jean-Pierre (2014), p.133.

27. Cassarino, Jean-Pierre (2014), p. 132.

28. Wolff, Sarah (2014), p. 72.

29. See: Cassarino, Jean-Pierre (2014), p. 133.

30. Kunz, Rahel (2013), Governing International Migration through Partnership, Third World Quarterly, Vol. 34, No. 7, pp. 1227–1246, p. 1236.

31. Reslow, Natasja/Vink, Maarten (2015), Three-Level Games in EU External Migration Policy: Negotiating Mobility Partnerships in West Africa, JCMS: Journal of Common Market Studies, Vol. 53, No. 4, pp. 857–874, p. 865.

32. Wolff, Sarah (2014), p. 93.

33. Reslow, Natasja (2012), The Role of Third Countries in EU Migration Policy: The Mobility Partnerships, European Journal of Migration and Law, Vol. 14, No. 4, pp. 393–415, p. 410.

34. Turkey focused during the negotiations on a readmission agreement on financial support until 2007, claiming the same treatment the Western Balkans, which had been given visa liberalization.

(published online mid-January 2016)

Le Triangle de Weimar avant le sommet de l'OTAN de Varsovie

Isabelle Maras

1. Introduction

À quelques jours du prochain sommet de l'Otan de Varsovie des 8-9 juillet, le danger de la « division, de la surenchère ou de la fuite en avant » guette[1]. À un moment-clé de son histoire, l'Alliance atlantique est en effet confrontée à deux défis majeurs : celui de la menace terroriste, doublé de l'impératif de gestion des flux de réfugiés arrivant sur le continent européen, ainsi qu'au retour d'une confrontation « dure » avec la Russie résultant de l'annexion de la Crimée en 2014 et de la guerre hybride menée depuis lors en Ukraine. Ce double défi est partagé avec l'Union européenne (UE), acteur-clé sur ces dossiers. À cela s'ajoute l'inconnue du futur de l'Union, suite au vote de sortie du Royaume-Uni de l'UE.

Le sommet de Varsovie devra aborder des questions-clé et trouver une voie médiane, entre rappel des fondamentaux de l'Alliance, de ses intérêts stratégiques (dont la question nucléaire) et le souci de maintien du dialogue par la voie diplomatique, après le sommet de Chicago en 2012 et celui du Pays de Galles en 2014 (centré sur le réarmement conventionnel de

---

1 Nathalie Guibert, « La dissuasion nucléaire au menu du prochain sommet de l'Otan », *Le Monde.fr*, 14.04.2016. Disponible à l'adresse : <http://abonnes.lemond e.fr/international/article/2016/04/12/la-dissuasion-nucleaire-au-menu-du-prochain-s ommet-de-l-otan_4900522_3210.html> (consulté le 19.06.2016).

l'Otan[2])[3]. En priorité, le sommet doit préserver l'unité politique de l'organisation. Cela implique l'expression d'une volonté collective claire de s'engager de manière équitable (les États-Unis demeurent le principal contributeur et pourvoyeur de troupes de l'Alliance). Les 28 membres de l'Otan doivent également trouver une position d'équilibre entre engagement et dialogue concernant les relations avec la Russie[4].

2. *L'état du monde avant Varsovie – les défis auxquels l'Alliance doit faire face*

L'Europe se trouve à la fin d'une phase de vingt-cinq années de paix consécutive. L'UE constitue une puissance mondiale de premier plan de par son histoire, sa culture, ses valeurs (démocratie, droits de l'homme, paix durable) et sa puissance économique. La phase post-1989 a été marquée par des avancées majeures pour la construction européenne[5]. La Charte de Paris pour une nouvelle Europe (1990) constituait l'un des fon-

---

2 En 2014, les pays de l'Otan ont décidé de renforcer la « Force de réaction de l'Otan » (NATO Response Force – NRF) en créant, en son sein, une « force fer de lance » baptisée « force opérationnelle interarmées à très haut niveau de préparation » (Very high readiness Joint Task Force). Ce renforcement de la NRF est une des mesures prises dans le cadre du plan d'action « Réactivité » (Readiness Action Plan – RAP), qui a pour but de répondre à l'évolution de l'environnement de sécurité et de renforcer la défense collective de l'Alliance. Voir Site internet de l'Otan, « La Force de réaction de l'OTAN », 12.06.2016. Disponible à l'adresse : <http://www.nato.int/cps/fr/natohq/topics_49755.htm> (consulté le 26.06.2016).

3 Afin de renforcer la sécurité des Etats d'Europe de l'Est et centrale face au voisin russe, l'Alliance a initié des mesures de réassurance en 2014. En réponse à l'arrivée de réfugiés sur les côtes méditerranéennes, l'Otan a lancé, entre autres, une mission de surveillance maritime en Mer Égée début 2016 afin de lutter contre les « passeurs ». L'Alliance a également développé une politique de cyberdéfense et de nouvelles méthodes combinant instruments militaires et non-militaires de la « guerre hybride ».

4 L'Otan reste en effet écartelée entre des pays sensibles et échaudés par la menace russe (Etats baltes, Pologne et Canada) et ceux qui sont davantage favorables à la réouverture des discussions avec Moscou (France et Allemagne).

5 Parmi ces avancées, on peut mentionner les élargissements successifs à l'Europe des Douze, puis des Vingt-cinq et Vingt-sept (1995, 2004-2007) ; l'accord de Schengen entré en vigueur en 1995 ; l'instauration de la monnaie unique, l'Euro (2002) ; la fin de la Guerre de Balkans et les débuts de la Politique européenne de sécurité et de défense (accords de Saint-Malo de 1999).

dements politiques sur lesquels reposait la coopération pacifique des pays européens après la chute du Mur de Berlin. Or l'annexion de la Crimée a rendu caduques de larges pans de l'ordre politique européen qui prévalait jusqu'alors.

La guerre hybride menée par la Russie en Ukraine, mais aussi la campagne de frappes aériennes russes (septembre 2015 - mars 2016) en Syrie ont gravement tendu les relations de l'Otan (et de l'UE) avec la Russie, obérant les initiatives diplomatiques prises par ailleurs. Ces tensions sont à replacer dans le contexte de la remontée en puissance de l'armée russe[6]. Tout projet de renforcement des capacités, de déploiement de forces de l'Alliance à l'Est ou les récents exercices d'envergure conduits par l'Otan (Anaconda[7], BALTOPS et Saber Strike) sont susceptibles d'être interprétés par Moscou comme une attaque frontale, ou pourraient tenir lieu de prétexte à une escalade militaire.

Par ailleurs, l'islamisme radical menace désormais directement, pour la première fois depuis les années 1990, les pays européens, et ne cantonne plus son offensive militaire à l'arc de crise s'étendant du Levant à l'Afrique de l'Ouest. L'auto-proclamé Etat islamique (EI) connaît depuis 2014 un énorme essor, favorisé par les déstabilisations politiques qui ont résulté des guerres menées en Irak et en Syrie. Ce mouvement est désormais en mesure de combattre des forces armées bien formées, comme en Irak, et de gagner du terrain, comme en Libye. Surtout, l'EI est parvenu à enrôler de nouvelles recrues au coeur de l'Europe et les encourage à mener des attaques terroristes[8]. L'afflux quasi-ininterrompu de réfugiés vers les côtes et frontières européennes résulte en grande partie des conflits

---

6 L'armée russe est en pleine modernisation suite aux conflits en Tchétchénie et en Géorgie. Outre les différents volets de la réforme de l'armée, une nouvelle doctrine militaire a été adoptée en 2014. Voir Isabelle Facon, « Que vaut l'armée russe ? », *Politique étrangère*, 1 : 2016, p. 151-163. Disponible à l'adresse : <https://www.ifri.org/sites/default/files/atoms/files/pe_1-2016_armee_russe.pdf> (consulté le 28.06.2016).

7 Sous le nom de code Anaconda, 31 000 soldats de 24 pays ont participé (6-17 juin) à cet exercice bi-annuel, sans précédent depuis la fin de la Guerre froide. La Pologne a déployé à cette occasion plus d'un tiers de ses effectifs (12 000 soldats). Outre les 19 pays de l'Otan, cette manoeuvre inclut des pays associés du Partenariat pour la paix, dont l'Ukraine.

8 L'organisation apparaît toutefois en difficulté dans les régions de Syrie, Irak et Libye. Elle connaîtrait des difficultés financières et aurait perdu 30% de la surface contrôlée en 2015.

sanglants et non-résolus de la région. Depuis 2015 en particulier, ces vagues de migration massive posent à l'UE un défi sans précédent.

3. Le Triangle de Weimar – chances et perspectives

Établi depuis vingt-cinq ans, le groupe de coopération trilatérale du Triangle de Weimar réunissant France, Allemagne et Pologne se doit de « transformer l'essai ». Sans pouvoir formel, le Triangle a bien joué son rôle dans la réconciliation de l'Allemagne avec la Pologne, en étendant le bilatéralisme franco-allemand à la Pologne et en présentant une expression visible de l'élargissement. Plus ponctuellement, le Triangle a pu faire figure de « tête de pont » politique européenne[9]. Cela ne saurait occulter l'asymétrie fondamentale de cette structure, au détriment de Varsovie. L'agenda du couple franco-allemand continue de déterminer les priorités du groupe, tandis que les relations entre la France et la Pologne forment le maillon faible[10].

Alors que l'on cherche à faire « repartir la machine » européenne, le potentiel de cette structure politique est toujours là – à condition que la volonté politique et le pragmatisme suivent. Les coopérations bilatérales germano-polonaise[11] et franco-polonaise sont déjà étroites[12]. Alors comment faire ? Le cadre de dialogue du Triangle pourrait permettre de répartir le

---

9   Au début de la crise ukrainienne, les trois pays membres ont affiché un front politique uni dans la volonté de promouvoir le dialogue entre l'Ukraine et la Russie.

10 Josef Janning, « What future for the Weimar Triangle? », *European Council on Foreign Relations*, ecfr.eu, 11.02.2016. Disponible à l'adresse : <http://www.ecfr.e u/article/commentary_what_future_for_the_weimar_triangle5097> (consulté le 9.06.2016).

11 La coopération germano-polonaise repose notamment sur la coopération entre armées (dont la subordination mutuelle des bataillons de combat), la formation conjointe d'officiers, l'achat de chars Leopard 2 en Pologne.

12 La coopération franco-polonaise recouvre notamment l'engagement commun depuis 2013 en faveur du renforcement de la capacité opérationnelle de l'Otan et de l'interopérabilité des mpreforces, une coopération militaire (système de défense anti-missile), une coopération nucléaire. Voir Isabelle Maras, « France, Allemagne, Pologne : au-delà du symbolique, concrétiser le potentiel », *in* Claire Demesmay, Hans Stark, « Repenser la géométrie franco-allemande : des triangles au service de l'intégration européenne », *Les Études de l'Ifri*, juin 2015, p. 24-29. Disponible à l'adresse : <https://www.ifri.org/sites/default/files/atoms/files/etude_ cerfa_repenser_la_geometrie_franco-allemande.pdf> (consulté le 23.06.2016).

poids du double défi posé à l'Otan – ainsi qu'à l'UE – au moyen d'une action concrète conduite par plusieurs États, selon un principe d'ouverture.

Cela ferait d'autant plus sens que l'UE a perdu son image de creuset de développement des capacités militaires au profit de l'Otan[13], l'organisation de sécurité « qui compte » face aux défis actuels[14].

La relance tant attendue de l'Europe de la Défense pourrait intervenir via un accord « post-Brexit »[15] recentré sur les domaines d'action clé de l'UE[16]– à condition que le couple franco-allemand en soit encore un, au vu des divergences entre Hollande et Merkel[17].

---

13 Le projet d'Europe de la défense est en « stand by », faute d'initiatives politiques de la part des Etats membres. Par ailleurs, plus aucun pays membre ne possède désormais la panoplie complète des capacités militaires.

14 À titre d'exemple, l'Allemagne a inscrit son « Initiative framework nation concept » dans le cadre de l'Otan, et non de l'UE. *In* Jean-Paul Maulny, « La France, l'Allemagne et l'Europe de la Défense », *Les Notes de l'IRIS*, mars 2016. Disponible à l'adresse :
<http://www.iris-france.org/wp-content/uploads/2016/03/Note-de-lIRIS-JPM-Mars-2016.pdf> (consulté le 23.06.2016).

15 L'Otan, l'UE et leurs Etats membres de taille critique poursuivront vraisemblablement de façon pragmatique leur coopération, y compris bilatérale, avec la Grande-Bretagne sur les dossiers de sécurité et de défense. Elle constituait jusqu'ici un acteur crucial de l'Europe de la défense, de l'Otan et un partenaire stratégique de la France, aussi bien en termes de capacités que de volonté d'agir au plan militaire. Le traité bilatéral de défense (Lancaster House), signé en 2010 pour cinquante ans et étendu à l'arme nucléaire ne semble pas remis en cause. Voir Thorsten Brenner, « Brexit is not Brexit when it comes to security », Opinion, *Deutsche Welle*, 21.06.2016.
<http://www.dw.com/en/brexit-is-not-brexit-when-it-comes-to-security/a-1934442 8> (consulté le 23.06.2016).

16 Le président Hollande, la chancelière Merkel et le président du Conseil italien Renzi souhaitent faire des propositions après leur récente rencontre. Voir *Le Monde.fr* avec *AFP* et *Reuters*, « Berlin, Paris et Rome en faveur d'une « nouvelle impulsion » pour l'UE », 27.06.2016. Disponible à l'adresse : <http://www.lemon de.fr/referendum-sur-le-brexit/article/2016/06/27/berlin-paris-et-rome-en-faveur-d -une-nouvelle-impulsion-pour-l-ue_4959257_4872498.html> (consulté le 27.06.2016).

17 Frédéric Lemaître, blog „Merkel: Acte III", « Merkel acte la fin du couple franco-allemand », *Le Monde.fr*, 25.06.2016. Disponible à l'adresse : <http://allemagne.bl og.lemonde.fr/2016/06/25/merkel-acte-la-fin-du-couple-franco-allemand> (consulté le 25.06.2016).

4. La situation dans les Etats concernés

a. Allemagne – davantage de responsabilités, mais comment ?

Ces dernières années, l'Allemagne a fait part de sa volonté d'endosser davantage de responsabilités en matière de sécurité internationale[18]. Après quelques années de « vache maigre » budgétaire (2011-2014) qui ont accompagné une profonde réforme de la « Bundeswehr » (2012), le ministère de la Défense a substantiellement augmenté son budget[19].

Au plan militaire (en parallèle avec une réflexion stratégique de fond), l'Allemagne a démontré depuis 2014 sa capacité à répondre au double défi actuel posé à l'Otan et à ses alliés. Sur le flanc Sud « élargi », Berlin s'est en effet engagé de façon significative au Mali (EUTM[20]), afin de lutter contre le terrorisme islamiste aux côtés de la France et de ses partenaires, et sur le continent africain. L'Allemagne a par ailleurs apporté une contribution décisive à l'adaptation militaire au nouveau contexte de sécurité opéré par l'Otan lors du sommet de 2014, en particulier sur le flanc Est[21].

---

18 Voir les discours du président allemand Gauck, de la ministre de la Défense von der Leyen et du ministre fédéral des Affaires étrangères Steinmeier lors de la 50ème Conférence de Munich sur la sécurité de janvier-février 2014.

19 Le budget s'élève à 1,39 milliards d'euros pour 2016. *In* Claudia Major, Christian Mölling, « Entre la crise et la responsabilité : Un premier bilan de la nouvelle politique de défense allemande », *Note du Cerfa 127*, Ifri/Cerfa, décembre 2015, p. 22. Disponible à l'adresse : <http://www.ifri.org/sites/default/files/atoms/files/ndc_12 7_major_molling_fr_0.pdf> (consulté le 26.06.2016).

20 Depuis début 2013, l'Allemagne participe à la mission de formation de l'UE « European Union Training Mission » (EUTM) au Mali. L'armée allemande en a pris la direction en août 2015 ; 350 soldats y ont été déployés. Dans le même temps, la « Bundeswehr » a déployé 600 soldats en Afrique. Le parlement allemand a également donné son accord à une mission limitée en Irak (jusqu'en janvier 2016) ainsi qu'à l'intégration d'un nombre réduit de soldats allemands au sein des états-majors de l'alliance internationale contre EI/Daech, en Irak et au Koweit. *In* Claudia Major, Christian Mölling, *op.cit.,* 2015, p. 26.

21 En 2015, l'Allemagne a pris la tête comme nation-cadre de la « Force opérationnelle interarmées à très haut niveau de préparation » (VJTF), avec 2 700 soldats sur les 5 000 déployés. Lors de la prochaine rotation de l'Otan, l'Allemagne doit jouer le rôle important de nation-cadre, aux côtés des Etats-Unis et du Royaume-Uni, en armant l'un des quatre bataillons « robustes » ou semi-permanents (en Lituanie) qui doivent être déployés en Pologne et dans les pays baltes. Elle s'est pourtant longtemps montrée réticente à stationner des soldats de l'Alliance dans la région, peu désireuse de froisser la susceptibilité russe.

Le pays est désormais le second pourvoyeur de troupes à l'Est de l'Europe après les Etats-Unis[22].

b. France – des responsabilités assumées, mais avec quels moyens ?

En dépit d'une marge de manoeuvre capacitaire limitée, la France démontre sa volonté politique et sa capacité d'agir, en priorité dans le voisinage sud-européen et au Sahel.

Si le budget français de la défense bénéficie en 2015, et jusqu'en 2019, d'une légère embellie fortement liée au contexte de menace terroriste[23], l'armée française arrive au bout de ses capacités militaires et humaines. Avec environ 30 000 militaires mobilisés en permanence, entre les opérations de sécurité intérieure (Sentinelle), la présence outre-mer et dans les bases militaires extérieures, et les opérations conduites au Sahel et en République centrafricaine[24], l'effort militaire est hors du commun, et appelé à se prolonger dans le temps. La menace terroriste, rendue aiguë depuis les attentats de Paris de janvier et de novembre 2015, a en effet entraîné une mobilisation considérable des forces armées terrestres aux côtés des forces de sécurité intérieures sur le territoire[25].

---

22 Le ministre allemand des Affaires étrangères s'est montré critique envers la politique menée par l'Otan à l'égard de la Russie dans un entretien publié le 19 juin par le quotidien *Bild*. Critiquant le déploiement des quatre bataillons de l'Otan, M. Steinmeier a recommandé d'éviter d'envenimer la situation avec des démonstrations de force militaire. *In* Burkhard Uhlenbroich, « Steinmeier kritisiert NATO-Manöver in Osteuropa », *Bild.de*, 18.06.2016. Disponible à l'adresse : <http://ww w.bild.de/politik/ausland/dr-frank-walter-steinmeier/kritisiert-nato-maneuver-und-fordert-mehr-dialog-mit-russland-46360604.bild.html> (consulté le 19.06.2016).

23 Après plusieurs années de baisse consécutive, le président Hollande a annoncé fin avril le maintien des crédits alloués au ministère de la Défense en 2015 (31,4 milliards d'euros) ainsi qu'une rallonge de 3,8 milliards d'euros sur la période 2016-2019. *In* Alexandre Pouchard, « En euros constants, le ministère de la défense a perdu 20 % de son budget en 25 ans », Les Décodeurs, *Le Monde.fr*, 29.04.2016. Disponible à l'adresse : http://www.lemonde.fr/les-decodeurs/article/2 015/04/29/le-ministere-de-la-defense-a-perdu-20-de-son-budget-depuis-vingt-cinq -ans_4625187_4355770.html#Cp4pS7O4LufPR1hC.99 (consulté le 26.06.2016).

24 Il s'agit de l'opération Barkhane qui mobilise 3 500 hommes dans la bande sahélo-saharienne et de l'opération Sangaris poursuivie en République centrafricaine.

25 Dans le cadre de l'opération Sentinelle, l'armée de Terre mobilise 10 000 hommes sur le territoire national (sites officiels, protection d'établissements publics et de personnalités, de sites industriels sensibles, etc.), ce qui représente près de 10 % de

c. *Pologne – un engagement réel, mais dans quel objectif ?*

La Pologne a, quant à elle, initié un processus de modernisation de ses forces armées depuis 2013[26]. Avec un budget de défense proche des 2 %, la Pologne fait en effet office d'exception dans une Europe dont les Etats membres ont été réticents à investir dans ce secteur ces dernières années[27]. Depuis les années 2000, les forces armées polonaises ont ainsi été déployées sur de nombreux théâtres d'opération, même si ces engagements militaires à l'étranger sont désormais en recul[28].

En octobre 2015, l'arrivée au pouvoir du parti national-conservateur et eurosceptique Droit et Justice (PiS) a ouvert une période d'incertitude marquée par un durcissement au plan intérieur et une distanciation, sinon une défiance affichée envers l'UE. Pour l'instant, la question de la fiabilité de la Pologne comme partenaire se pose donc au plan européen. Avec la dégradation des relations de la Russie avec ses partenaires occidentaux, Varsovie a désormais mis l'accent sur la défense du pays et des intérêts de l'Alliance[29].

---

ses effectifs. *In* Elie Tenenbaum, « La sentinelle égarée ? L'armée de Terre face au terrorisme », Focus stratégique, *Études de l'Ifri*, juin 2016. Disponible à l'adresse : <https://www.ifri.org/sites/default/files/atoms/files/fs68tenenbaum.pdf> (consulté le 14.06.2016).

26 Il consiste en un plan d'investissement d'environ 33 milliards d'euros sur une décennie dans des secteurs d'équipement prioritaires (sous-marins, hélicoptères de combat et de transport, drones ou encore défense anti-missiles). *In* Romain Mielcarek, « La Pologne, nouvel Eldorado des vendeurs d'armes », *rfi.fr*, 30.10.2015. Disponible à l'adresse : <http://www.rfi.fr/hebdo/20151030-pologne-defense-nouvel-eldorado-vendeurs-armes-europe> (consulté le 26.06.2016).

27 Le conflit de 2008 entre la Russie et la Géorgie aurait notamment encouragé cette évolution. *In* Maurice de Langlois, Barbara Jankowski (Ed.), « Dossier stratégique : La Pologne, un acteur de la défense européenne », *La Lettre de l'IRSEM*, mars 2014. Disponible à l'adresse : <http://www.defense.gouv.fr/content/download/269749/3369907/file/Dossier%20strat%C3%A9gique%20Lettre%203-2014.pdf> (consulté le 19.06.2016).

28 Les forces armées polonaises ont été engagées en Irak et en Afghanistan, dans les Balkans, au Moyen-Orient et en Afrique.

29 Le gouvernement polonais a souligné l'importance de son appartenance à l'Otan, et en particulier de la clause de solidarité de l'article 5.

5. Recommandations

Au sein de l'Otan, les pays sont libres de décider du cadre et des modalités de mise en oeuvre de leurs initiatives et axent leurs efforts sur les menaces qui les affectent directement. Dans le contexte actuel, le Triangle de Weimar pourrait ainsi permettre d'identifier de nouvelles modalités de « répartition du travail » entre ses pays membres selon leurs intérêts géostratégiques traditionnels[30].

La brigade franco-allemande (BFA), sous commandement binational[31], pourrait servir ce dessein politique en s'élargissant à la Pologne et en se déployant tour à tour sur les deux flancs régionaux de l'Alliance, à l'Est et au Sud. L'intérêt de la BFA est bien réel : elle peut être amenée à intervenir dans l'ensemble des missions de maintien de la paix et de la sécurité conduites sous couvert national, de l'Otan ou de l'UE[32]. Pourtant, les objectifs politiques fixés ont rarement coïncidé avec les possibilités réelles de cette structure militaire.

Selon les impératifs, la France et la Pologne pourraient tenir lieu respectivement de nation-cadre à l'Est ou au Sud du territoire de l'Alliance, tandis que l'Allemagne pourrait jouer le rôle de nation-cadre centrale étant

---

30 Les États situés au Sud ont jusqu'ici concentré leurs efforts sur les problèmes émanant de leur voisinage méridional – là où les menaces les affectent directement. Selon la même logique, les pays de l'Est de l'Europe agissent selon leurs intérêts de sécurité, sur le flanc Est. Enfin, les Etats « centraux » (ou qui ne sont pas situés en périphérie immédiate de ces zones, comme l'Allemagne, les Etats-Unis ; mais également des pays plus petits tels que le Danemark et les Pays-Bas) s'efforcent, de façon plus classique, de remplir les demandes politiques fixées collectivement au sein de l'Alliance.

31 Créée en 1989, la brigade franco-allemande est une unité binationale, sous commandement commun, mobile et opérationnelle de 5 000 soldats. La brigade s'est déployée dans les Balkans (en 2000), en Afghanistan (en 2004) et, plus récemment, en Afrique (en 2014, au Mali, où 250 hommes de la brigade franco-allemande ont pris part à des opérations de formation des forces terrestres au sein de EUTM Mali), mais aussi dans le cadre de missions nationales (aide aux réfugiés, opération Sentinelle, catastrophes naturelles).

32 La BFA peut en effet être déployée au sein de l'Otan (« Immediate response force ») ou de l'UE (« European battle group »), et dans certains cas aux ordres du corps de réaction rapide européen dont elle est généralement l'« Initial response force ».

donné son intérêt politique et son engagement sur les deux « fronts » d'intervention, dans le cadre de l'UE et de l'Otan[33].

La ligne d'horizon temporelle pour un premier déploiement de cette brigade trilatérale germano-franco-polonaise pourrait être fixée au prochain déploiement du « Very high readiness Joint Task Force » (VJTF), en 2020. La formation d'une BFA élargie devrait donc débuter d'ici le sommet de l'Otan de 2018.

6. Conclusion

Une expression commune forte existe au sein du Triangle[34], qui doit tenir lieu d'aiguillon – dans l'enceinte (UE ou Otan) au sein de laquelle une action concrète fait sens. Cette approche pragmatique permettra de contribuer à la solidité de l'« architecture de sécurité européenne » et à une Europe plus forte[35].

Un demi-siècle après sa création, le Triangle de Weimar n'a pas joué le rôle attendu de groupe dépassant les contingences nationales pour maintenir une volonté politique au long cours. Il est temps de faire de cette alliance « de fiction » une réalité. Cette initiative concrète pourrait ouvrir la

---

33 L'ouverture de la brigade franco-allemande à la Pologne permettrait à la France, lourdement engagée par ailleurs au plan capacitaire, de libérer un bataillon. Cette brigade élargie pourrait être déployée à l'Est, avec un engagement en rotation. Si nécessaire, la brigade pourrait être mobilisée au Sud, avec une participation française. Ainsi, les pays du Triangle pourraient renforcer ensemble les capacités de défense à l'Est tout en libérant des capacités supplémentaires pour la lutte contre le terrorisme dans le voisinage sud-européen.

34 En juin, les ministres des Affaires étrangères du Triangle de Weimar ont réaffirmé la nécessité de coopération et de renforcement mutuel entre l'UE et l'Alliance. *In* Ministère des Affaires étrangères de la République de Pologne, « Declaration of the Weimar Triangle European ministers : EU-NATO cooperation is needed », PAP dispatch, 14.06.2016. Disponible à l'adresse :
<http://www.msz.gov.pl/en/news/they_wrote_about_us/weimar_triangle_european_ministers__eu_nato_cooperation_is_needed__pap_dispatch_of_14_june__2016;j sessionid=8664CF1FB03389B1735CDE3EA3BA105B.cmsap5p> (consulté le 19.06.2016).

35 La nouvelle Stratégie globale de sécurité européenne (« A Global Security Strategy for the EU's Foreign and Security Policy »), présentée fin juin 2016 par la Haute représentante de l'UE Federica Mogherini, va dans ce sens.

voie, en démontrant comment l'Otan pourrait répondre au double défi actuel.

(publié en ligne début juillet 2016)

Troubled Times for Transatlantic Relations

Anna Dimitrova

Internal and External Challenges for Transatlantic Relations

One could hardly disagree that the transatlantic community today faces the "dim, if not dismal"[1] future that former US Secretary of Defense Robert Gates warned about in his 2011 farewell speech. Indeed, both sides of the Atlantic are currently grappling with serious problems starting with Europe's continued failure to maintain stable economic growth and strengthen its security, leading to an increasing mistrust in the European economic and political project. This has found its most obvious expression in the victory for the Brexit "Leave"[2] campaign and the rise of populist and Eurosceptic parties in France (FN), Austria (FPÖ), Germany (AfD), etc. Then there is the increasingly polarized 2016 US Republican and Democratic primary elections, personified by the unexpected rise of two anti-establishment candidates, the nationalist megalomaniac Republican candidate Donald Trump and the self-proclaimed democratic socialist Bernie Sanders, the latter still strongly defying the ultra-insider, former Secretary of State, Hillary Clinton.

Moreover, in addition to these internal challenges straining the transatlantic relationship, one should also add at least two external threats[3]: Russia's assertive and revanchist foreign policy, especially towards Ukraine, resulting in the annexation of the Crimea in 2014, and the breakdown of order in the Middle East caused by the fallout of the US military interven-

---

1 Thom Shanker, "Defense Secretary Warns NATO of 'Dim' Future", *The New York Times*, June 10, 2011, available at: www.nytimes.com/2011/06/11/world/europe/11gates.html?_r=0.

2 Avik Roy, "Victory for Brexit 'Leave' Shows Us Why Trump Is Succeeding in America", *The Forbes*, June 24, 2016, available at: www.forbes.com/sites/aviksaroy/2016/06/24/victory-for-brexit-leave-forces-shows-the-power-of-donald-trumps-message-in-america/#299d8aae1760.

3 Cf. Jeff Lightfoot, 'US View: Atlanticism at Risk », in: *New Challenges, New Voices: Next Generation Viewpoints on Transatlantic Relations*, LSE Ideas, Special Report, SR022, May 2016, pp. 6-16.

tion in Iraq (2003) and the Arab Spring popular uprisings. Especially significant is the civil war in Syria (2011), which has become the root cause for the current massive refugee flows to Europe and the rise of jihadist movements (ISIS) and Islamic terrorism.

In the face of the internal and external challenges outlined above, the future of the transatlantic community has never been as uncertain as today and its future course depends to a large extent on three essential questions.

The EU at Risk of Unraveling?

The first question is the unity of the European Union (EU) itself, today more problematic than ever, now that Brexit has become a reality. While it is still too early to speculate on the consequences the exit of the UK from the Union will have for transatlantic cooperation, in particular in the areas of economics and security, some analysts hasten to stress that "the EU is at risk of unraveling"[4] because Brexit might prompt other "exits" of EU Member States (MS), such as Poland, the Czech Republic or Hungary, not to mention the risk of sparking an independent movement and separatist initiatives inside the UK (Scotland and Northern Ireland), as well as in Spain (Catalonia) or Belgium (Wallonia).[5] Moreover, while calculating the cost of Brexit for the transatlantic economy seems to be complicated at the present stage, there have already been some studies, such as the detailed economic analysis of the Treasury published in April 2016, which revealed that if the UK left the EU, its GDP would be 6.2% lower and each British family would lose £4.300. Thus, the outcome of this economic analysis is that "the overall economic benefits of EU membership are significantly higher than in any potential alternative".[6]

---

4 Julianne Smith, Hearing on "Strains on the European Union: Implications for American Foreign Policy", *US Senate Committee on Foreign Relations*, February 3, 2016, p. 1.

5 Damon Wilson, Hearing on "Strains on the European Union: Implications for American Foreign Policy", *US Senate Committee on Foreign Relations*, 3 February 2016, p. 2.

6 Cf. "HM Treasury Analysis: the Long-Term Economic Impact of EU Membership and the Alternatives", April 2016, available at: www.gov.uk/government/uploads/system/uploads/attachment_data/file/517415/treasury_analysis_economic_impact_of_eu_membership_web.pdf.

On the US side, in a special statement about the UK decision to leave the EU, President Obama stressed that the US and the UK would continue to be "indispensable partners" and their "special relationship", along with the UK's membership of NATO, remained vital cornerstones of US foreign security and economic policy.[7] Despite having called on the British to remain in the EU by arguing in an article published in *The Telegraph* a few months before the British referendum, that "the European Union does not moderate British influence" and that "a strong Europe is not a threat to Britain's global leadership; it enhances Britain's global leadership"[8], Obama then said he respected their decision, but also evoked the challenges ahead.[9] While the presumptive Democratic presidential nominee Hillary Clinton sided with Obama's position, the Republican candidate Donald Trump welcomed the result of the Brexit vote by calling it a "great victory" that, according to him, would allow the British to take their independence back.[10]

Beyond the contrasting political reactions to the UK's exit from the EU, two main positions stand out in the academic debate. The first one is defended by those who consider that the US needs to renew its economic and political leadership in Europe because "a weak, fractured or failed EU would have devastating consequences for the Unites States, the global economy, and the wider region".[11] According to this view, strengthening transatlantic economic relations on the basis of free-trade agreements, such as the Transatlantic Trade and Investment Partnership (TTIP) currently under negotiation, is crucial for the economies on both sides of the Atlantic. In contrast, according to the second position, the absence of Britain in the EU, acting as an EU security pillar and a natural proxy in

---

7 "President Obama on the UK Decision to Leave the European Union", *The White House*, June 24, 2016, available at: www.whitehouse.gov/blog/2016/06/24/president-obama-uk-decision-leave-european-union.

8 Barack Obama, "As Your Friend, Let Me Say that the EU Makes Britain Great Again", *The Telegraph*, April 23, 2016, http://www.telegraph.co.uk/news/2016/04/21/as-your-friend-let-me-tell-you-that-the-eu-makes-britain-even-gr/.

9 Dan Roberts and David Smith, "US and UK Special Relationship Is 'Enduring', Obama Says after Brexit", *The Guardian,* June 24, 2016.

10 Even MacAskill, "Donald Trump Arrives in UK and Hails Brexit Vote as 'Great Victory'", *The Guardian*, June 24, 2016.

11 Julianne Smith, Hearing on "Strains on the European Union: Implications for American Foreign Policy", *US Senate Committee on Foreign Relations*, February 3, 2016, p. 1.

promoting US-UK interests, would further exacerbate the American disengagement from Europe.[12] In fact, this process has already started if one recalls the famous "US pivot to Asia" in the 2012 Strategic Guidance of the Pentagon. [13] This was announced as the new US defense strategy aimed at rebalancing the US military presence and investment from Europe to Asia Pacific in order to contain China's economic and military ascension. However, recent events in Ukraine could, to some extent, reverse this trend. As a result, in June 2014, the European Reassurance Initiative (ERI), costing Washington more than $1 billion per year, was put in place so as to increase the US military presence in Europe and assure military training and exercises with European NATO members.[14]

NATO: In A Quest for a More Balanced Burden-Sharing Alliance?

This brings us to the second issue concerning the future of the transatlantic community which is closely related to the first one as it is focused on NATO. It is a recognised fact that NATO is an asymmetrical alliance in which the US assumes the largest part of the burden-sharing. Pressure from Washington to make the European NATO members spend more on defense and increase their military capacity has had little or no effect, given that most of them still fail to meet "the 2% target" and continue to rely largely on the American security guarantee. As a result, the gap between the US and the European military capacity inside NATO has grown even more asymmetrical in recent years, with the defense budgets of European spenders, including the Big Three (France, Germany and the UK) being either frozen or decreased, mostly because of problems relating to public financial constraints. Thus, in 2015, the US share represented more than 75 % of NATO's total defense budget. Compared to the military budgets of France ($41.2 billion), Germany ($42 billion) and the UK ($54 billion)

---

12 Jeff Lightfoot, "US View: Atlanticism at Risk", in: *New Challenges, New Voices: Next Generation Viewpoints on Transatlantic Relations*, LSE Ideas, Special Report, SR022, May 2016, p. 7.
13 "Sustaining US Global Leadership: Priorities for 21st Century Defense", *Department of Defense*, January 2012.
14 "Fact Sheet: European Reassurance Initiative and Other US Efforts in Support of NATO Allies and Partners", *The White House*, June 3, 2014, available at: www.whitehouse.gov/the-press-office/2014/06/03/fact-sheet-european-reassurance-initiative-and-other-us-efforts-support.

in the same year, the US defense budget ($585 billion) was four times higher than the military expenditures of the Big Three taken together.[15]

Today the future of NATO seems blurred and hinges on two main issues on the European side: 1) the willingness, and 2) the capacity of European NATO allies to strike a more balanced burden-sharing alliance. With regard to the first prerequisite, the willingness of the European states to consolidate and strengthen their security and defense policy seems to be ever more present after the British referendum, as demonstrated by the new EU Global Strategy for Foreign and Security Policy (EUGS), presented to the European Council by High Representative Federica Mogherini on 28 June 2016, just five days after the British referendum.

Building on the 2003 European Security Strategy (ESS) and the 2008 Implementation Report, but also extending them in terms of strategy and priorities, the EUGS defines five goals: "1) the security of the EU itself; 2) the surrounding neighborhood; 3) how to deal with war and crisis; 4) stable regional order across the globe and 5) effective global governance".[16] The new EU foreign policy strategy of "principled pragmatism" put forward by the EUGS, represents, in fact, a "return to Realpolitik" but the Realpolitik in its original sense of combining realistic and liberal ideas[17] as stressed in the document itself – the strategy of principled pragmatism "stems as much from a realistic assessment of the strategic environment as from an idealistic aspiration for the advancement of a better world".[18] To implement this strategy, the EUGS affirms the need for a "closer Atlantic" by committing the EU to invest further in strong bonds across the Atlantic and maintain a solid transatlantic partnership through NATO, which "remains the strongest and most efficient military alliance in the world".[19] Additionally, the EUGS goes further by stressing the necessity for a "strategic autonomy" for the EU grounded on "the mutual and assistance soli-

---

15 Denitsa Raynova and Ian Kearns, "The Wales Pledge Revisited: A Preliminary Analysis of 2015 Budget Decisions in NATO Member State", *European Leadership Network*, February 2015, p. 9.

16 Cf. Sven Biscop, "The EU Global Strategy: Realpolitik with European Characteristics", *Security Policy Brief*, No. 75, Egmont Royal Institute for International Relations, June 2016, p. 2.

17 Idem, p. 1.

18 Shared Vision, Common Action: A Stronger Europe, *A Global Strategy for the European Union's Foreign and Security Policy*, June 2016, p. 16, available at: http://eeas.europa.eu/top_stories/pdf/eugs_review_web.pdf.

19 Idem, p. 37.

darity clause" (as defined in arts. 42.7 TEU and 222 TFEU) and the EU enhanced contribution to Europe's collective security closely related to its deeper investment in NATO.[20]

However, if the willingness of the EU MS to become further committed to NATO seems real this time (at the same time, they no longer have a choice because Brexit will inevitably weaken the European common security and defense policy, especially in terms of delivery, which in return could bring European states closer to NATO), the question of their capacity for achieving this remains open. Increased military spending should be coupled with making military capabilities more efficient at a bilateral level (the 2010 Franco-British treaties on security and defense cooperation), at NATO and EU level through "deeper industrial and operational cooperation, including the pooling of resources, specialization and sharing".[21]

On the US side, the future of NATO might be impacted by one specific factor worth mentioning here, namely the result of the US presidential election on 8 November 2016. In fact, Trump's position about NATO is quite extreme - for him, the alliance is "obsolete" because it was formed to combat the Soviet Union, whereas the main threat today is related to global terrorism, which is not necessarily state-bound. Trump has also repeatedly pointed out that NATO is "unfair economically" to the US because of the disproportionate share that his country pays.[22] He has also taken a very critical stance regarding the European NATO members describing them as "free riders" who stay aside from military intervention and conflicts and rely only on the US to defend the world. While the Republican candidate calls into question the need for NATO itself, he also advocates a non-interventionist approach and a light footprint in the world[23], which is in striking contrast with the Republican party's line generally focused on US interventionism abroad. If elected, Trump's isolationist populism would definitely represent a threat for the transatlantic community and NATO be-

---

20 Idem, p. 9.
21 Ben Jones, "EU View: Modern Dilemmas in the Old World", in: *New Challenges, New Voices: Next Generation Viewpoints on Transatlantic Relations*, LSE Ideas, Special Report, SR022, May 2016, p. 22.
22 "Transcript: Donald Trump Expounds on His Foreign Policy Views", *The New York Times*, March 26, 2016, pp. 10-11, available at: www.nytimes.com/2016/03/27/us/politics/donald-trump-transcript.html?_r=0.
23 Philip Rucker and Robert Costa, "Trump Questions Need for NATO, Outlines Noninterventionist Foreign Policy", *The Washington Post*, March 21, 2016.

cause "engagement and US attention rather than isolation" are the best means of pushing back illiberal political parties and movements.[24]

External Risks for the Transatlantic Community

Finally, the third question that will inevitably influence transatlantic relations is related to the two most challenging current external threats the transatlantic community is facing – Russia's aggressive foreign policy with regards to eastern Ukraine and the unchecked rise of ISIS in Iraq and Syria that brought about a wave of terrorist attacks in some EU members states, namely France and Belgium.

Dealing with Russia in the case of Ukraine needs a very smart strategy pursued by US and EU officials, given that Russia is a key player in the war against ISIS and an important "game changer" in the civil war in Syria. While the Obama administration's approach to Russia is based on pragmatism, restraint and efficient deterrence so as to avoid any escalatory response from NATO, this might change depending on the outcome of the coming US presidential election. Breaking again with Republican orthodoxy, Donald Trump advocates a rapprochement with Russia by stating that Putin is a "strong leader" whom he "would get along with very well" and calling on the US to disengage from Syria in order to "let Russia fight ISIS".[25] As for Russia's involvement in the conflict in Ukraine, Trump remains vague by stressing that the US has no vital interest in Ukraine and "that's really a problem that affects Europe a lot more than it affects us".[26] On the Democratic side, despite being one of the promoters of the "reset" policy in US-Russian relations, Hillary Clinton has now adopted a more hawkish position by claiming to strengthen sanctions against Russia for its

---

24 Jeff Lightfoot, "US View: Atlanticism at Risk", in: *New Challenges, New Voices: Next Generation Viewpoints on Transatlantic Relations*, LSE Ideas, Special Report, SR022, May 2016, p. 13.

25 Jeffrey Brown, "Making Trans-Atlantic Relations Great Again? A Look at US Front-runners' Positions on Europe", *Bertelsmann Foundation Brief*, March 21, 2016, p. 2.

26 "Trump on Putin, Russia in Syria: 'If He Wants to Fight ISIS, Let Him Fight ISIS'", *Fox News*, September 2015, available at: http://insider.foxnews.com/2015/09/29/donald-trump-putin-russia-syria-if-he-wants-fight-isis-let-him-fight-isis.

intervention in Ukraine, help Europe be less dependent on Russia's energy and expand US missile defense in Eastern Europe.[27]

That all shows that there might be a change in the US foreign policy towards Europe and its periphery after Obama's departure from the White House in a few months.

Conclusion

Based on the internal and external challenges the transatlantic community faces today, as outlined above, one can conclude that we really are living through troubled times today since we face a "new strategic moment perhaps less obvious but no less important than those of the last century".[28] The way of getting out of this crisis depends on the US and EU officials' willingness and capability to mitigate risks and act collectively by using responsible, pragmatic and appropriate means to deal with the numerous internal and external challenges. For the risky world we live in today needs not only a renewed US leadership of NATO to help Europe get out of the crisis, but also a stronger European Union, as rightly argued by EU High Representative Federica Mogherini: "A fragile world calls for a more confident and responsible European Union, it calls for an outward- and forward-looking European foreign and security policy".[29]

(published online early July 2016)

---

27 "Full Transcript: Democratic Presidential Debate", *The New York Times*, October 14, 2015, available at: www.nytimes.com/2015/10/14/us/politics/democratic-de-bate-transcript.html?_r=1.

28 Jeff Lightfoot, "US View: Atlanticism at Risk", in: *New Challenges, New Voices: Next Generation Viewpoints on Transatlantic Relations*, LSE Ideas, Special Report, SR022, May 2016, p. 13.

29 Federica Mogherini, Foreword in: Shared Vision, Common Action: A Stronger Europe, *A Global Strategy for the European Union's Foreign and Security Policy*, June 2016, p. 5.

International affairs

L'Accord de Paris après la COP21 : quelles perspectives pour la lutte contre le changement climatique?

Laurent Baechler

Parmi les multiples enjeux du développement durable, le risque climatique est souvent considéré comme le plus important, pour deux raisons bien justifiées. Premièrement le phénomène n'est pas réversible, contrairement à beaucoup d'autres trajectoires de détérioration de l'environnement qui peuvent être réajustées si les efforts nécessaires sont consentis (il en va ainsi par exemple de la reconstitution de la couche d'ozone ou de l'accès à l'eau potable). Il y aura une seule trajectoire de changement climatique, celle que la communauté internationale aura « choisie », au sens où le réchauffement climatique est désormais considéré comme étant largement le fruit des activités humaines, et du fait qu'il est maintenant question de faire des choix et de prendre des mesures pour le contenir. Le phénomène étant déjà en marche, il s'agit de limiter son ampleur pour l'avenir proche et lointain. Deuxièmement le changement climatique aura des impacts majeurs et essentiellement négatifs sur tout ce qui touche de près ou de loin à la vie sur Terre, impacts proportionnés à cette ampleur : perte de biodiversité, raréfaction de l'eau dans les zones déjà en stress hydrique, multiplication des phénomènes climatiques extrêmes, diminution de la productivité des activités agricoles, migrations humaines en masse, etc. La liste des impacts du changement climatique est interminable, avec son cortège de coûts humains et économiques.

On comprend ainsi l'importance accordée à la COP21 qui s'est tenue à Paris du 30 novembre au 11 décembre 2015. Comme son nom l'indique, il s'agissait de la 21ème Conférence des parties à la Convention Cadre des Nations Unies sur le Changement Climatique, le traité international adopté en 1992 lors de la conférence de Rio, qui constitue jusqu'à aujourd'hui le cadre institutionnel de référence pour les négociations internationales sur les questions climatiques. Les COP (l'organe suprême) se tiennent chaque année dans un pays différent, mais ne revêtent pas toutes la même importance. Celle de Paris venait après les échecs successifs des dernières COP (particulièrement celle de Copenhague de 2009) censées préparer l'adoption d'un nouvel accord international sur le climat, après l'arrivée à échéance en 2012 du Protocole de Kyoto, lui-même adopté lors de la COP3 en 1997. Il ne s'agissait pas véritablement de la conférence de la dernière chance, mais un échec renouvelé aurait considérablement décrédibilisé le processus de négociation, et aurait fait perdre un temps précieux dans la lutte contre le changement climatique. On comprend ainsi pourquoi l'Accord de Paris obtenu in extremis a été salué comme un succès retentissant, certains allant jusqu'à parler de tournant historique. Il s'agit de fait d'une prouesse diplomatique, consistant à trouver un consensus entre les 195 parties prenantes aux négociations dont les intérêts en la matière sont loin d'être convergents. Le plus surprenant a été l'ambition fixée par l'accord, qui va bien au-delà de ce qui était envisagé. L'Accord a été présenté par Laurent Fabius, ministre français des Affaires étrangères et hôte de la conférence, comme « différencié, équitable, durable, dynamique, équilibré et légalement contraignant ». Voyons de plus près ce qu'il en est.

Les observateurs n'ont pas manqué de souligner l'ambition de l'Accord, qui devra être signé prochainement, et qui sera à n'en pas douter ratifié par le quota minimum requis de pays pollueurs (au minimum 55 pays représentant au minimum 55% des émissions mondiales de gaz à effet de serre, GES), de manière à pouvoir entrer en vigueur à partir de 2020. Il est effectivement prévu de « contenir l'élévation de la température moyenne de la planète nettement en dessous de 2 °C par rapport aux niveaux préindustriels et de poursuivre l'action menée pour limiter l'élévation des températures à 1,5 °C par rapport aux niveaux préindustriels ». 2 °C est effectivement le seuil à ne pas dépasser défini par les scientifiques pour contenir le réchauffement climatique à des impacts « supportables ». Il n'a échappé à personne que la mention d'une action destinée à faire encore mieux, soit 1,5 °C, était une concession accordée aux Etats insulaires subissant déjà les impacts catastrophiques de la montée du niveau des mers. Mais un examen attentif de l'un ou l'autre de ces objectifs conduit rapidement à la conclusion qu'ils sont au pire utopique (1,5 °C) et au mieux largement irréaliste (2 °C).

Il suffit pour s'en convaincre de raisonner en termes de « budget carbone » pour la communauté internationale. Afin de limiter le réchauffement climatique à 2 °C (sans même parler de l'objectif de 1,5 °C) par rapport aux niveaux préindustriels, les études récentes stipulent que les humains peuvent se permettre d'émettre une quantité de dioxyde de carbone (le principal GES, et celui restant le plus longtemps dans l'atmosphère, pendant des siècles en fait) estimée à 3200 gigatonnes. Le total émis jusqu'ici est de près de 2000 gigatonnes, ce qui signifie qu'au rythme d'émissions actuel, le « budget » sera épuisé d'ici 30 ans. Sachant que les réserves connues d'énergies fossiles de toutes sortes (charbon, pétrole et gaz naturel) sont encore gigantesques, et elles-mêmes estimées à 2900 gigatonnes de carbone, l'enjeu d'un accord climatique contraignant est de faire en sorte qu'un tiers des réserves de pétrole, 50% des réserves de gaz naturel et 80% des réserves de charbon restent inexploitées. Il est peu probable que cela arrive, si l'on tient compte à la fois des efforts passés en matière de lutte contre le changement climatique… et des promesses faites par les gouvernements dans le cadre des négociations de Paris pour parvenir à l'Accord dont il est question ici.

Pour ce qui est des efforts passés, le bilan du Protocole de Kyoto, en vigueur de 2005 à 2012, suffit à s'en faire une idée. L'objectif qu'il fixait était extrêmement modeste, puisqu'il s'agissait de réduire de 5,2% les émissions de carbone par rapport à 1990. Cet objectif a été plus que largement atteint, puisque les émissions des pays ayant ratifié l'accord ont diminué de 24%, mais avec deux restrictions de taille. La première est que ce bilan ne tient compte ni des émissions des Etats-Unis qui se sont retirés du processus de négociations climatiques en 2001, ni de celles du Canada qui s'est retiré en 2011, alors que ces émissions ont augmenté respectivement de 4% et 18% entre 1990 et 2012. La seconde restriction est que les résultats obtenus par les pays ayant ratifié le Protocole sont largement dus à des événements fortuits n'ayant rien à voir avec des efforts particuliers réalisés dans le cadre de politiques climatiques ambitieuses : restructurations agricoles et industrielles en Europe de l'est après l'effondrement du système soviétique (les émissions de GES y ont diminué de plus de 40% entre 1990 et 2012…), changements de trajectoires énergétiques dans certains pays pour des raisons purement économiques (remplacement de centrales à charbon par des centrales au gaz naturel moins polluant en Grande-Bretagne par exemple), crise économique mondiale majeure en 2007-2009, sans reprise véritable depuis. De fait si l'on tient compte de ces éléments, les émissions de GES des pays ayant ratifié Kyoto ont réellement baissé de 4% sur la période, légèrement en-deçà de l'objectif fixé.

Au-delà, les émissions mondiales de GES ont accéléré entre 2000 et 2010 par rapport aux années 1990 et 2000, alors qu'il est question de les réduire de 85 à 90% d'ici 2050 pour atteindre l'objectif des 2 °C de réchauffement planétaire… Tout l'enjeu est donc d'atteindre un pic d'émissions globales très bientôt avant de les faire baisser graduellement par la suite.

Que proposent les parties prenantes aux négociations climatiques pour atteindre cet objectif ? Sur les 195 pays parties prenantes aux négociations, 187 ont proposé une contribution nationale à l'effort collectif, ce qui en soit est déjà un succès politique remarquable. Un problème est que les efforts proposés sont difficiles à comparer sur une base équivalente, dans la mesure où les pays ne choisissent pas toujours la même année de base pour fixer leur objectif de réduction des émissions nationales (invariablement le choix porte sur une année de pic d'émissions, de manière à faire apparaître l'objectif retenu sous un jour le plus ambitieux possible...), et où ils ne présentent pas leur objectif sous la même forme (certains proposent des objectifs quantitatifs de réduction de leurs émissions, d'autres de réduction de l'intensité énergétique de leur économie, d'autres encore d'investir massivement dans les énergies renouvelables, ...). Mais le décompte réalisé parvient à la conclusion que l'ensemble des contributions, si elles sont mises en oeuvre, mettent la planète sur une trajectoire de réchauffement de 3°C minimum, ce qui, étant donné la non linéarité de la relation entre réchauffement et impacts (un réchauffement de 3 °C au lieu de 1,5 °C ne signifie pas des dommages deux fois plus importants, mais potentiellement catastrophiques), pourrait correspondre à la différence entre le maintien des calottes glacières en leur état actuel (avec un réchauffement de 1,5 °C) et une montée du niveau des mers de près de 6 mètres en quelques siècles (avec 3 °C) ...

On peut retenir la valeur symbolique d'un objectif extrêmement ambitieux, qui marque la volonté des gouvernements de tourner le dos aux tergiversations passées. Au-delà, le grand mérite de l'Accord de Paris est d'entériner deux tendances déjà bien ancrées dans les négociations récentes, mais qui devaient être cristallisées dans un accord formel. La première consistait à amener la Chine et les EU (les deux plus gros pollueurs) sur un terrain d'entente, et par la même occasion à obtenir deux résultats collatéraux : l'acceptation par les autres pays émergents du principe que des efforts de leur part sont désormais indispensables (ce qu'ils n'auraient pas pu accepter sans engagement ferme de la Chine) ; la convergence progressive des obligations exigées des deux plus gros pollueurs, et ce malgré leur différence de niveau de développement économique, qui marque l'acceptation du fait que si les responsabilités doivent rester différenciées, il n'est plus question de ne plus rien exiger de la part des pays émergents ou en développement en matière de contribution à l'effort de lutte contre le changement climatique. La deuxième tendance est la reconnaissance progressive du caractère indispensable de transferts massifs de moyens financiers des pays riches (responsables de près de 80% des émissions de GES au cours des deux derniers siècles) vers les pays émergents et en développement, dont il faut obtenir rapidement des capacités de réduction des émissions puisqu'ils représentent déjà plus de la moitié des émissions totales actuelles, mais qui d'une part n'ont pas les mêmes moyens économiques et technologiques que les pays riches de faire face au problème, et d'autre part exigent un « droit » au développement économique qu'ils ne veulent pas voir pénalisé par des exigences environnementales trop contraignantes. Ce principe est acté dans l'Accord de Paris, avec le montant de 100 milliards de dollars annuels de transferts à partir de 2020, montant qui doit être reconsidéré en 2025. Les pays donateurs (car il s'agit bien de dons, chose en soi exceptionnelle étant donné l'ampleur) devront régulièrement informer leurs partenaires des sommes prévues ainsi que de leur destination. La majorité des fonds devra financer des mesures d'adaptation au changement climatique dans les pays en développement, et non pas de réduction des émissions de GES, ce qui peut se critiquer sur la base du principe qu'il vaut mieux lutter contre le phénomène que se résigner à devoir s'y adapter. Mais il est malheureusement de plus en plus réaliste de considérer que l'adaptation doit faire partie de la stratégie climatique, dans la mesure où le phénomène est déjà en marche, et qu'il aura des impacts surtout dans les pays en développement n'ayant pas les mêmes moyens d'y faire face que les pays riches.

L'Accord de Paris est donc conforme à ce que l'on pouvait attendre de mieux de cette conférence décisive, étant donné le contexte global des négociations climatiques. Il n'était donc pas usurpé de le présenter comme « différencié, équitable, durable, dynamique, équilibré ». Mais est-il aussi véritablement légalement contraignant ? Aucun mécanisme de sanction n'est prévu en cas de non respect par les parties prenantes des dispositions prévues par l'Accord, ce que l'on peut interpréter comme une concession collective supplémentaire pour faciliter l'obtention d'un consensus. Par ailleurs on ne peut exiger de ce nouvel accord qu'il soit plus efficace en la matière que le Protocole de Kyoto, ou que tout autre accord environnemental de ce genre qui, in fine, n'est respecté par les signataires que s'ils y trouvent leur intérêt. On ne peut donc qu'espérer que l'Accord de Paris sera le déclencheur d'une dynamique de coopération qui ne fera que se renforcer à mesure que les résultats de l'accord seront enregistrés.

(publié en ligne début février 2016)

Copper's Crisis and its Reciprocal Impact on Global Politics and Economy

Jean-Marie Rousseau

The year 2015 was marked by a series of political and economic troubles and turmoil of all kinds that played out across the globe, and more than ever, we realise that economic difficulties may adversely affect political situations... In the wake of the 2008 global financial crisis, many economies experienced some degree of turbulence and detrimental spillover effects, and conversely, advancements in technology continuously have been threatening to change the global deal. On the one hand, while China in particular is a major copper buyer, the US and the EU are essential players for the valorisation of copper. On the other hand, a significant portion of global supplies comes from South America, with the emergence of a new and increasingly aggressive competition from Asia, Australia and Africa. Eventually, as the third vertex of a triangular game in the global competitive intelligence, technological advancements have made possible substitutions for copper in certain applications.

Through this unstable equilibrium that is continually questioned or challenged, it is hereby proposed to distinguish a competitive intelligence approach, undoubtedly thanks to innovation processes and evolution of societies. Such a triangle leads to three stages of reflection about: 1) the inventory of the copper industry; 2) the game changing disruptions; and 3) the prediction of new horizons.

1. BACKGROUND AND STATE OF THE ART

Given the wide variety of the copper's applications, it is often suggested that the trends in its market are a useful leading indicator of the state of the economy. Because it acts as an effective conductor of heat and electricity, copper is used in the installation, the energy and the ICT sectors, in addition to a wide range of industries, including electrical appliances, electrical engineering, computers, and the transport equipment as well... Automobile production springs to mind it: a passenger car contains about 20-50 kilograms of copper, depending on the model. The construction sector is another major copper consumer, as the metal is used in several ways – on the walls and roofs of building – and as water pipes, and in infrastructure projects – the railway industry, for instance – as well as decoratively in the design of buildings. And finally, copper is also increasingly widely used in the medical sector, because of its strong anti-bacterial properties.

Main Demand Players and Fully Dependent Suppliers

In 1990, the US was the biggest consumer of copper, accounting for 20% of global copper consumption, while China accounted for only 5%. But nowadays, as the world's largest consumer, China accounts for 42% of global copper consumption. The US has the second biggest slice with 9% of the world's consumption, followed by Germany's 6% and Japan which was the second in 1990 and is now the fourth. As the global manufacturing hub, China has overtaken all the other countries as the premier manufacturing location and its demand therefore proves a key driver of global trade in copper.

Copper reserves are highly concentrated. This is unlike other basic metals such as iron ore and bauxite that are dispersed, while Latin America is accounting for almost half of global copper reserves. Chile has the highest reserves, followed by Peru, but Australia has the third biggest reserves of copper. China has the sixth biggest copper reserves, but it is the second largest copper miner behind Chile while Peru holds the third rank, and the United States ranks fourth in terms of copper mine production.

Copper Price as a Leading Indicator

"Dr. Copper" is therefore regarded as a reflection of the global economy's health. The diversified nature of copper's end usage contributes to its bellwether status and then the drop in copper prices can be largely attributed to the global slowdown. The production of copper is capital-intensive and dominated by three components: the price and quality of raw materials, energy costs, and labour costs. The growing dependence on energy across the chain underlines the strong correlation with the oil and electricity prices, since when the oil price rises, energy costs will go up, and the copper price will therefore rise. Normally the US$ rate is inversely related to the copper price, and since copper is traded in US$, a stronger dollar will depress demand for copper as this translates into higher costs in the buyer's currency, and thus adversely affects demand. Conversely, when the dollar weakens against other currencies, demand for copper used to increase, although a regression analysis on a daily basis shows that there is no long-term correlation between the two. Trends in Chinese GDP growth – that is, at the moment, and consequently the world trade – plays a major role, and it is hardly surprising that economic developments in China are very closely tied to the copper price. By 2015, the stock price index combining construction and farm machinery companies and industrial machinery companies continued its downward spiral and made the largest negative contribution to the net decrease in the leading index. Declining production and other shocks – such as workers' strikes – also have an impact on pure copper prices, despite many analysis show that long-term correlation between Chilean copper ore production and the price of pure copper is less strong. Stock levels do have an impact on the copper price over time, since when stocks are low, the price will be relatively high, and for high stocks, the price will be low.

The copper price also responds strongly to macro-economic figures, which may disrupt the correlation with fundamental factors and may somewhat affect price volatility. In addition, the more intangible factors can have an impact on the copper price over time, because it is also affected by investor sentiment and other intangible factors, such as speculation, the use of copper as collateral issues, etc.

SWOT Analysis and Geostrategic Outlook

A comprehensive approach, by systematic signals' exploration help consider the real state-of-the-art as well as particular zoning rules of the copper in view to anticipate and face challenges head on.

Strengths and advantages

- Copper has a wide range of applications, as it is used in water pipes.
- Skilled workforce, strong supply chain capabilities, with quite good research infrastructures.
- Major copper mines and deposits that are often poly-metallic.
- Copper offers major advantages for new and developing technologies.

Weaknesses and gaps

- Slowing construction industries limit demand.
- Copper is a limited resource and like many metals can be recycled, as an alternative.
- High operating costs, and difficulties in raising capital for exploration and development.
- Environmental constraints due to the international commitment in terms of pollution and climate change are more and more time-consuming, and often lead to an increase in costs.
- Limitations on water and power supplies in remote and deserted regions with difficult access.

Opportunities and enhancements of understated or unexpected results

- Copper reclamation may emerge from the middle class population in emergent countries.
- Copper's natural germicidal and fungicidal effects may expand its uses.
- Replacing stainless steel hospital fixtures with copper could dramatically hamper the spread of antibiotic-resistant "superbugs" such as Methicillin-resistant Staphylococcus aureus (MRSA)...
- Discovery of exceptional new copper deposits, while stepping up production in operating mines.
- Capitalisation on technologies and infrastructure from other industries and research technologies reducing OPEX (Operational expenditure) and CAPEX (Capital expenditure).
- Emergence of technologies to create "clean" ore and meet social and ecological requirements.

Threats and risks

- A lower supply would eventually increase the price as product becomes scarcer.
- Sensitiveness to macro-economic factors such as interest rates and income levels.
- Loss of risk-taking appetite for investors, with uncertainty in future for research funding.
- Impurities unable to be removed at competitive cost at the expense of the price-quality relationship and the best value-for-money.
- Loss of expertise and knowledge with changing economic landscape.

- Substitution of copper by other products and new technologies.
- Provision for Historical Comparison
- Products, materials, technologies and technical processes can abruptly turn obsolescent.
- Mistakes of the past should not be traumatic, but should not be forgotten in what would be a culpable carelessness or a guilty recklessness, as regards the history of Salitre in Chile.
- Copper's extractive countries may fear the progressive deterioration of their economy through a creeping deindustrialisation, that is, "Dutch disease."

When creativity and innovation are applied to every aspect of the current business, there are opportunities to stay ahead of a changing marketplace and enter a new system of competition and a new mode of society. Such a competitive intelligence allows the society to adopt another world vision.

2. PERMANENT ENDANGERMENT F(OR) CREATIVE DESTRUCTION

Joseph Schumpeter (1883-1950), in his work entitled "Capitalism, Socialism and Democracy" (1942), introduced the concept of "creative destruction". It consisted of something new killing something older that denotes a "process of industrial mutation that incessantly revolutionises the economic structure from within, incessantly destroying the old one, incessantly creating a new one." This concept is now firmly entrenched in our minds and does not go forward without sweeping away the preexisting order. Starting from 1997, the work of Christensen should also be regarded as seminal since some companies and countries succeed in exploiting disruptive shifts, while others fall victim to these changes. The key question then is whether the existing policy frameworks with their 'conventional' instruments are adequate to address the implications of disruptive innovation. Because investors face obstacles in betting against stock futures, they have turned to the copper market as they seek avenues to bet on a deepening slowdown in the advanced economies, including China.

Growing Anxiety towards China

In recent years, Chinese investors who used physical metals as collateral for bank loans were credited with driving up demand for copper, zinc and nickel and contributing to higher global prices. Now, the heavy selling of copper futures in China could have skewed prices so much that they no longer accurately reflect the supply and demand for a metal used in everything from iPhones to refrigerators. China's economy is still strong, but its ascendancy can't last forever, and yet China has grows important enough that its domestic vulnerabilities now roil the world at large, about three elements: 1/ China is facing a productivity challenge, particularly for State-owned-enterprises (SOEs); the drop in profits has been larger than the drop in revenue, pointing to a rising cost base; 2/ The industrial capacity has been kept too high; industrial value-added has been growing, and output has held up on average, and using credit to prop the heavy industry up is merely delaying the pain; 3/ China's industrial sector is exporting low prices elsewhere, while local buyers are reaping additional margin from the divergence between producer and consumer prices.

If China chooses the "long-termist" strategy for the 'Rest of the World', this means: (1) no devaluation of the RMB; (2) a major weakness of the Chinese economy in the short term, which will obviously weaken the capacity of exporting toward China; (3) a forward upmarket of China, which will led to a new competition for sophisticated goods, aerospace, IT services... China is a resource-rich country and is not analogous to Japan with its almost total dependence on foreign supplies of oil and gas imports. However, its rapid economic growth, allied with its growing role as the most important site of global manufacturing, has led to increasing demand for externally-sourced oil, gas and minerals so as to meet the exponential growth in domestic demand. As a result, China will be accounting for a major share of both the consumption and production of copper.

When Copper Flops, Suppliers Come Cropper

Recovering and recycling copper for reuse helps meet global demand, conserves natural resources, and improves sustainability by reducing environmental and social externalities. The process of recycling copper uses far less energy – up to 85% less – than mining production. Based on the global copper stocks and flows model recently developed by the Fraunhofer institute, it is estimated that two-thirds of the 550 million metric tonnes of copper produced since 1900, are still in productive use. This copper is largely unavailable for recycling because it is still productively employed in buildings, equipment, generators, ships and other built capital

assets. During these past 25 years, the Chilean economy slipped into negative territory only twice – in 1999 and again in 2009 – and after hitting a
peak of 45% in 2006, the percentage currently stands at 35%. Although
Chile has a stable democracy and macroeconomic stability, it is not trou-
ble-free. Copper used to provide 20% of Chile's GDP and 60% of its exports. Poverty rates had tumbled and public services were mostly improving... But more recently, the shifts in the copper price made Chile concerned about its future. Towards the end of 2008 during the height of the
financial crisis and decline of the housing market, copper struggled more
than most metals. Rising copper prices during the middle of the 2000s
eventually led to advanced uses of aluminum as a substitute in power cables, electrical equipment and refrigeration tubes. Nevertheless, the major
issue is its dependence on copper exports for revenue. The Chilean economy slowed down in 2014, at 1.9%, in part due the end of a commodities
super-cycle, which has depressed prices and cooled investments, and the
growth of copper mining supplies at a faster pace than demand.

Beneath and Beyond the Dutch Disease, Risks & Challenges

Comparative advantages work where price is a primary differentiator between the various suppliers of a particular product. Simply put, it refers to
a "given" advantage of situation where one country can produce a certain
product more efficiently than the other. But in the current global marketplace, more focus is placed on the other components of what is known as
differential advantage and, further down the value chain, in the supply of
cheap labour sufficiently to make one country attractive to manufacturers.
As a country moves up the value chain, in order to retain its comparative
advantages, it must continue to seek improved efficiencies, such as a high-
ly-trained workforce. Investment in R&D on technologies will reduce
marginal production costs while increasing production volumes and making a significant differentiation, if possible by industrialization and up-
grading in the value chain. The dependent copper's countries should be
concerned about the economic volatility that comes with commodity
wealth. The question is whether copper could translate into a virtue or a
curse.

In economics, the "Dutch disease" is the apparent causal relationship
between the increase in the economic development of a specific sector –
for example natural resources – and a decline in other sectors, such as

manufacturing or agriculture. In the country's exports becoming more expensive for other countries to buy, while imports becoming cheaper, making those sectors less competitive. The term was coined in 1977 by The Economist to describe the decline of the manufacturing sector in the Netherlands after the discovery of the large Groningen natural gas field in 1959, and the subsequent formation of a massive partnership between Esso, Royal Dutch Shell, and the Dutch government in 1963, translated into a substantial decline in the Dutch manufacturing sector. When the copper industry suffers, the entire nation feels the effects, despite efforts towards commodity diversification. In fact, as the copper industry boomed, Chile for example, operating under a system of flexible exchange rates, should have observed an appreciation of the domestic currency due to the influx in foreign exchange. Particularly in medium-income countries such as Chile, it is as difficult to control it – since there is often pressure to spend the boom revenues immediately to alleviate poverty, while ignoring broader macroeconomic implications. As for the extended Dutch disease, economic growth always depends on transfer of labor to sectors with higher value-added per capita, which is impossible since the more sophisticated manufactured goods necessarily use more skilled labor force.

The Salt of the Earth2 and the Salary of Salitre

By the end of the nineteenth century, the demand for the so-called "Salitre" was beginning to outstrip supply. In 1900, Chile provided two thirds of the nitrogen fertiliser used around the world, and in 1913 Germany bought about one-third of the total Chilean production. Exports of Salitre that reached a maximum of nearly 3 million metric tonnes during WWI, temporarily declined afterwards and then again increased by 1928. Meanwhile, Germany however started producing synthetic nitrogen compounds as soon as 1915, and then surpassed the production of Chilean Salitre in the early 1930s. From 1830 to 1930, the Chilean nitrate deposits were the world's chief source of fixed nitrogen for explosives, fertiliser, and a large variety of chemicals. Within hundred years the Chilean position deteriorated from domination of the world market to a state of not being able to supply the global market for more than one or two years.

In 1913, the Salitre production supplied 54.7% of the world consumption of nitrogen, and by 1923, the figure had gone to 32.2%. By 1950, they accounted for only about 15% of the world market. In the 1990s their share was down to less than 0.1%, but as soon as 1978, only four operating facilities were left, many of the original producing sites and their accompanying living quarters had already become ghost towns. Thus, this Salitre can serve as an excellent example how a chemical technology can arise to create a very large and almost exclusive market, to be sent then almost into oblivion by competing technologies: a discrete invention and technology, the so-called Haber-Bosh process, resulted in the crash of the dream and a serious economic crisis for Chile, practically overnight...

3. REGARDING POSSIBLE FUTURES & EVEN

IMPREDICTABLE 'FUTURIBLES' Raw materials and technology substitutions aim to strongly reduce or totally eliminate the cost connected to the importation while keeping productivity, efficiency and industrial scalability. Companies and copper supplier countries invest in R&D projects in order to create full mechanisms and develop complete value chains. Some advanced economies are fully mobilised and attempt through private-public partnerships, to boost or revitalize the copper sector, while encouraging a responsible approach of innovation strategy and territorial intelligence. However, there is also, out of the box, many ways to escape an overflow by surprise as it previously occurred for the Chilean Salitre.

Why Demand Players Are Not Looking For Other Products?

Fortunately, as for many applications, at the moment, copper is a difficult material to replace because it performs so well as a power and heat conductor and up to now there was no satisfactory substitute for copper. Large-scale substitutes such as aluminum wiring, Pex plumbing, or optic fiber, claim to be actually more sustainable than copper. But, copper is also 100% recyclable, without any loss in performance, and can therefore be reintroduced again and again into the material cycle. Recycling prolongs the use of the earth's natural resources and saves the energy otherwise consumed to process primary raw materials. There are now many stakeholders in the recycling of End-of-Life Vehicles (ELVs): Original Equipment Manufacturers (OEMs) design vehicles for production and recycling, dismantlers remove components form ELVs and make parts available for reuse, and forward it to those who process it into raw materials for new vehicles.

Carbon nanotube conductor cables, currently under development, show promise. They have been shown to carry four times as much current as copper wire of the same mass, but at a fraction of the weight. If price-competitive carbon-based nanocomposite products can be produced at a large enough scale, then the demand for copper in power distribution cabling could be reduced. According to a report by BCC Research, "Global consumption of nanocomposites [was] expected to grow [...] at a Compound Annual Growth Rate (CAGR) of 21.1% for the period of 2014 to 2019." Thus currently, growth represents the application of nanocomposites to far more than copper replacement applications.

Where Could the Real Danger Come From?

Copper mining has significant social and environmental impacts and risks of mining include displacement of communities, water contamination, and damage to downslope communities from waste rock and tailing. Nevertheless, the catastrophic misadventure of Chile with Salitre – as stated above – seems sufficiently instructive. "Graphene" is a material with an extraordinary combination of physical and chemical properties. Conducting electricity better than copper, stronger than steel, the Graphene's structure is remarkably strong and efficient, even self-repairing – thanks to nano-technology, it is essentially two-dimensional and endowed with unique optical properties. Even though many experts still underestimate its capacity to replace copper, we should not doubt its ability – perhaps in shorter terms we otherwise are expecting, given the dazzling progress made since its discovery. Therefore, it is not absurd to regard Graphene as able to first complementing, and then ultimately replacing copper, for a series of applications. At the moment, the price to and hassle of switching to Graphene need to make sense financially, but the bottom line is that Graphene is too good to be ignored and may yet prove to be too good to be true. The European Commission Vice President Neelie Kroes has announced the "Graphene" flagship initiative, with one billion euro in funding over a period of ten years from the Future and Emerging Technologies (FET) scheme as well as national and industrial sources. The "Graphene" flagship initiative is led by Prof. Jari Kinaret, from Sweden's Chalmers University; it involves over 100 research groups, with 136 principal investigators, including four Nobel laureates. Graphene research has long been supported by the Materials Unit of the European Commission's Directorate for Research and Innovation. There are at present eight research projects related to Graphene running, and several others are currently being evaluated.

According to Constantinos Markides (2006), early pioneers that create the new products markets are "very rarely the ones that scale them up from little niches to big, mass markets." This requires a knowledge of what future markets will demand, while it is rather uneasy, if not impossible, when a potentially disruptive technology, such as Graphene, is still in its infancy.

When You Hear the Bullet, You Have Already Been Hit3...

Researchers have been hard at work experimenting with Graphene compounds for batteries that can be scalable, cost-efficient, but most of all, powerful. Researchers also recently found that Graphene mixed with vanadium oxide can create battery cathodes that recharge in twenty seconds and retain more than 90% of their capacity, even after 1,000 cycles of use.

As recently stated ('Wonder Material' Graphene to push TESLA performance to the next level", David Smith), TESLA's critically acclaimed all-electric Model S sedan can travel roughly 265 miles on a single charge, according to the EPA, but CEO Elon Musk last month said "it will be possible to have a 500-mile range car," adding "in fact, we could do it quite soon." According to China's Xinghua News Agency and Clean Technica), TESLA could soon achieve this 500-mile battery thanks to a development in Graphene-based anodes that can reportedly quadruple the density and output of lithium-ion batteries. Actually, it may take years before TESLA can create Graphene-based batteries on a large scale, but if it ever happens, electric car critics would suddenly have little to gripe about. Copper has always been recognised as the preferred material for conducting electricity, which is why it is used universally in motor windings. But Graphene could change and outperform any raw material in this industry. Additionally, the U.S. Department of Telecommunications and Cable (DTC) is developing its important transition from traditional copper based landline telephone service to fiber optic based landline technologies. Specifically, in the US, Verizon is replacing its traditional copper network in certain communities and migrating customers to a fiber network. Advanced materials ventures are most likely to achieve success if they develop an IP claim on a long-term, emerging market application with major potential. As a matter of fact, not only the big automotive companies are preparing for this disruptive shift, but also new entrants to this market are taking the leadership of this potential revolution, if not a likely announced disaster for the lagging behind industries and territories. A common feature of many disruptive technologies is that their development requires expertise – both in terms of technologies and markets – from different industries. Current forecast methodologies are generally incapable of predicting extreme scenarios, especially those in which the most beneficial or catastrophic events occur. Concepts of 'disruptive technology' describe such competence-destroying discontinuities, and the inertia that prevents incumbents from recognizing the potential of an emerging market or a new product feature.

Copper mining companies and, consequently, fully-dependent-copper countries, can't be immune to the emergence of a new sector, that is to say, neither the emergence of new markets, nor disruptive enhancement of substitute products. They therefore can't afford just reactiveness or retro-activeness, but should instead anticipate and constantly monitor the evolution of competition, the advance of new technologies, and then the needs of societies that may occur at any time. Most industries fed by copper components are ripe for disruption, while many more new players – especially start-ups, cash-rich high-tech companies and smart territories – will be likely to empower and literally shape new markets. But, when latecomers and laggards will realise that something occurs and is there, it will be already too late and might be fatal… implacably lethal!

References

1. Most part of the information and data are hereby derived from the weekly informative watch – free and open to access – of Mr. Jean Grisel (CPU informative watch) on behalf of the Conférence des Présidents d'Université – CPU (France). <https://listes.cpu.fr/sympa-/arc/veillecpu>

2. Matthew 5-13: "You are the salt of the earth; but if the salt has become tasteless, how can it be made salty again? It is no longer good for anything, except to be thrown out and trampled underfoot by men."

3. "We all think that we will have time to react when we see it coming. Like a bullet, it hits before it's heard." Mike Elliott, Leader, Ernst & Young, Global Mining & Metals, October 2015

(published online mid-February 2016)

Turkey in the changing world; what to expect in 2016

Emre Gür

There is good reason for pessimism when considering the state of the world today, despite all the apparent progress we have been going through we do not see this translating into real life.

The world is not in a good state. In the foreword of Amnesty International's report for 2014-2015, the introduction reports the period must be seen as an ultimate low point from which we can only rise up.[1] But the following year 2015-2016 portrays a much more pessimistic situation with state level violation of Human Rights all over the world. Examples are many but among the most serious ones are; war crimes being committed in at least 19 countries, torture and ill treatment in at least 122 countries, 60 million displaced people...[2] The number of countries with declining democratic standards has risen dramatically over the last 9 years, as seen in the graphic below.[3]

The performance of democracy is poor, civil society is under threat, the media is censored in many countries. This applies to European Union member countries and even liberal democracies like the USA in some respects. The authoritarian attitudes of politicians, even within the EU such as Poland and Hungary, are having serious implications in terms of international relations.[4]

There are growing risks of crises and conflicts all around the world. In 2014, there were 40 armed conflicts were active in 27 locations worldwide, representing an increase of 18% when compared to the 34 conflicts reported in 2013. This is also the highest number of conflicts reported since 1999.[5] The nature of these conflicts however demonstrates well the changing trends in the nature of international relations. Large-scale interstate conflicts have declined. Only one was active in 2014, the conflict between India and Pakistan, which led to fewer than 50 fatalities. On the other hand, the trend toward international conflicts is still on the rise, with 33% - the highest recorded since the post World War II period.[6]

There are of course various risk factors which have contributed to these trends. However the outlook in this regard doesn't seem very promising either. Despite COP21, global warming continues to be a great concern.

January 2016 figures were well above the average, marking the highest measured since records began 137 years ago.[7] The risks associated with global warming are not as visible as in other crises but in the near future they are predicted to increase problems for all countries. IPCC puts forward a clear correlation between the future implications of climate change and several issues like armed conflicts, food security, migration and geopolitics.[8] The estimated number of people that are projected to be displaced will reach 150 million by 2050, according to some predictions.[9] Some also argue that global warming is partly responsible for the Arab Spring.[10] In particular, the phenomenon known as "agflation" (inflation resulting from agricultural produce price increases) is an interesting factor to observe before the outbreak of war in Syria.[11]

The structural crises inherent to capitalism complete the picture. While the USA is about to recover from the 2008 financial crisis, the EU still has not managed a full recovery. Especially issues like Greece's finanical situation and the future of the Euro have complicated the picture. There is a slowdown of trade in Japan and a slowdown in China's growth which are affecting the global markets. The radical fall in oil prices are also complicating international relations with implications such as Russia becoming increasingly aggressive and the Iran deal opposed by many other countries in the region.

However the trend in the USA is making matters difficult for emerging countries like Turkey. As the Federal Reserve starts to increase its interest rate, this in turn leads to less liquidity for emerging countries like Turkey in particular. On the other hand, while there have been fears pertaining to China's growth, especially when it comes to its military ambitions, similar fears have started to emerge with regard to its fall in growth rate.[12]

In its 2016 Economic Outlook report, the IMF lists "a general slowdown in emerging market economies, China's rebalancing, lower commodity prices, and the gradual exit from extraordinarily accommodative monetary conditions in the United States" as determining factors for the world economy, and as has become evident, they are all quite imminent.[13] The slowdown in trade is still a concern for many as stated in the IMF report "Some five years after the global financial crisis, global GDP is about 4.5 percent below what it would have been had post-crisis growth rates been equivalent to the pre-crisis long-term average".[14]

The territorial claims of China in its region is also contributing to these challenges[15] along with North Korea's inexplicable situation with regard to the missile launches. [16]

Turkey in this global context

Actually Turkey represents a good example of how a crystallization of all these pessimistic scenarios can occur.

Taking into consideration the wave of reform after the 2001 crisis, and adding to this the EU memberships talks opening in 2005, Turkey made incredible progress in terms of its democratic and economic development over a number of years. But for the last 7-8 years this trend has been reversed due to several factors and this experience is well worth observing when we consider the real challenges of today's world.

Located at the very center of critical conflicts in the Middle East, bordering Syria, on the corner of the Ukraine and within the zone of Russian influence, Turkey is in the middle of all the hottest crises that exist today and inevitably everything that is happening has implications for Turkey's interior affairs.

If we consider the country's record of positive change to be the result of the Europeanization of Turkish Foreign Policy as seen by many, looking at how Turkey and EU relate to each other might be significant, especially at the moment.[17] Membership of the EU has been seen as the most critical issue for the democratization and development of Turkey. This is especially true of the first years of the AKP's term, with the pursuit of a more peaceful foreign policy and better relations with the transatlantic system.

In addition, it is possible to witness a change in Turkey's foreign policy towards its Middle Eastern neighbors from a hard power approach to one that also utilizes soft power instruments.[18] TIKA (Turkish Agency of International Cooperation and Development) has been strengthened with the delivery of aid to imminent crisis points around Turkey such as the Syrian Civil War and while the development aid of Turkey comprised about 85 million USD in 2002, this amount reached 3 billion 591 million USD in 2014, according to figures from TİKA'S website and confirmed by OECD, ranking Turkey as the 4th biggest donor in 2014 after the USA, EU and UK.[19] Along with TIKA the so called Yunus Emre Cultural Centers that serve as Turkish culture centers similar to the Instituts Français, or Goethe Institute in their most known form, constitute contact points in various countries and emphasize the importance of cultural interaction and cultural representation in foreign policy and bilateral relations.[20]

As Kaya&Tecmen suggests that Turkey wants to be a middle power but there are discrepancies between the ways in which the ruling party (AKP) and pro-Europeans perceive the way forward for Turkey becoming a regional player - on the one hand, the ideal of the Pax-Ottomana, and on the other hand, empowerment via an alignment with Europe.[21]

Developments since 2010 have shown that the politics of Turkey has been shaped more or less by the views expressed above rather than lining up with the EU and Turkey's traditional allies. Turkey wanted to be a game changer by testing its capabilities in the context of a regional war that is, in fact, shaking the whole of Europe and the World right now, faced with the obligation to host around more than 2,5 millions refugees.[22]

Of course there have been a lot more other factors shaping the relationship between the EU and Turkey. The EU has paid little attention towards Turkey as internal concerns within the Union have prevailed and serious debates have been ongoing with the economic crisis in Greece and the Brexit issue also being debated. Turkey on its side, has also been deeply preoccupied with its home affairs, debating a change in the political system, consolidating more power in the hands of a highly controversial president, the Kurdish conflict with a small pause for peace talks and social movements leading to a high polarization of Turkish Society.

But now with the so called imminent refugee crisis In the EU, the relationship between the EU and Turkey has been highlighted by many leaders and taken out of the refrigerator it's been stored in. EU intentions came at a time when Turkey's polity was also looking for an exit from its complicated situation in the international arena and from the not so shiny economical climate prevailing up until 2010. A closer look at the reasons behind this thawing in relations and willingness to explore possibilities for the near future could be an important factor in shaping these relations, especially with regard to policy-makers on adopting the proper approach.

A bitter anniversary; 2015:

2015 was a critical year that marked 10 years of EU candidacy status. It also marked the relaunch of the vicious debate concerning the nature of Turkey's membership. With the EU already having discussions within its membership about differentiated levels of integration, Turkey could not escape this, constituting as it does, one of the biggest pieces to swallow and digest for a Union that is the subject of heated debate. At this time, Turkey had to come to terms with discussions around open-ended membership talks, customs union without membership and even a "privileged partnership", the concept put forward by the Merkel and Sarkozy duo at that time. Even though Turkey has appeared on the international stage at events like the G20 and those promoting further values such as women's empowerment with the introduction of W20 for the first time, it is still disappointing to see these tools having limited effect on its own policies, as seen with the controversy of ranking 130 out of 145 on the Global Gender Gap Index.[23]

2015 was also an important year for Turkey as it experienced two consecutive elections after the first one could not reach a majority for the AKP to govern, taking the country to a second tour. During this process there was also a breakdown in the peace process that had lasted for 2 years and had actually worked in favor of the AKP by guaranteeing nationalist votes. This was of most significance to the Kurdish political movement in Turkey which has been squeezed in between terrorist groups such as the PKK and the Turkish state, since they were forced to choose a camp. It finally resulted in the loss of votes for the HDP, the main political party relying on Kurdish votes in the second tour of the elections. The continuous postponing of a resolution to the Kurdish conflict in Turkey's southeastern area has now been further complicated by the new twist in the Syrian conflict, as one of the very important components in the fight against ISIS is carried out by the PYD which entertains close relations with the PKK. This constitutes a breakdown in Turkey's relations with almost the entire world, confirmed by the UN Security Council decision on 16th of February, which managed once more to reunite all countries against the shelling of PYD targets – including China, Russia and the USA. Turkey failed to get onto the Security Council in 2014 the way it had in 2008, demonstrating a significant fall of votes in its favor. This is in line with the concept of "precious loneliness" as mentioned by Erdoğan when criticizing the UN System and defending Turkey's idealist foreign policy.[24] However one should not forget how fast the dynamics of the Middle East can change and that political expediency requires a willingness to adapt. That's why not meddling into Middle Eastern politics has been seen as a refuge for Turkish foreign policy at the expense of avoiding relations with the region as a trend for the last few years.

Foreign policy failures:

Turkish foreign policy has gone through a period of idealism with no strong background in terms of power shifts but mainly from a desire for a political ideology that has proved very costly under Davutoğlu who has shaped the whole of Turkey's foreign policy since the time he began his term as a respected minister of foreign affairs at his term in Erdoğan's cabinet.

The good and ambitious start with a policy of so called "zero problems with neighbours" didn't pan out well, setting Turkey at loggerheads with all its neighbours. Armenian relations did not improve, with Iran the conflict with Syria has always been ongoing. The relationship with Iraq has never reached a stable position, with the Iraqi central government more recently making threatening demands for Turkey to withdraw its soldiers from Northern Iraq that Turkey claims to deploy for military training reasons Kurdish peshmerga of Northern Iraq.[25] Not to mention the tensions with Greece that still remain unsolved, overshadowed by the past - most importantly Cyprus and the refugees.

The attempt to take advantage of the Arab spring to be a regional player, especially its close relations with the Muslim Brotherhood, didn't pay off well and relations with Egypt and Tunis didn't improve while some assets have been lost with regard to Turkish business investments in the region. So the soft policy tools of trade and cultural ties have also been jeopardised.

However this reversal in foreign policy has not only seen a return to old historical conflicts but has also created a shift with regards to Turkey's allies. Traditionally, since the foundation of the Republic, Turkey has been keenly sidelining with the Transatlantic alliance - except for one special case; Cyprus intervention.[26] Being a member of NATO and ally of the US with accession hopes to EU has been an enduring trend.

On the other hand, a recent political shift is worth observing, since Turkey's efforts to acquire Chinese missiles despite NATO being vocal in its opposition, is a significant development. Improved relations with Qatar and Saudi Arabia, taking direct sides by creating a military base in Qatar and collaborating with Saudi Arabia on military bases (the first non-NATO country to send out its planes from an Incirlik airbase) are signs of Turkey's increasing shift to a different understanding of foreign policy. There have been signs that a rupture might be possible, with Erdoğan even mentioning membership of the Shanghai 5 as an alternative to the EU, during this friendly phase with Putin's Russia.[27]

Unprecented developments in the past year have, of course, pushed Turkey to reconsider its position towards the EU. The disagreement over Syria with Russia escalating to a level where a Russian plane was shut down, the fight against ISIS and refugee problems are among the most important ones.

Turkey and Israel have been negotiating an agreement to restore diplomatic relations which were cut off in 2010 after an Israeli naval raid on the Turkish Mavi Marmara ship which was seeking to break Israel's blockade of the Gaza Strip. If one factor of the rapprochement process reflects the changing security dynamics in the Middle East, especially in Syria, pushing Israel and Turkey to a closer cooperation, the second one would be a energy deal.[28]

In the light of these developments, a more likely scenario would be the cancellation of Chinese missile deals, reconciliation starting with Israel, improved cooperation with NATO, and efforts to work more closely with the USA and EU despite disagreement on certain issues like YPG.

3 important perspectives for 2016 to observe

One can state 3 main areas that will be most decisive for both Turkey and EU in this framework, and for the moment only one of them seems to have a positive outlook.

Cyprus

The stalemate in Cyprus that continued since 1974 was very close to being solved in 2004 with the so called Anna plan which was designed to unite the country prior to the admission of Cyprus to the EU. In the referendum despite 67% of favorable votes from the Turkish side, 76% of Greek Cypriots voted against it and that was the moment when the Cyprus conflict became an EU problem by bringing in an unsolved issue.[29]

Of course this has radically impacted on the nature of relations, as the EU requires the application of the Ankara agreement's rule to all member countries while Turkey doesn't recognize Cyprus and is not willing to get into a relationship unless the negotiations are completed. This has led to the blocking of 6 Chapters unilaterally by Cyprus in the accession talks with Turkey, thus causing another controversy.[30]

Since then tension has been on the rise at various periods, especially with regard to Cyprus's efforts to exploit the use of natural gas. But for the first time since 2004 we might be a lot closer to a real solution.

1. Political conjuncture is quite promising in both parts of Cyprus, with the new Turkish president who is a pro-unification person seen as a catalyst[31], daring to take on Turkish opposition despite strong dependency. The same signs are also coming from Cyprus seeking o diversify its regional ties, especially after the financial crisis that also impacted its economy.

2. Turkey is willing to get closer to the EU and having already meddled with Middle Eastern politics doesn't seem likely to block any talks as long as its interests are respected. Despite criticism from the leaders of Greece, Cyprus and Israel, the door is left open to Turkey's new policy towards this new geopolitical bloc.[32] The first time visit of the Foreign Minister of Northern Cyprus in this context was an act that was not warmly welcomed by Greek Cypriots, but can be considered as an important signal for the involvement of Turkey in the resolution of the conflicts.[33]

3. To continue to a third point, and a very important point in the agenda is the fact that the most cost efficient way of delivering Israeli gas to the Turkish Market seems to be via the Exclusive Economic Zone of Cyprus. This could be an important synergy for the export of gas found in the Aphrodite reserve with a volume that is not viable enough to support a pipeline project in the context of the low commodity prices of today.[34][35]

Alignment with the EU

Even though a very first and separate chapter is needed for Cyprus it is not possible of course to separate it from relations between Turkey, the EU and the world.

The main focus of EU & Turkish relations in 2016 seems to be constituted by the Refugee Crisis. And in order to solve this issue Merkel is pursuing a very proactive policy complementing even the point above with regard to Cyprus by pushing not only Cyprus but also Greece to reach an agreement on blocked chapters.[36][37][38]

Actually both sides have reasons to reignite the long stalling accession talks. Refugee issues have added more fuel to the crises of EU countries that have been going through difficult times internally. Austerity measures made conservatism and extreme right parties win a lot of popularity, accentuated with a touch of Islamophobia as a reaction to ISIS actions. The EU's reactions show a greater solidarity when it comes to the financial crisis in Greece and other austerity measures but also on the repartition of refugees with quotas. Finally Brexit has been on the agenda for a very long time - another issue calling the Union into question. Merkel has recognised the need to take an action and has taken advantage of her popularity at home compared to other leaders to do so. She has been the one leading negotiations with Turkey on refugee issues, along with the European Commission.[39]

From Turkey's side its much more critical to decide on the future of the country. It is hard to predict whether the implications of Syrian refugees are seriously considered. But there is one thing that most of the actors could agree on: Turkey has lost its shine since 2010. A period that reversed democratic evolution, bringing a change in the constitution and continuing with the negative effects of the Arab Spring on the „soft-power" policy Turkey aspired to in the region. The shooting of Russian military jet was a milestone. It has finally led Turkey to a point where it is at odds with both Russia and the United States at the same time.

This is why the EU offer has come at a good time to meet the needs of both parties, even though it doesn't represent a great win for either of them. But one important aspect where the EU has come under criticism is the fact that the values that must predominate the accession negotiations are being neglected in favour of the gains in the negotiations with regard to refugees. While the EU has some chance of enforcing a peaceful solution to theKurdish problem, and continue promoting democracy by enforcing conditionality, it is revealed that even accession reports have been postponed following demands from the Turkish authorities, leading to a loss of hope in liberal and pro-EU circles in Turkey.[40] [41]

Turkey's domestic politics

The domestics politics in Turkey could be in one of its worst stages under constant pressure from foreign policy developments and the high polarization of society on almost every matter that is subject to public debate.

There will be two main areas to observe in Turkish domestic politics in 2016. The first one is the change in the constitution or the so called presidential regime debates. The second one is the tension associated with the increasing polarization of society which will be more concretely seen in the public debates realting to the first point and lastly but most importantly to the Kurdish problem.

1. Presidential Regime or Democratic Governance:

Erdoğan's willingness to push for a presidential regime is interpreted as a move towards a further consolidation of power into his own hands by many observers. This is especially true of the foreign press covering Turkey who are critical about Turkey's role and positioning in terms of its ties with the West that has not been witnessed before.[42]

At the moment, according to the numbers present in the parliament a change in the constitution requires a coalition with at least one of the three other political parties that are all against a presidential change.43 Despite efforts to present the context as a new constitution, the substance of this discussion is of course the presidential regime, and there are signs that Turkey might face a new parliamentarian election or referendum now that the main opposition party CHP has stated that it will not negotiate anything related to a regime change in this direction. As already put forward, Erdoğan and the AKP have shown themselves remarkably adept at spinning security concerns into political support. This was not clear to see after the voting turnout spiked after June to the November parliamentary elections with 9% giving back absolute majority to the AKP. [44]

However there is a great opposition to the political moves, both from inside and outside Turkey. The researches carried out show the level of polarization in Turkish society. The people identify themselves more and more with their political engagement and they declare negativity towards the "other side" to the point that they do not want their kids to marry the opposition's kids (83,4%), they do not want to do business with them (78,4%), nor do they want to be their neighbours (76%).[45]

Any problem that Turkey is experiencing cannot be solved though without the addressing challenges of democratization including the very pertinent Kurdish problem.

2. The Kurdish problem

Turkey is a good example of how postponing the resolution of a country's problems is not good for long term results. When the framework of a peaceful agreement was open it was not possible to resume the peace talks with the PKK.

In 2005 Erdoğan was hailed as the first leader to acknowledge the Kurdish question.[46] That stance was strengthened by the introduction of optional Kurdish lessons at schools, opening of a public TV channel broadcasting in Kurdish and similar moves since the beginning of this acceptation. However after the 2015 events, the government has declared a unilateral approach towards resolution of Kurdish issue with Davutoğlu's so called Mardin plan, that is seen by many a vain effort not having counterparts and doomed to fail.[47]

Now Syrian branch of PKK called as PYD is the most successful army on the ground battling against ISIS making them indispensable for the coalition. This is on the others side against all game setting in the AKP's Syria policy also having implications in the interior affairs.

The harsh reaction of the state against PKK's organizations in some cities of Southeastern Anatolia has come under the spotlight of the international arena because of the mainly civilian casualities. Erdoğan was really close to a peaceful settlement, then suddenly changed direction most likely because of public reaction. This has stopped the ceasefire, changing the result of the ballot box again in favour of the ruling party.

The change in the constitution and even a regime change towards a presidential regime is again on Turkey's agenda. It is an important time for Kurdish politicians to also be involved but it is difficult to bring this about, given the ongoing tension and military conflicts in the southeastern borders. On the other hand, Kurdish politicians are losing their momentum given the fact that they stayed in between the PKK and State authorities, a very difficult situation to manage peace talks especially in a context like this.

Conclusions

It won't be wrong to say that the relationship between Turkey and EU will be driven mainly by their own interests rather than shared common values. The actual setting that has just been described cleraly shows the seriousness of the situation.

But this serious situation is creating a window of opportunity for Turkey in which EU can be a convincing choice if the following steps are taken:

First of all the EU should play a more active and supporting role in creating a solution for the island of Cyprus. This will not only help to revitalize accession talks with Turkey, but also normalize an anomaly created by the EU itself by accepting Cyprus without resolving its disputes.

Secondly, it would be wiser to improve coordination in terms of Foreign Policy. For Turkey this could only be achieved by pushing again for a normalization of Kurdish problems and going back to peace talks that might have also positive implications for relations with the PYD in Syria, also putting an end to the misunderstandings with the USA. Otherwise Turkey might be left out of solutions a very undesirable situation given the importance of the bordering regions.

Thirdly, the EU has its role to play in this, supporting Turkey in the refugee crisis open heartedly would not only contribute to the well being of Turkey but also stop the uncontrolled flux of refugees. But doing this by closing its eyes to what is really happening with the democratization in Turkey would not be the solution. The EU must not simply focus its interest in cutting down the number of refugees approaching its borders, but in contributing to a more stable regional balance with a truly democratic and strong country by its side. This is why accountability and transparency in the management of this cooperation package is indispensable and requires engagement from all stakeholders such as international organizations, Civil Society, etc.

And of course finally, Turks must do their homework, and collaborate more with the international community and march towards a more democratic way that embodies more international democratic values and human rights.

References

1. The State of the World's Human Rights Report 2014-2015, Amnesty International http://www.amnestyusa.org/pdfs/AIR15_English.PDF
2. https://www.amnesty.org/en/documents/pol10/2552/2016/en/
3. Freedom in the World 2015, Discarding Democracy: Return to the Iron Fist, Freedom House p.5 https://freedomhouse.org/sites/default/files/01152015_FIW_2015_final.pdf
4. Willy, Craig; Towars Putinisation of Central Europe https://euobserver.com/opinion/131884
5. Therése Pettersson and Peter Wallensteen Armed conflicts, 1946-2014 Journal of Peace Research July 2015 52: pp: 536-537
6. idem p. 537
7. https://www.ncdc.noaa.gov/sotc/global/201601

8. http://www.ipcc.ch/pdf/assessment-report/ar5/wg2/WGIIAR5-Chap12_FINAL.pdf

9. http://ejfoundation.org/sites/default/files/public/EJF_climate%20change%20and %20migration%20%282011%29.pdf

10. Global Warming and the Arab Spring, from the Arab Spring and Climate Change: A climate and security correlation series February 2013 https://cdn.american-progress.org/wp-content/uploads/2013/02/ClimateChangeArabSpring.pdf Sarah Johnstone and Jeffrey Mazo pp.15-22

11. idem, Climate Change Before and After the Arab Awakening: The Cases of Syria and Libya Francesco Femia and Caitlin Werrell pp. 23-28

12. http://www.wsj.com/articles/china-economic-growth-falls-below-7-for-first-time-si nce-2009-1445221368

13. http://www.imf.org/external/pubs/ft/weo/2016/update/01/pdf/0116.pdf

14. http://www.imf.org/external/pubs/ft/weo/2016/update/01/pdf/0116.pdf

15. http://www.theguardian.com/world/2015/oct/27/tensions-andterritorial-claims-in-th e-south-china-sea-the-guardian- briefing

16. http://www.bbc.com/news/world-asia-21710644

17. Müftüler Baç&Gürsoy, Is There a Europeanization of Turkish Foreign Policy? An Addendum to the Literature on EU Candidates, Turkish Studies - Vol. 11, No. 3, 405–427, September 2010, Routledge Taylor Francis Group

18. İdem p. 406

19. http://www.tika.gov.tr/en/page/about_us-14650

20. The Role of Common Cultural Heritage in External Promotion of Turkey: Yunus Emre Cultural Centres, p.17 Kaya, Ayhan&Tecmen,Ayşe, European Institute Working Paper No:4 2011, Bilgi University

21. idem p. 19

22. http://data.unhcr.org/syrianrefugees/country.php?id=224 data by 16 February 2016

23. http://reports.weforum.org/global-gender-gap-report-2015/rankings/

24. http://www.ft.com/cms/s/0/ef238938-c1a1-11e4-8b74-00144-feab7de.html#axzz40 sTVHuwC

25. http://www.theguardian.com/world/2015/dec/04/turkishtroops-iraq-train-forces-fighting-isis

26. http://www.haberturk.com/yazarlar/soli-ozel/1193259-oyuna-gelmek

27. http://www.hurriyetdailynews.com/turkish-pm-erdogan-toputin-take-us-to-shangha i.aspx?pageID=238&nID=58348&News- CatID=359

28. Gumbatov, Akhmed; Prospects of Delivering Israeli Gas to the Turkish Market http://turkishpolicy.com/blog/10/prospects-of-delivering-israeli-gas-to-the-turkish-market#.Vqii3lPjS88.facebook

29. Yakinthou, Cristilla, "The EU's role in the Cyprus Conflict, System Failure or Structural Metamorphosis?" p.309 Ethnopolitics, Vol. 8, Nos. 3–4, 307–323, September–November 2009

30. http://oldweb.ikv.org.tr/icerik_en.asp?konu=muzakeremevcutdurum&baslik=Current

31. http://www.bbc.com/news/world-europe-35522456

32. http://www.haaretz.com/israel-news/.premium-1.700464?-v=9707B6E9F6D6634E0C6FA0F10556052C

33. http://www.timesofisrael.com/for-first-time-senior-officialfrom-turkish-northern-cyprus-in-israel/

34. Gumbatov, Akhmed; Prospects of Delivering Israeli Gas to theTurkish Market http://turkishpolicy.com/blog/10/prospects-of-delivering-israeli-gas-to-the-turkish-market#.Vqii3lPjS88.facebook

35. http://www.timesofisrael.com/israel-mulling-twin-gas-pipelines-to-turkey-greece/

36. https://euobserver.com/enlargement/130735

37. http://cyprus-mail.com/2015/10/22/under-pressure-to-openchapters/

38. http://www.sigmalive.com/en/news/greece/137776/tsipras-positive-on-opening-cyprusblocked-chapters-turkey39. http://www.ft.com/intl/cms/s/0/fe07dfce-c41d-11e5-b3b1-7b2481276e45.html#axzz411psjYNH

40. A greek news portal has released the transcripts of Erdoğan's and EU leaders negotiations on Refugee issues where it is mentioned that progress report's publishing has been postponed to after elections inTurkey

41. http://www.economist.com/news/europe/21693243-turkey-where-european-foreign-policy-went-die-graveyard-ambition?force=scn/tw/te/pe/ed/agraveyardofambition

42. Calls for getting Turkey out of NATO and western camp have been frequented as seen in the following article; http://www.huffingtonpost.com/david-l-phillips/losing-turkey_b_8922912.html

43. http://www.independent.co.uk/voices/erdogan-is-on-the-brink-of-ultimate-power-but-turkey-is-falling-apart-a6853416.html

44. http://time.com/4231009/turkey-syria-war-refugees/

45. http://kssd.org/wp-content/uploads/2016/02/Kutupla%C5%9FmaAra%C5%9Ft%C4%B1rmas% C4%B1-Sonu%C3%A7lar%C4%B1.pdf

46. http://www.independent.co.uk/voices/erdogan-is-on-the-brinkof-ultimate-power-but-turkey-is-falling-apart-a6853416.html

47. http://www.radikal.com.tr/yazarlar/cengiz-candar/mardinsakasi-halep-ciddiyeti-1506456/

(published online early March 2016)

From China to Greece - on track for the New Silk Road

George N. Tzogopoulos

Whither Sino-Greek relations?

The beginning of 2016 finds the relationship between Greece and China in a better status in comparison to the same period of 2015. The recent decision of the Greek Asset Development Fund to call COSCO the 'preferred investor' to buy the Piraeus Port Authority[1] can theoretically pave the way for a win-win co-operation. Such a collaboration based on investments and common economic interests constitutes the core of a pragmatic approach in the Sino-Greek partnership. It also contradicts illusions of last year that China could provide bilateral loans to Greece challenging the country's Euro-Atlantic orientation and its stay in the eurozone. As Vice-President of Greece Ioannis Dragasakis said in an interview during the pre-election period of September 2015 his government had unsuccessfully attempted to find a loan in third countries before the so-called 'Agreekment'.[2] Former Finance Minister Yanis Varoufakis goes even further suggesting that a phone call from Berlin blocked an alleged Sino-Greek financing deal.[3]

The 'Dragon's Head'

China has followed a careful and systematic policy vis-à-vis Greece since 2009 when COSCO started its investment in Piraeus. Prioritising its relations with major EU powers such as France and Germany, it has not sought to become critically involved in the Greek debt crisis and unilaterally provide liquidity. Considering the problem a European one per se, it highly supports Greece's stay in the eurozone and has only played a secondary role. According to an interview given by former Greek Prime Minister George Papandreou in the pre-election period of January 2015 Beijing had bought Greek sovereign bonds worth of 6 billion euros at the beginning of the economic crisis.[4] This amount is not insignificant but much lower compared with loans provided by Greece's creditors when the first bailout was agreed in May 2010.

China's interest in Greece is interwoven into the port of Piraeus at the economic and geopolitical level. The management of piers II and III in the port of Piraeus by COSCO has contributed to an increase of its profits. Its revenue from the terminals business rose by 13.6% in 2014 and this - according to the Chinese company - was attributed to three of them, namely Piraeus, Guangzhou South China Oceangate Container Terminal and Xiamen Ocean Gate Container Terminal.[5] Furthermore, the Piraeus port is a key point for China's 'One Belt and One Road' policy.[6] It marks the passage from the maritime Silk Road in Europe to the land-based one (Economic Belt) towards the Old Continent. Specifically, Beijing seeks to establish trade links from Greece to Central and Eastern Europe via the Balkans. This strategy was made straightforward during the '16+1' meeting in Belgrade on 16 December 2014.[7]

Sino-Greek relations have slowly but steadily improved since 2009. COSCO's profits along with the announcement of the Silk Road plan by President Xi Jinping in September 2013 paved the way for a deeper cooperation. In June 2014, China's Premier Li Keqiang visited Athens and discussed with the then Prime Minister of Greece Antonis Samaras the possibility for further collaboration in infrastructure projects including shipping, logistics, ports, airports and maritime affairs.[8] From a Greek perspective, a stronger co-operation with China could also boost tourism as well as the real estate sector. The number of Chinese tourists visiting Greece was 12,203 in 2012 and went up to 28,328 in 2013 and 37,196 only in the first nine months of 2014.9 As far as real estate is concerned, foreign citizens have since 2013 the opportunity to acquire a long-term entry visa in Greece, if they decide to buy a property worth of 250,000 euros or more.

The misunderstanding

In January 2015 Antonis Samaras inaugurated the beginning of works by COSCO to extend Pier III in the port of Piraeus confirming the spirit of solidarity between Greece and China. Nevertheless, after the victory of SYRIZA in the election 25 January 2015 and for a period of approximately six months Sino-Greek relations entered a new period of relevant misunderstanding. Before the snap election and in its immediate aftermath, some ministers of the new cabinet and other members of the governing SYRIZA party started to put into question the necessity of the policy. Merchant Marine Minister Theodoros Dritsas, for example, said that the Greek government would be prepared to renegotiate the already signed agreement with COSCO. Then Minister of Economy, George Stathakis announced that the process for the privatisation of a 67,5 percent stake of the Piraeus Port Authority would be cancelled.10 Subsequently, the Chinese Ministry of Commerce responded by asking Greek authorities to protect the legal interest of companies including COSCO. Also, for the first time during the ongoing economic crisis, Chinese media – traditionally positively predisposed toward Greece – raised doubts on the motivations of the new leadership of the country.[11]

The initial ice between Greece and Chinese authorities broke after some meetings between Greek politicians and China's Ambassador to Greece Zou Xiaoli. Greek Prime Minister Alexis Tsipras spoke on the phone with his Chinese counterpart Li Keqiang on 11 February and eight days later he publicly said that he was 'ready to support China's links to Europe, with Greece serving as China's gateway into Europe.'[12] Further to this, during his meeting in Beijing in March 2015 with Chinese Vice-Premier Ma Kai, Ioannis Dragasakis attempted to put an end to the confusion by asserting that the privatisation of the Piraeus Port Authority would take place as usual and by calling interested companies, including COSCO, to submit offers.[13]

In every occasion Beijing was clearly communicating to Athens that COSCO would be the 'Head of the Dragon' in its investment policy in Greece in the framework of the revitalisation of the ancient Silk Road. COSCO's potential expansion in Piraeus was one of the reasons why the Chinese leadership was highly concerned about the risk of a Grexit.[14] The Chinese company - along with APM Terminal and International Container Terminal Services – were preselected to submit binding offers for the sale of the Piraeus Port Authority. Nonetheless, the privatization could not be implemented as long as the Greek government was failing to find common ground with its creditors.

The privatisation of the port

The 'Agreekment' of 12 July 2015 gave an end to Grexit fears. From that day onwards and especially after the new snap election of 20 September 2015, the SYRIZA-Independent Greeks government started to employ a completely different approach in carrying out privatisations. Despite ideological opposition and some new delays leading to the partial amendment of the concession agreement of the Piraeus Port Authority, the sale had already entered its final phase. The deadline for the submission of bids by interested companies was set for 21 December 2015. The withdrawal of APM Terminals and International Container Terminal Services facilitated the attempt of COSCO. A few days later, the Greek Privatisation Fund confirmed that the Chinese company had been the only candidate investor but asked it to improve its offer.[15] COSCO improved its offer indeed and on 20 January 2016 it became the preferred bidder offering 368,5 million euros.

In a detailed statement the Greek Privatisation Fund presented the benefits of the agreement for the concession of the Piraeus Port Authority.[16] According to the Fund's assessment, the total value could amount to 1,5 billion euros, including future investments by COSCO in the port. The Chinese company offered a higher price in comparison not only to the share price of the Piraeus Port Authority on the day of the agreement but also to that of two independent appraisers. In fact, COSCO agreed to pay 22 euros per share while the price range of the independent appraisers was from 18.4 to 21.2 euros per share and the share price at close of trading was 12.95 euros on Wednesday 20 January 2016.

Following the recent decision by the Greek Privatisation Fund the tender envelope will be directly filed with the Court of Auditors for a pre-contractual control. The Greek Parliament will also have to approve the concession. The way ahead is not without obstacles. Greece is already under pressure by a recent conclusion made by the European Commission. In particular, the Commission argued in March 2015 that Greece had granted COSCO some benefits - such as tax exemptions and preferential accounting treatment - providing the Chinese company with an undue advantage over competitors in breach of EU state aid rules. Therefore, it asked COSCO to pay back the advantage received to the Greek state and encouraged the latter to avoid further distortions of competition.[17] In parallel with the recommendation from the European Commission, Athens will be also encountered with reactions by trade unions operating in the port of Piraeus as they are losing their privileges and are not prepared to accept new labor conditions.

The sale of the Piraeus Port Authority is an obligation of the Greek government in the context of the bailout agreements. Therefore, the beginning of a debate on whether this decision is wise or an alternative could exist, leads nowhere. What matters more is that after the conclusion of the deal and the expansion of Chinese investments, the Piraeus port can be transformed into a transshipment hub, boosting trade, attracting new domestic and foreign investors and strengthening the geopolitical and strategic importance of Greece. In that regard, several local actors and businessmen have endorsed the agreement and expressed their optimism.[18] All in all, as President of the Piraeus Chamber of Commerce and Industry Vassilis Korkidis puts it 'the impact of the recent agreement will be safely in the future' when potential investors will be specified and tangible results will be apparent.[19]

Last but not least, the amount of 368,5 million euros to be offered by COSCO might seem sufficient taking the ongoing financial crisis and the stock market continuous fall into account but is certainly much lower than the real value of the Piraeus Port Authority under normal circumstances. If this privatization had taken place earlier, economic benefits for the Greek state would have been much higher. Thus, the important lesson learned is that politicalinstability constitutes a negative factor not only averting foreign players from investing in Greece but also reducing the cost of their future transactions. Unavoidably, the two-year delay in proceeding with the sale of the Piraeus Port Authority has had serious repercussions on the Greek national interest.

Looking towards the future

After the Piraeus port sale Sino-Greek relations are expected to improve. Increased high-level meetings will be high on the agenda of both countries. An official visit of Greek Premier Alexis Tsipras to Beijing is expected to take place soon on the invitation of his Chinese counterpart Li Keqiang. If this happens, Mr Tsipras will be escorted by a group of Greek businessmen looking for new deals with Chinese partners. Further to this, the Greek side is elaborating on a three year plan of bilateral co-operation with China. This idea was first suggested in March 2015 during the meeting between foreign ministers Nikos Kotzias and Wang Yi in the Chinese capital.

The development of close relations between Greece and China creates some skepticism in Western circles regarding potential geopolitical implications. That is because the latter has the opportunity to access Europe via the former by obtaining control in critical infrastructures. However, as Thanos Dokos puts it, even when it comes to the geopolitical consequences of having close relations with China, Greece does not consider its position as fundamentally different from that of other European Union states.[20] In the final account, Greece – as opposed to several European states including Germany, France, Italy and Britain – does not participate in the Asian Investment and Infrastructure Bank (AIIB). Further to this, international media have proven to be wrong in speculating Greece's hypothetical adhesion to BRICS New Development Bank.

In the coming months Greece will insist on combining the privatisation of the Piraeus Port Authority with potential future benefits for its national economy. Pillars of this strategy include the launch of additional investments by Chinese companies around Piraeus, principally in ship building, maintenance and logistics as well as the increase of Greek exports towards China. Additionally, the significant rise of tourists visiting Greece having China as their country of origin is another objective. The launch of new Air China flights connecting Beijing with Athens from 1 June 2016 outlines the will of the Chinese administration to respond to the logic of a win-win co-operation.

To sum up, China's New Silk Road - as it is developing via Piraeus – is not a panacea for the Greek economy. But it can contribute to Greece's growth, also sparking new infrastructure projects in Europe. Financing can be guaranteed by a new European instrument, Juncker's Investment Plan where China participates.[21] In that regard, the role of Piraeus will be central. It is not a coincidence that China's Ambassador's to Greece Zou Xiaoli publicly emphasizes - after the port deal - the Sino-Greek future collaboration 'to build the China-Europe Land-Sea Express Route to connect the maritime Silk Road with the Silk Road on land'.[22]

References:

1. Press Release of the Hellenic Republic Asset Development Fund, 1 January 2015, available at: http://www.hradf.com/sites/default/files/attachments/HRADF%20Press %20Release_PPA200116B.pdf [accessed 1 February 2016]

2. Ioannis Dragasakis interview with euro2day, 9 September 2015, available at: http:// www.euro2day.gr/specials/interviews/artiprivatisationcle/1359826/dragasakhs-s-afth-th-fash-h-aftodynamia-einai.html [accessed 15 January 2016].

3. 'Varoufakis speaks about Plan X and its rejection', ekathimerini.com, 20 January 2016, available at: http://www.ekathimerini.com/205218/article/ekathimerini/news/ varoufakis-speaks-about-plan-x-and-its-rejection [accessed 1 February 2016].

4. China bought Greek sovereign bonds worth of €6bn at the beginning of crisis', chinaandgreece.com, 21 January 2015, available at: http://chinaandgreece.com/china-bought-greek-sovereign-bonds- worth-6bn-euros-beginning-crisis/ [accessed 15 January 2016].

5. COSCO Pacific 2014 Final Results, 24 March 2015, available at: http://www.cosco-pac.com.hk/en/news.php?action=content&-class_id=16&id=375, [accessed 10 January 2016].

6. For a detailed discussion on the investment of China in the port of Piraeus see: Frans-Paul van der Putten , 'Chinese Investment in the Port of Piraeus, Greece: The Relevance for the EU and the Netherlands', Clingendael Report, 14 February 2014, available at: http://www.clingendael.nl/sites/default/files/2014%20-%20Chinese %20investment %20in%20Piraeus%20-%20Clingendael%20Report.pdf [accessed 3 October 2015]. And on the investment of China in foreign ports including Piraeus see: Frans-Paul van der Putten and Minke Meijnders, 'China, Europe and the Maritime Silk Road',Clingendael report, March 2015, available at: http://www.clingendael.nl/sites/default/files/China%20Eu-rope%20and%20the %20Maritime%20Silk% 20Road.pdf [accessed 10 January 2016].

7. The Belgrade Guidelines for Cooperation between China and Central and Eastern European Countries, Ministry of Foreign Affairs of the People's Republic of China, 17 December 2014, available at: http://www.fmprc.gov.cn/mfa_eng/ wjdt_665385/2649_665393/t1224905.shtml [accessed 15 January 2016].

8. George Tzogopoulos, 'Cultural and economic ties draw China and Greece closer, Global Times, 18 June 2014, available at: http://www.globaltimes.cn/content/ 866362.shtml [accessed 12 January 2016].

9. Data are based on the Association of Greek Tourism Enterprises (SETE) and refer to Chinese tourists coming directly to Greece from China.

11. George Tzogopoulos, 'Greece takes realistic approach to Chinese investments after election wobble', Global Times, 4 March 2015 available at: http://www.global-times.cn/content/910227.shtml [accessed 18 January 2016].

11. Liu Zhun, 'Greece betrays principle of contract by halting port sale', Global Times, 29 January 2015, http://www.globaltimes.cn/content/904648.shtml [accessed 30 January 2016].

12. Tzogopoulos, 'Greece takes realistic approach to Chinese investments after election wobble'.

13. George Tzogopoulos, 'Greek government looks to reassure Beijing over port sale', Global Times, 2 April 2014, available: http://www.globaltimes.cn/content/ 915148.shtml [accessed 30 January 2016].

14. George Tzogopoulos, 'Stake high for China in possible Grexit', Global Times, 23 July 2015, available at: http://www.globaltimes.cn/content/933442.shtml [accessed 20 January 2016].

15. Press Release of the Hellenic Republic Asset Development Fund, 21 December 2015, available at: http://www.hradf.com/sites/default/files/attachments/HRADF_O LP211215eng.pdf [accessed 15 January 2016].

16. Press Release of the Hellenic Republic Asset Development Fund, 20 January 2016, available at: http://www.hradf.com/sites/default/files/attachments/HRADF%20Press %20Release_PPA200116B.pdf [accessed 25 January 2016].

17. European Commission Press Release, 'State aid: Commission orders Greece to recover incompatible aid from Piraeus Container Terminal', 23 March 2015 available at: http://europa.eu/rapid/-press-release_MEX-15-4650_en.htm [accessed 23 January 2016].

18. 'This is how Piraeus actors have seen the sale of the port', 20 January, available at: http://www.naftemporiki.gr/finance/story/1057009/pos-eidan-tin-polisi-tou-olp-for-eis-tou-peiraia [accessed 1 February 2016].

19. Press Release of the Piraeus Chamber of Commerce and Industry, 21 January 2016, available at: http://www.pcci.gr/evepimages/-press210116_F9292.pdf [accessed 1 February 2016].

20. Thanos Dokos, 'The geopolitical implications of Sino-Greek relations', Clingendael article, 10 June 2013, http://www.clingendael.nl/publication/geopolitical-impli cations-sino-greek-relations-0?l ang=nl [accessed 25 January 2016].

21. George Tzogopoulos, 'China and Juncker Investment Plan', ELIAMEP Briefing Note, 41/2015, November 2015, available at: http://www.eliamep.gr/wp-content/upl oads/2015/12/Briefing-Notes_41_November-2015_Tzogopoulos-George.pdf and Lihua Zhang and Trigkas Vasilis, 'Can China's New Silk Road End Greece's Economic Tragedy?', Carnegie-Tsinghua Center for Global Policy, 11 May 2015, available at: http://carnegietsinghua.org/2015/05/12/-can-china-s-new-silk-road-end-gree ce-s-economic-tragedy/i8e5 [accessed 10 January 2016].

22. Address by Ambassador Zou Xiaoli at the 'Happy Chinese New Year' Celebrations- Performance by China Anhui Art Troupe, 28 January 2016, available at: http://gr.china-embassy.org/eng/zxgx-/t1336087.htm [accessed 1 February 2016].

(published online mid-March 2016)

Some comments on the Chinese Development Model

Ryszard Piasecki

Visiting China after a long period of absence cannot fail to make one reflect on the reasons behind this country's success. Paradoxically China's economic success story has neither deepened media interest in the European Union, nor has it provoked any serious reaction from neoliberal economists. Meanwhile, developments in China during the last 25-30 years, require serious reflection on the part of economic theorists and practitioners of business. One should note that for more than a quarter-century, western specialists have focused on the effectiveness of the neoliberal model.

In the Washington Consensus, which was adopted in late 1980's and at the beginning of the 1990's by many developing and former socialist countries, deregulation, liberalization, openness, privatization and democracy were seen as the most significant factors, apart from capital inflows (mainly foreign direct investment). Openness and privatization strategies in the last 25 years have become worldwide processes covering many countries. This process had many elements of universal significance, but there were also many elements specific to the group of countries with similar socio – economic structure and a certain position in the world economy. The Washington Consensus development model was implemented in some 40-50 countries of the world. Unfortunately, the results were rather mixed and a lot of countries ended up strongly disappointed.

China is a special case of economic success not fully understood by economists from the so called mainstream economics. They took for granted the main development paradigm which embraces liberalization and privatization in the context of full western style democracy. In the case of China's success, we have instead the Beijing Consensus, which is the adoption of a market economy and a strong state (with limited democracy).

The Beijing Consensus (also sometimes called the "China Model" or "Chinese Economic Model") refers to the political and especially economic policies of mainland China after the death of Mao Zedong and the rehabilitation of Deng Xiaoping (1976) and are thought to have contributed to China's spectacular growth in gross national product over the last 25 years. The phrase "Beijing Consensus" was coined by Joshua Cooper Ramo (the former editor of Time magazine) to pose China's economic development model as an alternative — especially for developing countries — to the Washington Consensus of market-friendly policies promoted by the IMF, World Bank and U.S. Treasury.

The term (Beijing Consensus) has been described variously as the pragmatic use of innovation and experimentation in the service of "equitable, high-quality growth", and "defense of national borders and interests" as well as the use of "stable, if repressive, politics and high-speed economic growth". There are 3 main guidelines according to Joshua Cooper Ramo:

- The first guideline involves a "commitment to innovation and constant experimentation."
- The second guideline states that GDP/per capita should not be the sole measure of progress. Rather, Joshua Ramo feels that the sustainability of the economic system and an even distribution of wealth, along with GDP, are important indicators of progress.
- The third guideline urges a policy of self-determination, where the less-developed nations use leverage to keep the superpowers in check and assure their own financial sovereignty. This includes not only financial self-determination, but also a shift to the most effective military strategy, which is more likely to be an asymmetric strategy rather than one that seeks direct confrontation. Unlike the Washington Consensus, which largely ignored questions of geo-politics, Joshua Ramo argues that - particularly in China - geo-politics and geo-economics are fundamentally linked.

You don`t need to be a very keen observer to see the huge leap forward this country has taken in the period since 1990 (at least an 8-fold increase in GDP in this period). At every step one can see the huge amount of investments, thousands of cranes, skyscrapers, a vast network of high-speed rail (10000 km), the rapid development of the internal market and consumption. All young people talk on iPhones, the largest global brands are present in the cities of China, there are plenty of well-stocked shops etc. Such a major turnaround in overcoming the underdevelopment of China could only be possible under the conditions of a long-term, continuous very high economic growth rate at 8% -12% per year. Of course, these achievements are most apparent in the cities, and much less in the countryside. Many western economists accuse the Chinese authorities of having created several different Chinas (rich east and poor west).

The development of each country has its historical roots. The development of China must be observed with increasing attention, because the transformation of economic and social life in this country seems to be much more durable than many Western experts previously believed. The main features of this transformation can be listed as follows:

1. Incremental reform (as opposed to a Big Bang approach),
2. Innovation and Experimentation,
3. Export Led Growth,
4. State Capitalism (as opposed to Socialist Planning or Free Market Capitalism),
5. Authoritarianism (as opposed to Democracy).

In other words, China joined the free market in a very successful way, as a strong state.

In the West there still remain a number of negative myths about the country with regard to the falsification of statistics, "impermanence development," the weakness of the private sector, overinvestment (too many roads, bridges, buildings, etc.), little innovation, environmental degradation and growing social inequality. In reality, the situation looks much better. There is no evidence that there is a real threat to the sustainability of development in China. The share of the state sector decreased from 78% in 1978 to 22% in 2015, and the development of the private sector is impressive. The economy is becoming more innovative (2% of GDP devoted to R & D). Chinese authorities are, slowly but surely, caring more about the environment (eg. in large cities electric motorcycles and scooters now dominate, which has clearly improved air quality). Growing inequality is not just a problem in China, but also in the USA, and in many European countries.

Moving around the country by train at a speed of over 300 km per hour (Shanghai Maglev even reaches 431 km per hour on a stretch of 40 km), one tends to forget that only 30 years ago it was still a country of starving people. The past is gone. It is too pejorative today to say that "the Chinese people work for a bowl of rice." A young person out of college receives 3000 yuans, nearly 500 euros per month (lunch in the canteen employees is 1-1,5 euros), a good professional earns 1000-1500 euros, and a high-class manager or engineer in Shanghai up to 4500 euros per month. On the congested streets in many cities mostly new and modern automobiles can be seen, such as BMW, Audi, Volkwagen etc. China produces more than 18 million vehicles, the same as Japan and the US combined.

China's economic success is the result of firstly, opening itself up to foreign direct investment. Whereas in the initial period, investors were arriving in this country in search of cheap labor, now they are benefitting from strong demand in the internal market which is becoming wealthy. Secondly, China has become a world export centre. Thirdly, the policy of the state is coherent, thoughtful and far-sighted. Fourthly, we must not forget about the hard-working Chinese citizens.

It is understandable that an important issue for the West is the lack of (the limited nature of) democracy in China. In fact it is a separate topic, inspiring a lot of emotion. Given the historical particularities of the country, the diversity of ethnic and regional disparities, social inequalities, but also cultural conditions and a tradition of strong central government for more than 2 thousand years, one should not expect major adjustments to government policy in this regard. One thing is for sure: The undeniable economic success of China is a major challenge to many largely accepted and even "sacred" paradigms of mainstream economics (eg. regarding privatization, property rights and democracy).

(published online early June 2016)

References

Gerard Strange, Towards a New Political Economy of Development, States and Regions in the Post-Neoliberal World, Macmillan 2014, pages 41-87

Naughton B., China: Economic Transformation Before and After 1989, University of California, 2009

List of Authors – Liste des auteurs

Laurent Baechler est économiste, Directeur du Master in European Studies and International Relations (MAEIS) du CIFE filière anglophone, et rédacteur en chef de « L'Europe en formation ». Il est spécialisé dans les questions de développement durable, liées en particulier aux problématiques énergétiques, climatiques et hydriques.

Roland Benedikter, Dr. Dr. Dr., is Research Professor of Multidisciplinary Political Analysis at the Willy Brandt Center for German and European Studies, University of Wroclaw, Senior Research Scholar of the Council on Hemispheric Affairs Washington D.C., Trustee of the Toynbee Prize Foundation Boston and Full Member of the Club of Rome. His publications include nation studies on Europe, the USA, China and Chile. Corresponding author e-mail: rolandbenedikter@yahoo.de.

Katrin Böttger est Directrice adjointe de l'Institut de la Politique européenne (Institut für Europäische Politik, IEP, Berlin)), où elle dirige le projet de recherche « La politique européenne à l'égard de l'Europe orientale et de l'Asie centrale : un rôle clé pour l'Allemagne ». Ses champs de recherche principaux à l'IEP sont la politique européenne de voisinage, l'élargissement de l'Union européenne, les relations de l'UE avec l'Asie centrale et le processus constitutionnel de l'UE.

Anna Dimitrova is Associate Professor and Researcher in International relations at ESCE International Business School (Paris.) Holder of the Master in Advanced European and International Studies (MAEIS) of CIFE and a PhD in Sociology at the University Nice of Sophia-Antipolis, she also did a post-doctoral research in Political Science at CNRS (Paris). Her research interests and publications are mainly focused on US foreign policy, transatlantic relations, Euro-Mediterranean relations, and geopolitics and conflicts.

Eddy Fougier est politologue. Il est enseignant invité à l'Institut européen (ie-ei) et chargé d'enseignement dans les Institut d'études politiques (IEP) d'Aix-en-Provence et de Lille et à Audencia Business School (Nantes). Il est chercheur associé à l'Institut de relations internationales et stratégiques (Iris).

Helgard Fröhlich is director of CIFE's Berlin office and CIFE's e-learning Master programmes. She teaches at the University of Vienna and is an expert in Early Modern European History, in particular British and the history of Constitution building.

Cristian Ghinea est le directeur du Centre roumain de politique européenne (Romanian Center for European Policies (CRPE)), un organe de réflexion basé à Bucarest et disposant également d'une agence à Chisinau, en République de Moldavie. Il coordonne le projet « Coopération régionale Roumanie-Moldavie-Ukraine, la clé de la stabilité de l'ancienne région Crimée/mer Noire », financé par la fondation Black Sea Trust for Regional Cooperation. Cristian possède une longue expérience des médias, il écrit depuis 15 ans une rubrique hebdomadaire dans le magazine roumain renommé « Dilema veche ». Il est spécialisé dans le concept institutionnel de l'UE, les réformes du secteur public et les politiques anticorruption. Il a récemment commencé à s'intéresser à ces thèmes dans les pays du Partenariat oriental, en accordant une attention particulière à la Moldavie.

Emre Gür is CIFE Representative in Turkey and CIFE Alumni Manager.

Ireneusz Pawel Karolewski is Professor of Political Science at the Willy Brandt Centre for German and European Studies, University of Wroclaw and Adjunct Professor at the Chair of Political Theory, University of Potsdam. His publications include European Identity Revisited (2016, Routledge) Extraterritorial Citizenship in Postcommunist Europe (2015, Rowman & Littlefield), Nation and Nationalism in Europe (Edinburgh University Press, 2011) Citizenship and Collective Identity in Europe (Routledge, 2010), Nationalism and European Integration (Continuum, 2007). Email: karolewski@wbz.uni.wroc.pl.

Frédéric Lépine is Deputy Director General at CIFE and Lecturer in "Federalism and Governance" . His research focuses mainly on federalism in political philosophy. His latest published articles are about theories of federalism and federalism in Belgium.

Isabelle Maras est chercheuse associée au CIFE depuis janvier 2016. Elle est spécialiste des questions de sécurité et de défense ainsi que de la politique étrangère de l'Union européenne. Elle dispose d'une expérience professionnelle approfondie dans le domaine des affaires européennes et de la recherche acquise à Bruxelles, Hambourg et Berlin. De 2013 à 2016, elle a été chargée de projets « Dialogue européen » à la Fondation Genshagen en tant qu'experte technique du Ministère des Affaires étrangères français.

Hartmut Marhold is CIFE's Director of Research and Development. He is Honorary Professor at the University of Cologne and teaches at the Turkish-German University, Istanbul. His research covers European integration history, EU institutional developments and Germany's European politics.

Ryszard Piasecki is a Polish economist and diplomat, professor at the University of Lodz, recently Ambassador in Chile, member of the board of CIFE.

Dagmar Röttsches is Center Manager at the Graduate School for Economic and Social Sciences at the University of Mannheim. She holds a PhD in political science and was a DAAD Lecturer at CIFE for five years.

Jean-Marie Rousseau is currently working as an independent consultant in Brussels in Territorial Intelligence and Regional Strategies [TAO-ITINeRIS] and yet actively contributed to many reports for international institutions and national or regional governments all over the world, including Europe, Mediterranean countries, South-America and China. He is member of CIFE's Scientific Council

George N. Tzogopoulos, CIFE Alumnus, is a journalist and media-politics expert. He is founder of chinaandgreece.com and the author of the books US Foreign Policy in the European Media (IB TAURIS 2012) and The Greek Crisis in the Media (ashgate 2013).

Jean-Claude Vérez, économiste, maître de conférences habilité à diriger des recherches, responsable du module Economie et Mondialisation à l'Institut Européen de Nice.

Isabelle Weykmans, Minister for Culture, Employment and Tourism of the German-speaking Community of Belgium, Master in political science and international law, CIFE Alumna and member of the Board.

Franziska Wild is intern at the political section of the EU Delegation to the Republic of Cape Verde. Her primary research interest is the European foreign and migration policy. She is currently doing research on the Mobility Partnership of the European Union with Cape Verde.

Sebastian Zeitzmann is Director of Studies and Academic Coordinator at the European Academy of Otzenhausen (Germany) and lecturer in European Law and European Integration at Saarland University. He is also member of the editorial board of ZEuS (Zeitschrift für Europarechtliche Studien) and a freelance translator at the Court of Justice of the European Union. He spent three years in the United Kingdom in total.